W9-BIQ-368

COLTRANE

A Biography

COLTRANE

A Biography

by

Cuthbert Ormond Simpkins, M.D.

Black Classic Press
P.O. Box 13414
Baltimore, MD 21203

Copyright © 1975 by Cuthbert Ormond Simpkins, M.D.
All rights reserved
First Published by Black Classic Press 1989
ISBN—0933121-20-2

Many thanks to my darling wife Diane Simpkins, for preparing the enlightened index which accompanies this volume.

C.O.S.

For a complete list of Titles
Published by the Press Write:

Black Classic Press
P.O. Box 13414
Baltimore, MD 21203
c/o List

To My Family

In Memory of the great warrior, Harold Wade Jr.

Acknowledgements

Living within this book are the vibrant spirits of many persons. Without their giving of themselves this book would have been less than a wish. I am deeply indebted and sincerely grateful to all of you.

Hassan Abdullah
Chris Alexander
Jeru Alexander
Rashied Ali
Gene Ammons
Shela Anderson
Gary and Maxine Bartz
Ernest and Karen Baxter
Bernadette Beekman
John Blair
Art Blakely
Arthur Bonner
James Boyd
Rocky Boyd
George Braithe
Ras Brancato
Franklin Brower
Marion Brown
Dr. Roy Brown
Dr. Burford
Zita Carno
George Coleman
Ornette Coleman
Johnny Coles
Naima Coltrane
Saida Coltrane
Harold Cottman
Dr. Gerald Deas
Craig Dellimore
Charles Drake-Long
Sonny Fortune
Richard Freniere
Alpha Phi Alpha, Columbia U.
Phi Psi, Amherst College
James Garrison
Dizzy Gillespie
James Golden
Mr. Granoff (Granoff Studios)
Carl Grubbs
Roy Haynes
Jimmy Heath
Oliver Henry

Dr. Hicks
Mr. Hoover
Freddie Hubbard
Mrs. Hughes
Hank Ingram
Mrs. Ingram
Raymond Johnson
Elvin Jones
Orin Keepnews
John O. Killens
James Kinzer
Rahsaan Roland Kirk
Steve Kuhn
Pete LaRocca
Michael Lawson
Harold Lewis
Mr. Lewis (Granoff Studios)
Harold Lovette
Mary Lyerly
Majumdar
Calvin Massey
Warren McLennon
Jymie Meritt
Hank Mobley
Thelonious and Nellie Monk
Dr. Morgan
Bob and Marie Neloms
Michael Olatunji
Jimmie Oliver
Pat Patrick
Odean Pope
Sun Ra
Max Roach
Sonny Rollins
George Russell
"Big" George Russell
Sulieman and Aisha Saud
    (Mr. & Mrs. McCoy Tyner)
Pharoah Saunders
Tom Sellers
Archie Shepp
Wayne Shorter
Prentice Taylor

Joe Termini
George Turner
Mal Waldron
Jack Walker
Mrs. Wilson
Mr. and Mrs. Williams
Walter Williamson
Mr. Witted
Rev. William M. White
Reggie and Elaine Workman
Khalid Yasin
    (Larry Young)
Nok Publishers
    Che Ude
    James Hazel

Contents

Cover by Elroy Williams

COLTRANE

A Biography

I

Equinox

Moments. Moments of great emotion never die. They are like purple diamonds swirling through the ages, or lavender pulsation burning, magnificently, about the mortal universe.

Through art come bursts of true life. Love and hope fly upward, like red and orange birds, into the chilled beauty of night. Yet, most of our lives are spun in lonely glass tunnels. Each in his own tunnel struggles through the pilgrimage from birth to ashen death. Frantically our heads turn toward each other. We want each other. We reach to touch. But the deceiving glass presses only harder against our trembling hands.

Tragically, it is the rare person who can transcend the walls. This person works a juju that spirals our lives to a higher plane, with joyful shaking, eyes closed tight, mouths open wide, jumping, twisting. Then, we may share a tear, or steal away to cry alone.

Through courage comes freedom. It takes courage to express what you feel, to meditate as you need. Emotional depth and mastery of technique rarely throb within a single pulsation. John Coltrane possessed, and was possessed, by this gift. His story begins with his ancestors.

Heart pushing outward, fists shaking high, Reverend William Wilson Blair could set the people on fire — make them shout, make them weep, make them thunder the floor with stomping feet. Then he talked about them, told of their sins and gossip, while always preserving their clinging hope of sustaining any hardship.

He preached more than fire and brimstone, though his admonitions burned many souls, more than sweet chariots though they sang the song, and more than the straight and narrow path, though he stuck to it himself. Like a Malcolm X or James Foreman of the 1920's, he denounced the white man from the pulpit, teaching that we should work together for *our* common advancement. Some Blacks thought being so straightforward with "important" white folks was improper, and that conditions for Blacks need not be improved. Others shuddered as he unleashed attacks with all the fury of the holy ghost.

A cook was once so frightened, she ran to her white employer revealing what Rev. Blair had said. Indignant the white man called, threatening in twangy redneck tones, "Did you say . . . ," Rev. Blair interrupted, "Yes, I said it! And I'm going to say more!" slamming down the phone. The "Old Man" didn't bite his tongue for anybody, and was quite influential.

He had been a state senator representing the area around Edenton, N.C. Later he became a proud forceful minister of the African Methodist Episcopal Zion Church. He had a highly successful pastorate in Hamlet, N.C. until 1926, when he was promoted to presiding elder. In this new capacity he had to evaluate and preach in churches within that district. Upon receiving this promotion he and his family moved to High Point, N.C.

There his energy flamed the community into movement. Before his arrival there were no public schools for Black children. Instead there was a Quaker boarding school, to which the city paid a yearly sum, for the children's instruction. However by the 1920's, the community had outgrown the school's facilities and the Quaker administration was giving more attention to the tuition paying out-of-town students. Reverend Blair organized several Black men to go before the mayor, city council, and school board and demanded that the city construct and maintain schools for Blacks. This demand was so forceful (and Rev. Blair may still have had some influence from his senatorial days) that the city built a new brick structure, the Leonard St. Elementary School, and took control of the Quaker School, converting it to the William Penn High School.

Reverend Blair sent his daughter, Alice, to Livingston College where she studied music and teaching. She was dark complexioned, not very talkative and had the tall stature and dignified bearing of the Blair family. She wanted to be an opera singer. However there was no one in High Point to teach her and her family felt it was unsafe for a young single woman to be in a distant city alone. Because of these and other considerations Alice sang and played piano for her father's gospel choir.

At Livingston, she met John R. Coltrane, a short, good looking, brown-skinned man, who dressed neatly. He, like Alice, was a quiet person. He liked to joke a lot and had a pleasant smile. His father was also a minister of the AME Zion Church, the Reverend John Coltrane from Sanford, N.C. Alice and John married, eventually moving to a second floor apartment, at the corner of Hamlet Street and Bridges Avenue in Hamlet, N.C. There on September 23, 1926, the equinox; the day when the sun crosses the equator, when night and day are of equal length throughout the earth; the day between Summer and Fall, between Virgo and Libra; with a rising sign between Pisces and Aquarius; and a moon in Aries — John William Coltrane was born, with the help of a midwife.

In Hamlet, the earth sent broad, white reflections of the sun's rays, revealing the small grains of sand that made up the soil. It appeared that the town, with its rigid brick and wooden structures, had been built on a beach, where the air smacked of the sweet smell of barbecue, brightly colored balls bounced happily from hand to hand, and mouths were wide with laughter. There was, however, much distance between image and reality. Black women sweated each day before the ovens in the white man's kitchen. Sidewalks ended abruptly, and still do, at the edge of the Black section. White folks could do pretty much as they pleased with Black lives.

More than fourteen trains passed each day through this small but important town where they were repaired. This railroad presence made a "good" job for Black men, that of Pullman Porter. However, little John never knew much of Hamlet. Two months after his birth, Rev. Blair moved to High Point, and his family followed.

The name of the city originated from the 1850's. At that time the state built the North Carolina and Midland Railroad, and built a town at the highest point on the line between Goldsboro and Charlotte. This new town was named High Point for its geographic characteristic. In the 1920's, High Point was considerably larger than Hamlet, consisting of about 6,000 Blacks and 24,000 whites. Instead of sand, the soil was clay, red, and stuck to your shoes after a mighty rain. At the edge of the Black neighborhood yawned a wooded area where friends could take long quiet walks.

The Black community valued education highly and was very religious. There was only one dance hall and most of the social activity centered around the church. Young people in their twenties or early thirties would go to nearby Greensboro to hear their favorite bands.

Many Blacks voted, but politics and the system of oppression were infrequent topics of discussion. There were few if any of the overt acts of violence by whites common in other towns. So-called "racial etiquette" was not enforced. This consisted of moving from the sidewalk onto the street when a white man approached, or waiting at a shop until the whites were helped. A large segment of the population drank from water fountains marked "colored," sat in the park, and took the long walk up to the "buzzard's roost," i.e. movie balcony, without a second thought.

There were no policemen from the all white force in the Black community, except for a plain-clothesman who raided bootleg stills or searched the woods for five-gallon cans of corn liquor. The Blacks of High Point, at least the segment that Alice and John Sr. belonged to, were a small and religious group that had its liquor, had reached an unequal equilibrium with the whites, prayed to God, and strived to send their children to college.

Eight persons shared what was called "Rev. Blair's house": John Sr., Alice, their son John William, Alice's sister Betty, her husband Goler, their daughter Mary, Mrs. Blair, and Rev. Blair, when he wasn't away on church business. It was a wooden two-story house sitting near the top of Underhill St. Like a gentle river, this street curved gracefully downward. Broadly branching trees rooted in the air, holding up the toy-laden front and backyards where John and Mary played. The area was called "the Hill" for three reasons. One was the high position of part of the street, two, because of the name, Underhill, and three because the best homes owned by Blacks were there. At a time when there were only dirt roads through most of the Black section, Underhill Street was paved.

However, there was no social snobbery. Many of the home owners on the street were maids, chauffeurs or laundry workers. The only significance living on Underhill had was that your family was lucky enough to get a nice place to live. Even on Underhill most of the sidewalks were unpaved. The city left it up to individual homeowners to pave their walks. Most, including Rev. Blair's family, didn't bother.

Those living in Rev. Blair's house made up one of the most prominent families in High Point. They were proud. Much of this pride emanated from Rev. Blair, who spoke what he felt. Not many ministers of that time, or now, would have dared challenge the power of the whites. Even fewer linked, in the traditional minister's language,

The Blood of the Lamb

Cherubim and Seraphim

and the holy trinity

to fighting a vicious system — a typical minister

would have,

sweated and ranted

twisted and danced

pointing

to the promised land in the sky. He would not have mentioned the dismal schools which kept his flock from that land here on this earth.

Though proud, the family was not chained to the self-hatred shown by disdain for those less well-off financially, or those of a dark hue. They spoke to Miss-Lucy-down-the-street and gave a warm reply to anyone who said hello. Alice and John were quiet, friendly people who didn't socialize much, and stayed close to home. Those who lived in "Rev. Blair's house" formed a closely-knit family.

When John Sr. first arrived in High Point, he worked in Deacon Johnson's tailor shop. Within four years he had his own busy pressing club, where tailoring and cleaning were done. Sometimes he would prop up his feet, get a couple of shots of whiskey in him, but never much more, and sing country music for hours, playing the violin or ukelele he had taught himself. Customers would walk by and see a mountain of dirty clothes, climbing toward the ceiling. He would just keep on singing. But his work always got done, and he was known as one of the best tailors in the area. Each day Alice would walk with her small son to take her husband's dinner to the shop.

John was a chubby little boy, who carried raisins in his pockets, and loved to roller skate in the driveway with his cousin Mary. He and Mary were more like sister and brother than cousins, playing up and down the curving, sliding board street. Sometimes they would tease and play games on the other children. Once a girl from across the street annoyed John. To get back at her, he prepared a dookey sandwich from which she took a greedy bite. Whenever James Kinzer came by they would tease him because his mother would always be holding his hand.

James "Pochey" and Franklin Brower were John's two best friends. The three boys lived on the same street. They were together so much that folks thought they were brothers. But neither John nor Mary had any brothers or sisters.

John and his friends did all the things most boys did – boxing, wrestling, football, baseball. His favorite position was first base. Hustling all over the field, John enjoyed being a good athlete. He was bigger than most boys his age. When they played top-of-the-hill, a game in which one boy would run with the football toward the top while the others tried to stop him, he usually made it. The others were afraid to tackle him. He also proved to be a good runner in the neighborhood races.

Roller skating was one of their favorite things. Even high school kids and adults roller skated in High Point. Instead of riding a bicycle to a friend's house they would often skate there. Because it was paved. Underhill St. was one of the places where many skated. John and his friends would go to the top, start downward and - snap! around to skate the rest of the way backwards. At that age it seemed a daring thing to do.

When they weren't on Underhill St. they would be in the park where they heard Ella Fitzgerald sing "A Tisket A Tasket" and Jimmy Lunceford playing "Margie." Mr. Steele, the boy scout leader, would take them on weekend trips through the woods. Sundays after church John and his friends would go on walks among the rustling trees.

Some Sundays they decided to walk in a different direction, down Washington St. towards the main business district called, "uptown." This walk would take them past William Penn High School with its spacious campus. The "colored folks' " library was also on this campus. Next they would come into the Black business district which was only about fifty yards long. Here there were, among other things, a pool hall, cafes, a taxi stand, a drugstore where you could get a soda or ice cream cone, and the Kilby Hotel. Walking further on the right they crossed Fourth St. and entered the white neighborhood. On the left, Perry St., a little more distant, was the dividing line. In this part of the white neighborhood were big plantation houses where old rich families resided. Finally reaching uptown the boys could refresh themselves with fruit from one of the many stands.

Hints of achievements in later life appeared in many of the childhood interests of John and his friends. He and Frank's preferences for movies and comics manifested such hints. Their minds were engaged by subjects that involved logic and imagination. Sunday evening might be spent at the movies watching Dick Tracy logically piecing together a crime, or the fantastic world of Flash Gordon with his ray gun and ability to fly.

Their favorite comic series was "Doc Savage." Doc Savage was the leader of a group which solved crime using scientific knowledge and logic. In one story the criminals made it snow in the summer to create confusion and divert attention from the scene of their crime. The more unusual and difficult the situation, the more John and Frank were interested. Once they tried to write their own book based on Doc Savage. Frank did the writing and John did the illustrations. Both boys loved to draw human figures, animals, but most of all sleek, futuristic, streamlined cars. They would compete to see who could draw the most advanced car. Most children preferred the wild west comics but none held John and Frank's interest like the intriguing Doc Savage.

II

The Family

After work John Sr. would come straight home, passing up the amusements and aimless conversation on Washington Street, to be with his family. He would take John and Mary on long car rides through the country, to the County Fair, or anything else going on around High Point. When they returned he would sit on the side of his bed, pick up the violin, and sing as though no one else were around, while John and Mary watched and listened.

Even though a religious influence was ever present in the household, there weren't any rules such as no smoking, no dancing, no drinking. John and Mary felt free to do as they pleased, skipping the main church service if they wanted and even playing games at the dinner table. They went to dancing class but poor John seemed to have two, or three, left feet. Maybe he wasn't really trying. There were other things on his mind.

In Christian Endeavour, a church religious training class, he seemed to know more about the lesson than the teacher. He would ask questions about God — perceptive questions — not challenging but striving for more understanding. At home he would show an ability to concentrate, spending hours constructing model airplanes. He was a quiet, thinking boy.

But not withdrawn. Whenever there was a fight at school John would lead the other boys to help break it up. If two students decided to meet after school for a battle John would tell Mr. Witted, the principal, who rushed to separate the little warriors. At this early age he demonstrated a desire for harmony. Also his desire to know more of the Creator and his ability to concentrate long hours, would characterize his later life.

In elementary school little girls began to interest John. He and his friend, Frank, always seemed to like the same one. In the fourth grade they both liked an out-of-town girl named Annie Legrand. They were disappointed when she preferred another boy. Later Eloise Monroe, another out-of-towner caught their budding fancy.

As a student John was always near or at the top of his class. He excelled on the annually given state board of education exams. A vigorous student, he was involved in almost all school activities including the patrol boys. It was a big event when the patrol boys took a train ride to Washington. Few children had been on a train before.

Selection of a child for the patrol boys was based on teacher's opinions. A student had to have a good scholastic record, good manners, and a neat appearance, all of which John easily met. His personality tended not to offend anyone and all the teachers liked him. They put him in school plays and May Day parades. School was out on May Day to allow the children to participate in marches, programs and other activities. Parents would come to watch their children perform to the sound of a piano placed outside, especially for the day. For the boys dressed in white pants, shirts and socks, it was just a lot of marching, stopping, and standing in the hot sun. His mother followed his school progress closely. She was one of the first presidents of the Leonard St. School PTA. Mary's mother, Mrs. Betty Lyerly was also very active. On the outside John, like his parents, was quiet but inside he burned with the energy of Rev. Blair.

He was 12 when Mr. Steele formed a community band composed of boys of all ages. Mr. Steele liked to work with children and knew much about music. He led a city band of adult men, and taught choirs in many of the local churches.

When he brought in some beat up old instruments, John chose a clarinet. He also played an E-flat horn but his primary instrument was clarinet. Like the other boys he didn't care that the instruments were in bad condition. All they considered was 'Here is a man who is going to teach us to play.' Mr. Steele taught them the staff, time signatures, techniques on the instruments and other basics. When they practiced in the basement of his grandfather's church a piano was there to accompany them. This was John's introduction to chords.

Mr. Steele was a good teacher. If one of the boys was having difficulty with a part he would stand beside him, pointing to each note, while the others played. Homework and penalties for tardiness were unnecessary. These boys *wanted* to play. They were always on time and voluntarily practiced exercises at home.

And did John practice — day and night! Sometimes the neighbors complained, especially when he practiced in his backyard at three or four in the morning. His family learned to live with it. They just walked, around, over or between with life as usual while he blew with all his strength. He was steadily advancing, practicing, playing, thinking — feeling the life in his horn.

> "little boy on his
>   sailing red bike
> speeding up the hill with
>   all his might
> smoothly he travels
>   to a world
> he dreams of
> anchoring a direction
> right here above the
>   clouds
> like an airplane
>   or jet soaring
> way above
> far away he rambles
> into his world of
>   wind and sea"[1]

III

Young Man

It was 1939. The minister stood in the grass incanting, enchanting, trying to soothe the broken faces in the somber crowd. She wasn't one to scream — but a storm of heavy emptiness raged inside, and all that showed was a few, slowly, dropping tears. Still twelve, little John patted her softly but affirmatively on the shoulder, "Don't worry mom. I'll take care of you." Death had taken his father at the age of thirty-eight.

Time determined to destroy this family. Only a few months later Rev. Blair died. Soon afterwards, Aunt Betty's husband was taken. Mrs. Blair had been ill for sometime. It would only be a few years before she too would pass. The suddenness and sadness of these deaths made the apprehensive survivors appreciate each other even more, and band together in a protective warmth of closeness.

With the adult males gone, alternate sources of income had to be found. Lucrative work was scarce in High Point. Still John's mother found a job at the white country club.

For Rev. Blair, the very idea of women in his family working in the white man's kitchen was repugnant. Now there was no recourse. The country club job paid better than many others available to Blacks, like the laundry where many Black women labored from seven to five each day for four dollars a week.

Superficially, John and his family were not affected by the financial crisis. The fact that there were only two children probably helped make this possible. In the midst of the depression his family never had to take in roomers as others did. John didn't have to be without shoes or receive fewer gifts at Christmas as did many of his friends, nor did he have to work as a shoe shine boy, caddy, or grocery delivery boy. His mother recognized his talent and encouraged him to practice as long as he wished. The neighbors still complained, but behind closed doors they discussed how everything about young Coltrane said, "I'm going to be a top musician someday!"

Resembling a large church, the steepled main building of William Penn High School, stood handsomely on a smiling campus. Via well beaten paths five smaller buildings connected themselves to the door of the main building. These structures were the library, two classroom buildings, a cafeteria, and a cottage. The cottage had been inhabited by Mr. Griffith, the first principal after the city took control of the school. Now in 1939, only his daughter, the school librarian, lived there. Professor Griffith's picture hung in the auditorium where the community gathered for concerts of European music or gospel groups like "Wings Over Jordan." Scholastically, William Penn was an "A" rated school.

As small boys, John and Frank had played in the halls and read in the library. They looked to the day when they would finally be students there. Now on the first day they stood on the steps of one of the classroom buildings, feeling good that they had made it, while watching the girls go by. Especially interesting were those they hadn't met from Fairview Elementary School in South High Point. For some reason the most attractive were the older girls from sophomore class up. They were soon disappointed to learn that these girls were neatly paired off with boys their age or older.

As a young man of 13 John was calm, easy-going, and took everybody as a friend. He wouldn't say anything if he didn't know you. But if you spoke to him he would answer warmly. He was popular almost as soon as he entered the doors of the church. It wasn't because of a pumping handshake or an automatic smile that he was well liked. His popularity was based on his playing an instrument and a warmth which made him pleasant to everybody. As a result he rarely, if ever, had a fight, though he would make his point.

Around this time John began going to parties at the community youth center, or in private homes. There Billy Eckstine cried,

> Jelly Jelly Jelly
> Jelly stays on my mind
> Ooooo Jelly Jelly Jelly
> Jelly stays on my mind
> Jelly O killed my pappy
> And it drove my mama stone blind.[1]

Avery Parish played his mellow "After Hours" and the fellows could hold the girls close, moving to an easy groove. But John was more in the party than of it. He danced very little and would sit quietly thinking.

By this time, the interests of the three friends, John, Frank and James, began to diverge. James became involved with athletics. Frank was absorbed in his studies and in sports writing. He could quote the vital statistics of each football team and knew the names of almost all the players. John could care less. Music had begun to possess him. Frequent trips were made to the music store on Lane Street in the uptown district, for sheet music and equipment for his instrument. Around 1940 he began reading *Downbeat*, a "Jazz" magazine, paying close attention to the advertisements for instruments.

Through *Downbeat* John was exposed to the music industry which was white controlled and unfortunately reflected many of their racial and artistic biases. It was ironic that John, a young, aspiring Black musician, had to read a magazine in which few Blacks were featured. White bands dominated the reader's polls in spite of the fact that we had created the music. An insignificant white accordion duo would receive more publicity than the important experiments Black musicians were involved with in Kansas City. A music labeled "Swing" was widely publicized. Since most of the publicity went to white musicians, some of the oldest European musical traditions became widely disseminated.

One prevailing idea was that the drum should be "felt not heard." It was common practice in recording studios to put a cloth over the drum — mocking and muting the mighty instrument that was once the most eminent voice in our music. An alternative reason for the cloth was that the electronic equipment could not handle the full sound of the drum. Still the cloth was a suitable solution that fit the idea of chaining the strength of the drum to a minimum.

Barrelhouse Dan, who was the *Downbeat* record critic, further imposed European sentiments, arrogantly and ignorantly objecting to the "advancement of percussion instruments into the solo field," and referring to the "African savage" in an article from *Downbeat* June 1, 1940.[2]

Few Blacks broke through to be pushed by the publicity machine. Many of the records produced by us were put into the category of "race disc." Records of this category were only mentioned, receiving (maybe fortunately) very little critical attention. Throughout the magazine there were few pictures of Blacks. These distortions were so constant that someone not told otherwise, or from another planet, might think it was whites who had created the music. It was no surprise that whites dominated the polls.

Also, there were stories of recording sessions and the conflict between ASCAP and CBS. Another article complained of the decline in the number of bands. This was blamed on the upsurge in jukeboxes. There were articles criticizing critics. There was a story of a band which lost a job because it had Black and white musicians. Also, in the September 15, 1940, issue there was this cartoon.

Chicago. September 15. 1940   **NEWS**

"My Lip's Still Giving Me Trouble."

Looking through the pages of *Downbeat*, it seems as though it considered itself "liberal" on racial matters. There were articles denouncing the prejudice against mixed bands and later articles protesting police harassment of clubs with a mixed clientele. *Downbeat may have* been liberal in a relative sense. But it reflected all too well the self-interest and racial arrogance of whites. The effects of the music industry reached even the smallest cities.

A typical High Point teenager, listening to the radio in the morning before school, would hear Harry James playing "You Made Me Love You," records by Charlie Barnet, the Dorsey Brothers, and very much Glenn Miller, playing tunes like "Chattanooga Choo Choo" and "Flight of the Bumblebee." Less frequently he would hear Duke Ellington, Count Basie, Lucky Millender, or Cab Calloway singing "Hidey Hidey Ho."

However, at church or special concerts the teenagers would be exposed to rich gospel music sung by groups like the "Golden Gates" who sang without instruments.

> "Religion is a Fortune
> I really do believe
> Religion is a fortune

> I really do believe
> Religion is a fortune — yes!
> I really do believe
> That Sabbath
> Sabbath has no end"[4]

Blues was also heard in High Point though not as much as gospel. Jazz[5] was looked upon with disdain. To the old folks it was "devil's music." Whenever a jazz record was put on they would shout, "Take off them reels. Take off that devil's music." But this was not the dominant attitude in the Coltrane household where John was free to play and practice records by popular musicians.

He sought others with the same interests and met a man named Charlie Haygood. Mr. Haygood owned a big, clean restaurant on Washington St. When business was lean he would sit in the kitchen, or at one of the dinner tables, blowing his saxophone. From this older man John may have been informed of musicians he might not have known through *Downbeat* and of techniques in playing the instrument.

High school progressed and it was becoming evident that neither John nor Mary was going to reach the academic potential they had shown in elementary school. They became students who simply passed their courses. John no longer cared to excel, but knew well that he could if he wanted to. Two reasons may have contributed to his lack of production in school — the deaths in his family that were continuing into the early high school years, and his love for music which surpassed any sense of duty to standard subject matter.

Frank, involved with his studies, began to feel somewhat superior to John. He had become the highest ranking boy in William Penn. But John's mind still bristled. Once he and Frank argued over whether or not a man was an animal. Frank felt he wasn't and John felt he was. As his logic faltered and John's points began to pierce, Frank tried without success to twist and manipulate the argument, to maintain his superior image.

The once close relationship between John and Frank was not the same. They became sarcastic in their greetings. Yet there was no enmity. John, usually quiet, could still talk endlessly with Frank, shoot pool with him on Washington St., or hang out in front of the drugstore. The bond was altering, not breaking.

One subject that John was interested in was civics, the content of which was much like social studies. He and the teacher, Mrs. Hughes, would have engaging conversations after class. He wanted to know everything that had to do with people − on an abstract level − what made them function, trends of society, sociological changes, and the achievements of Black people. Mrs. Hughes became a good friend of the family's and came to know John well. In him, as did many in the community, she saw a "strong-willed, determined, and creative young man, who in any conversation, always expressed his desire to do something in music."

In John's junior year a school band was formed. The fact that for uniforms they had only ragged capes didn't stop them from playing exceptionally well. John's first musical influence was Lester Young, or "Pres," who after recording with the Count Basie quintet of 1936 began inspiring a rising number of young musicians.

At ten, Pres played drums in his father's band which traveled with a minstrel show. At thirteen he switched to saxophone because the drums were too bothersome to carry around, and by the time he packed them up after a show, all the pretty girls in the audience would be gone. Frankie Trumbauer was one of the most popular saxophonists of Pres's early years. He liked Trumbauer's light sound on C melody saxophone and also liked him because he " . . . always told a little story. And I liked the way he slurred his notes. He'd play the melody first, after that, he'd play around the melody."

Pres also listened very carefully to singers. "Most of the time I spend listening to records is listening to singers and getting the lyrics to different songs. A musician should know the lyrics of the song he plays. That completes it. Then you can go for yourself and you know what you're doing."

By the time Pres developed, his playing was much different from that of his idols. His search for individuality was guided by an independent personality, for example, the way he dressed. He wore a wide, flat-brimmed, porkpie hat, sometimes backwards. Once a friend took him to Brooks Brothers, selected and paid for some suits, which Pres never picked up.

His speech was a language all its own. At the end of a sentence he would say "Ding Dong" or "Bells." Someone he disliked would be greeted with "Bells," meaning that the conversation was over before it began. Once he criticized a pianist for not playing enough with his left hand. Checking periodically on his progress Pres would ask him how his "left people" were.

His term for policemen was "Bob Crosbys" and for playing an

instrument "Voncing." His personality came out on his horn. Pres played or "vonced" in a deceptively easy-going manner, with a free sense of time that made him seem to lag behind the beat. But Pres was also wild. Over a pounding drum he would break out with weird exciting phrases like human emotion, rough on soft mixed with lagging laughter, or sadness in blue. The simplicity and excitement in Pres's phrases matched John's energetic inner spirit.

Like his idol, John wanted a tenor saxophone. But his mother took the advice of his band instructor, Mr. Steele, who suggested that an alto saxophone would be easier for a youngster to handle. Since John didn't get the tenor his idol became Johnny Hodges, an alto saxophonist who played with Duke Ellington and whose musical concept was much different from Pres's. Hodges' sound was large and smooth. Many musicians declared that no one could play sweeter than Rabbit (Hodges' nickname). To many of his friends, including Mary, John sounded just like him.

In class, John began noticing a tall, slim girl who had a sunniness about her and an outgoing personality. She was also the best student in the class. As usual, Frank also liked her. One night they stood in front of John's house discussing Doreatha Nelson. John prodded Frank with,

John: "I know somebody who likes you."
Frank: "Who?"
John: "Doreatha."
Frank: "When you gonna tell her?"

Frank was apprehensive and embarrassed that his feelings might be exposed to Doreatha before he was ready. John pursued,

"Well, if you don't, then I'll tell her."

Frank was beyond help now. John went on,

"I'll give you a week."

Frank asked for more time but John only reminded him that his time was short. As the week passed John would say,

"You ain't got much time left."

Frank never met the ultimatum and John had at least one competitor out of the way.

Doreatha wouldn't tell John where she lived. He knew the neighborhood she was from and on Sundays would walk with James "Pochey" looking there for a house that might be hers. One day they followed her home from school. They knocked on the door after waiting for her to enter. Doreatha answered and upon seeing them fell into tears. She didn't want them to know she lived in a poor neighborhood, especially since they were from a comparatively rich one

In High Point in 1942, going with a girl consisted of nothing more than walking her home from school. You might take her to a movie. If you were bold, you would drop by her house on a Sunday and stay for a while, if her mother liked you. Though John and Doreatha "went together" in the context of High Point, he never pushed the relationship as close possible. He confided in Frank that he had told her, "Outside of books you don't know nothing."

In John's junior year a school football team was formed The boys had been playing during the twelve o'clock break but this was the first official team. They were given second-hand uniforms from the white schools, but in spite of this they became the best team in the area. In his senior year, John tried out for the team. During practice he was kicked in the lower spine and paralyzed. His family suffered through a week which seemed like a year before he regained complete control of his muscles. He went back to playing anyway, but a little more cautiously this time, and made a strong tackle on the second string team.

En route to a game the coach was annoyed by the bad language the boys were using. In desperation he shouted, "Can't you boys do something else?" So they began to sing. Next thing, many of them wanted to join the school chorus, but the music teacher only wanted students whom she felt could sing. This somehow left the football players out. They felt discriminated against and protested to Mr. Burford, the principal, stating that they too enjoyed music and should be given a chance to express it. Mr. Burford solved the problem by forming and teaching a boy's chorus himself. The boys did so well that they were able to perform in other cities.

The summer after his junior year, John went to Philadelphia to visit an aunt. It was probably during his senior year that his mother left for Philadelphia to find more lucrative work. With the war came an acceleration in the economy and many Blacks went north to get some of that war money. Aunt Betty was left to take care of John and Mary. In February 1943, Aunt Betty and Mary went to Newark leaving John with the Fair family who paid rent to live in the Coltrane house. With his mother and her watchfulness gone, John took on a new group of wine drinking friends. They and a group of girls would have parties every Friday night and a part of John's conversation became like the others — how much wine he had drunk, with variations. In the context of High Point drinking even a little liquor was disapproved of. Frank really looked down on John now. But secretly Frank was jealous because he would like to have done the same things, but felt they were forbidden. Still, their friendship remained intact and they could talk for long periods of time. The high regard for John held by those in the community was affected only slightly, if at all.

It was most likely sometime in his last semester that John got a job as a sodajerk in the drugstore on Washington Street. Being selected for this job was an indication of how well one was thought of in the community. Drs. Lemon and Greenwood selected only those for whom they had high regard. Among the boys it was a very desirable job because of the good pay, and the fact that you could sneak a couple of dollars from the cash register without anyone saying anything. There was no indication that John ever took advantage of this extra benefit.

Most of the boys were clothes conscious. School attire much of the year consisted only of a shirt, pants and no jacket, because of the warm weather. Pants were called "drapes." These big pants actually draped over your leg. They were baggy at the knee and narrow at the ankle. With his new job John no longer got his suits at Jacob's like the other boys but had them tailor made at the more exclusive Schackleford's.

John, 16 years old, graduated from William Penn on May 31, 1943. His early experiences, in many aspects, had been those of most children. He laughed, ran, played, dirtied his clothes, and wondered about girls. Yet there were many unique factors. There was the heavy religious influence and his concern for God, unusual even for a minister's grandson. There were the music he heard in High Point, his insatiable love for and possession by music, and his ability to concentrate for long periods. His non-involvement in fights and efforts to stop other children from fighting revealed a desire for harmony. He had a calm exterior, with an intense inner spirit. The deaths in his family, the futuristic drawings, the logical, imaginative Doc Savage stories, and even the raisins in his pockets, had great though unsuspected significance. All would become important as time unfolded its plan. But the path was strewn with deterrents. The strength and love experienced in his family, combined with some innate quality, as well as chance, would have to carry him past the clear crystal daggers of life.

IV

African Gifts

On June 11, 1943, John, Frank and James left on the 10:30 p.m. train for Philadelphia. James wanted to find a job there to pay for tuition at Wilberforce College. Frank also wanted to attend Wilberforce. John, unlike the others, had not been talking of college since the beginning of senior year. He was determined to go to music school.

During wartime, trains were usually crowded with soldiers. But the car that the three friends were in was crowded with other Black folks going north for jobs, or to visit relatives. Six-thirty a.m. the train arrived in Washington, where they transferred from the Southern Railroad to another line. Suddenly, the seating was racially mixed. Frank took a seat, got up for a brief period, during which John slipped jokingly into it. Frank was surprised that John had taken his seat but quietly sat elsewhere. Both had a serious demeanor and a joke like this would come unannounced and unexpected. About 8:30 a.m. they arrived at the North Philadelphia station.

From there they took a cab to the home of Frank's brother. Soon work would have to be found, but this first day work wasn't on their minds. They decided to walk to City Hall where the tall statues had caught their attention. They didn't realize how long the distance was. Beginning near 1600 N. Park St. they proceeded down Broad Street toward City Hall. On their walk they noticed the rows of houses stuck together with little yard around them and none in between. The streets crowded with people caught their attention, as well as all the fine, fine girls. They imagined how good it would be if a pretty one came up to talk to them. But this didn't happen. The walk to City Hall was too long, so they turned around and got lost, becoming even more confused by the directions folks gave.

A few days later they went to the state employment agency. John got a job at a sugar mill. James and Frank got other jobs. At the employment agency Frank was surprised to see a Black man in charge with a white secretary under him. Settling in Philadelphia, Frank stayed at his brother's house. Frank's aunt told them about an apartment on the fifth floor of the building in which she lived. John and James moved into this apartment.

John didn't waste much time in applying to the Ornstein School of Music. He was accepted but stayed only a minute, transfering to the Granoff Studios. Even at this early date he was experimenting with his horn. At Granoff it was readily seen that he had exceptional talent and the school eagerly gave him a scholarship for the study of clarinet and saxophone. A few months later John showed his teachers some writing he had done, after which they just as readily gave him a scholarship in composition.

He became known as a "brilliant, sensitive and receptive" student who listened very carefully and was always willing to learn. He was always prompt. Whenever he had a class at 9 a.m. he would be there at 8:50 and rarely missed a day. As in high school, he was very popular and respected by the students. The teachers were enthusiastic, sometimes giving him three or four lessons a week when only one was required. John came to be called a "tenant" of the school because he would be there ten to twelve hours each day, practicing his instrument or studying composition.

His mother would call occasionally, to ask about his progress. Mr. Granoff would only tell her that he looked promising, and would be a good saxophonist, but one could not say too much in the early stages. John was confident and determined to express his ideas in music. He would say, "You watch, Mr. Granoff, one day you'll be proud of me." John became one of the best students in the history of the school. After graduation he took post-graduate courses over a period of eight years, beyond which time, the instructors would feel the school had no more to offer him.

His mother's support was very important. By playing "jazz" and going directly into music school instead of college, he was breaking some of the strongest traditions of the High Point community. If a child didn't go directly into college after high school, laments of "Oh, what waste" would be heard. Even Mr. Steel's community band played only marches. Being in Philadelphia away from these community pressures might have made it easier for both John and his mother. He was probably determined enough to continue even if his mother had objected. Still, her encouragement made the feeling he had to express through music easier to reach. In 1944, Mary and her mother came from Newark to Philadelphia. Around the time of their arrival John changed jobs to work in a Campbell's Soup plant. Most of the places where music was played in Philadelphia wanted cocktail music. So John's first professional job was with a cocktail lounge group in 1945.

But World War II was taking many young men. To avoid the draft John took a job at the Naval Yard with the signal corps. But he was drafted anyway, and sent off in Navy bell bottoms to one of the Hawaiian Islands. There he spent a year playing clarinet in a band called the *Melody Masters*. The band was very popular and the other musicians admired his skill. As the war ended he contributed a unifying spirit in trying to keep the band together, which had made a great impact on the island. This effort was noted in an article about the island's bands, from a military paper called *The Mananan*.

"This the last of Manana's bands, has done much to break down the racial barriers around the island. Lovers of fine swing are not prejudiced against who gives it to them, and the Melody Masters gave fine swing. Playing for dances all over the 'rock,' these music makers left a fine opinion of themselves and they also left pleased audiences.

"Yes, we have witnessed the official decommissioning of the band, a band which has held on to the end and done their job well, even in the face of overwhelming circumstances. Much of this 'carry on' spirit can be attributed to Coltrane who sought to keep the band together in the waning hours.

"It is with a feeling of loss that we bid 'goodbye' to the last of Manana's bands; for the history of the bands on Manana has been a colorful one; one filled with true entertainment, not only for the Men of Manana but for everyone on the island of Oahu."[1]

The band was one thing and the Navy was something else. When John returned to Philadelphia he told a friend it was a drag and that he'd never go back.

John returned home and found that a musical upheaval had finally crumbled the walls of Europeanized swing. It was 1946 and Charlie "Yardbird" Parker was becoming the idol of young musicians. Several stories explain the origin of the name "Yardbird." One begins with him in a car with other musicians riding to a gig. Lazily the car rolled the miles away until suddenly, a chicken took a chance and scampered

across the road. Charlie shouted to the driver "Speed up! Speed up!"
S-C-R-E-E-C-H! the chicken was struck. Grinning, Charlie jumped out,
picked up the unlucky fowl and held it until they reached the night
club, where he asked the chef to prepare it. Soon he sat down to a
delicious and free meal. After this he was called "Yardbird" which was
often shortened to "Bird."

But there was more to Bird, the alto saxophonist, than funny tales.
His music *is* a marvel of all time — highly emotional with ideas leaping
at an astonishing rate. There are moments of soaring fitful beauty,
rhythmic voodoo, and down home hollers. Other musicians would sit
on edge with mouths hanging open until Bird walked off the stage.
After the trance was broken, some could only shake their heads and
utter a breathful "Shit!", because there seemed to be no hope that they
could ever reach the standard he set. Bird was a phenomenon and like
most phenomena he was a summation and extension of elements from
the past. An understanding of this past begins with the blues.

> I'm a big fat mama, got the meat shakin' on my bones
> I'm a big fat mama, got the meat shakin' on my bones
> And every time I shake, some skinny gal loses her home.[2]

or

> Did you ever wake up in the mornin'
> Just about the break of day
> Reach over across the pillow
> Where your baby used to lay.
>
> Then you got the blu - ues
> I'm gonna tell you that's the blues
> It'll make you feel so bad
> You could lay right there and die[3]

This no bullshit blues scared a lot of Black folks. They didn't want to
hear this "lowly" music so full of "bad taste." The cries of their people
reminded them of slavery, which they considered a shameful origin, and
brought forth images of low down, wine breath "niggers" not ready to
make the step into the "respectable" American melting pot.

"Swing," originally a Black conception, had been completely
appropriated by whites by the 1940's. They made it into a big business

and played from their cultural frame of reference with soft tones, restraint rather than fervor, and fewer slurs and screams. This music was much more acceptable than blues to Blacks who wanted to forget their origins and the stereotypes of themselves.

But there were others who could walk that walk, talk that talk, and snap their fingers to the blues without a damn for the thin tones of the swing orchestras. These people were the preservers of the gem — a part of which was the blues. They were the bearers of the musical legacy of dynamism, forthrightness, shouts, African rhythms and melodic patterns which make up the unique African-American conception.

Swing no longer expressed the attitudes of the people who created it. The attitudes of Blacks were rapidly changing. A pattern of raised hopes followed by abysmal disillusionment prevailed. During the war jobs were abundant and there was more money among Black people than ever before. The number of Blacks attending high school and college rose sharply. Those who had participated in the war expected doors to open for them upon their return home. They were brutally surprised. Lynching, torture, land-stealing and madness continued.

Many didn't have to wait to get out of the army before whatever illusions they may have had were wrecked. Black papers had frequent stories of fights between Black and white servicemen.

Lester Young, whose life before entering the army had been optimistic and carefree, spent twelve of fifteen months of his time in the military, in jail. There he suffered greatly. After this experience, his outlook was more cautious and distrustful, especially of whites.

Social protest seethed. A. Philip Randolph threatened Roosevelt with a march on Washington. Roosevelt responded by signing an executive order forbidding discrimination by government contractors. William Hastie, a Black member of the War Department, resigned in 1943 after his office had been bypassed in an effort to establish a segregated training facility. Race riots burned in Detroit and later in Harlem.

In Kansas City seeds of a new music more expressive of the Black rage began to flourish. In the 30's great bands such as those of Bennie Moten, Walter Page and his Blue Devils, and Count Basie relied heavily on the blues legacy.

"Kansas City style began as a grass roots movement and retained its earthy, proletarian character to the end. In the beginning it was plain, rather stiff and crude, but aggressively indigenous and colloquial. It drew from two main sources, folksong and ragtime. From folksong with its grab bag of country dances, field hollers, ballads and work songs —

and from the blues — both the old country and the newer urban blues — Kansas City extracted much of its material.[4]

From Africa, musical sounds beyond the scope of the European system are preserved abundantly in the blues. These sounds are often seen as attempts to reproduce the human voice on instruments.

> "The golden link that bound the jazzman to the blues tradition was the concept of vocalization. When the jazz musician understood the blues men, observing the great variety of devices at the disposal of his model — vibrato, variable pitch, microtones, fast turns, and the many sliding, slurring, leaping effects — he found it only natural to try to reproduce these efforts on the instrument of his choice . . . "[5]

Like a precious jewel hidden and preserved by its people, these African sounds were carried from generation to generation. In addition to a unique tonal quality, the jewel held within it richness of rhythm, exuberance of emotion, and distinctive patterns of phrasing. The Count Basie band originally based in Kansas City was an important bearer of this treasure.

It was a hard driving band which employed strong rhythms that pushed the horns outward to fervent improvisation. For melody the band used a riff, i.e., a brief melodic idea that is stated in forceful rhythmic terms. Lester Young was a member of the Basie reed section, extensively using the overtones, screams, honks and leaping effects that were a part of the jewel. It was in the setting of this rhythmically powerful band that many musicians were inspired by Young. The bands of Count Basie and others also provided a heavy training ground for young musicians.

Charlie Parker grew up in the years of these Kansas City bands. Born and raised there, his mother bought him an alto saxophone when he was eleven. At fifteen he would pass from club to club, listen, and try to imitate what he heard. His favorite saxophonist was Lester Young. But Charlie, at fifteen, was very much a musical neophyte. After an embarrassing attempt to jam with other musicians he was spurred to intensive practice and study. He spoke of this incident which occurred at the Hi Hat Club.

> "I'd learned the scale and learned how to play two tunes in a certain key, the key of G for the saxophone, you know, F concert. I'd learned the first eight bars of *Lazy River* and I knew the complete tune of *Honeysuckle Rose*. I didn't stop to think about any different kind of

keys or nothing like that. So I took my horn out to a joint where the guys, a bunch of fellows I'd seen around were, and the first thing they started playing was *Body and Soul*, so I go to playing my *Honeysuckle Rose* and they laughed me off the bandstand, laughed at me so hard I had to leave the club."[6]

He wasted no time in learning more. After this incident he took a job with the Tommy Douglass band, at the Paseo Ballroom. Douglass was well versed in harmony and technically proficient on his clarinet. He knew of passing tones, substitute chords, and double time concepts that Charlie would later extend. Douglass recalled,

"When I was blowing, he'd be sitting there smiling and tapping his foot . . . and digging. I took a Boehm system clarinet (I played both Boehm and Albert) over to him one day and he came back the next and played all the parts, he was that brilliant. It wasn't long before he was playing all the execution, . . . "[7]

Nevertheless his education was not yet complete. He tried to jam again. After hearing him, drummer Jo Jones was so infuriated that he took off his cymbal and slung it clear across the room. Humiliated, Charlie had to leave the club again.

Next he took a job with George Lee's band booked to work a summer at a resort. Two members of the band came to his attention. One was Efferge Ware, a guitarist and the other Carrie Powell, the band's pianist. Both were known for their knowledge of harmony and good musicianship. Charlie made a packed schedule for himself.

At night he worked with the band, then caught a few hours sleep, and rose early to study harmony with Powell and Ware. Study of scales, arpeggios, and saxophone drills were carried out during additional time. Lester Young solos were played on a record player at slow speed over and over again so he could play along, committing each solo to memory. In the fall of 1937 he was ready.

"When he came back, only two or three months later, the difference was unbelievable . . . He was the most popular musician in Kansas City . . . "[8]

Eventually he worked his way to a job in a band co-led by Buster Smith and Jesse Price at the College Inn. Buster Smith remembers,

"He used to call me his dad, and I called him my boy. I couldn't get rid of him. He was always up under me. In my band we'd split solos. If I took two, he'd take two; if I took three, he'd take three, and so forth. He always wanted me to take the first solo. I guess he thought he'd learn something that way. He did play like me quite a bit, I guess. But after a while, anything I could make on my horn, he could make something better out of it. We used to do that double-time stuff. I used to do a lot of that on the clarinet. Then I started doing it on alto and Charlie heard me doing it and he started playing it . . . "[9]

Later Charlie joined Jay McShann's band. The McShann orchestra was one of the best of the Kansas City bands. It utilized much from the blues and it was intellectually fertile. Many of the band members were experimenting with musical concepts. Charlie was also seeking his own voice.

In 1939 the band went to New York. While jamming with guitarist Biddy Fleet at a Harlem Chili parlor, Charlie found part of what he was seeking.

"I remember one night I was jamming in a chili house (Dan Wall's) on Seventh Avenue between 139th and 140th. It was December, 1939 . . . I'd been getting bored with the stereotyped changes[10] that were being used all the time, and I kept thinking there's bound to be something else. I could hear it sometimes but I couldn't play it. Well, that night, I was working over 'Cherokee,' and, as I did, I found that by using the higher intervals of a chord as a melody line and backing them with appropriately related changes, I could play the thing I'd been hearing. I came alive."[11]

"Biddy would run new chords. For instance, we'd find you could play a relative major, using the right inversions, against a seventh chord, and we played around with flatted fifths."[12]

In Harlem there were half a dozen places where musicians could jam after hours. Two of the most popular were Minton's Playhouse and Monroe's Uptown House. Many musicians jammed together, Charlie Parker, Dizzy Gillespie, "Lips" Page, Roy Eldridge on trumpets, Thelonius Monk, Allan Tinney on piano, Sid Catlett, Kenny Clarke, and Max Roach on drums, guitarist Charlie Christian and others.

Collectively these musicians with their exchange of ideas and creation of new ones formed a fertile ground of musical development. From this confluence of musical voices emerged a new form which changed music on almost every front.[13]

Like an endless horizon of creativity and at the forefront of these developments was Charlie Parker, presenting depth of emotion, new ideas, and technical facility that astounded musicians and non-musicians. Bird's composition, *Confirmation* is an example of his achievement.

Confir - MA - tion

Drums	that	LEAPS	riches
boom	continues	riding	of
filling	laying	the	emotion
the	a	steady	trembling
cave	carpet	boom	thrashing
of	for	of	purple
your	Bird	the	moons
body	and	bass	he
Rhythm	Dizzy	cutting	calls
section	to	caressing	straining
pushes	play	caring	reaching
smoothly	the	cursing	opening -
into	rhythmically	Bird	both
a	exciting	THRILLS	doors
magical	theme	with	of
pulse	Bird	unbelievable	time[14]

In 1944 Bird went with singer Billy Eckstine's band on a tour of the south. There he was constantly confronted with racially motivated abuse and just as constantly Bird was intolerant of it. In St. Louis the management objected to the band entering through the front door, telling them that they had to come through the back which was the entrance Blacks were supposed to use. After rehearsal, Bird went to the tables where the other musicians were relaxing and asked each man if he had drunk from the glass in front of him. When they answered "yes" he broke each one explaining that, of course, the management would not expect customers to drink from the same glass as Blacks. A good number of glasses had been clanked to small pieces when the owner, a well-known gangster, arrived. Violence was narrowly avoided and the engagement was canceled. The band was re-hired at a Black club in town, the Riviera.

Do you hear what I'm saying?

Two streams ran through the Black consciousness. One caused people to turn their backs on their own music and try to adopt the music of their oppressors. The other led people to appreciate their own music. With this latter group lay the preservation of the African gem which had been passed precariously onward from generation to generation. The music was not, strictly speaking, like that in Africa. Rather it was an honest expression of African people who had been wrested from their homelands. With them they carried a way of feeling and playing music and from America they took those elements that agreed with the way they felt music should sound.

During the 1940's the frustration and rage of Blacks, always present, boiled over so that it became visible to the white man and became widely known through his news media. Concomitantly, Black musicians formed a new music which drew from the African gem and was an honest expression of themselves and their times. The music was emotionally forthright and honest. It was many steps upward from the commercialism and European values that had been imposed by the late 30's. The new music provided the technical and emotional foundation for a later surge of creativity.

Returning from the Navy in mid-1946, John found himself in a musical environment that had changed radically from what had existed before. Entranced also by Bird, he would listen to his records, playing each note to better understand what Bird was doing. There was a whole realm of musical education that he could not get from "formal" schooling, but would obtain from other musicians past, present and those to come. Many musical concepts were introduced to him during this period. "I was first awakened to musical exploration by Dizzy Gillespie and Bird. It was through their work that I began to learn about musical structure and the more theoretical aspects of music."[1]

However, John was able, at least to other musicians, to do more with the music than imitate it. The name Coltrane became legend among Philadelphia musicians. To them it was evident that John was inspired by Parker, but he didn't play Parker cliches and had a tone all his own. Charlie Parker was a formidable presence, but John had an individual, personal approach.

At twenty years old he was about 5'11", 180 lbs., with the long fingers of a born saxophonist. The fresh look of youth had not left his face. His voice was deep, resonant, and sincere. He loved to eat. If his Aunt Betty cooked a pan of rolls, he'd eat the whole pan. If she fried a chicken, he'd eat the whole chicken. And if she baked a cake, he'd eat the whole cake.

He often said that he thrived on people, and there were always people at his apartment. Yet, he rarely showed his emotions, except through his horn. He was a quiet person who said very little. But when he said something, God damn it, it weighed a ton. Someone who had just met him might have become disconcerted by his quietness, until they learned that nothing really had to be said.

He presented a cool, relaxed exterior. He disliked anything restrictive and wore loose clothing. Since the age of 18, he had stopped wearing underwear and rarely wore socks.

He rarely went to parties or sports events, and spent little time with women. Much of his time was devoted to music. The remainder was for his family whom he loved dearly. He was wide open musically and would listen humbly to musicians less skilled than himself, feeling he could learn something from anyone — and wanting to miss nothing. John felt strongly about the oppression of Black people in the south. He began to realize why his grammar school and high school books were second-hand, and why the football uniforms were so ragged. He had made two or three trips back to High Point because he missed his friends, but decided after the last trip that the south was not for him.

He had a subtle sense of humor, often forming jokes by varying words and phrases. His laughter was high, country, and natural, but his usual mood was serious and pensive. At these times he would stroke the constant precursor of a moustache, with his head bent slightly to one side, eyes downcast, looking only at his thoughts.

Refreshing blues, browns, and greens of High Point had become the cramped grays of Philadelphia. Red clay soil that stuck to shoes were now slabs of unyielding concrete. The graceful, downward curve of Underhill St. was now the cold straightness of monotonous city blocks. There were no longer any upstairs, backyards, or even soft beds. Instead, there was only an apartment with a kitchen, and a bigger room where Mary, Aunt Betty, John and his mother lived. The bathroom was down the hall. A partition divided the apartment, leaving a small narrow space for John, with a cot to sleep on, a record player, and only one picture — that of Charlie Parker.

The apartment was at 1450 N. 12th Street between Jefferson and Masters Streets. Directly below there was a radio shop owned by a Black man named Tyfer, for whom Mary worked as secretary. John's mother worked away from home during the week as a domestic. She would return on Saturdays to be with her family, and to attend Sunday services at the storefront church down the block. Aunt Betty stayed home to do the cooking. John practiced all day and into the night. He had learned to make his night practice compatible with those who wanted to sleep, by moving the keys while not blowing into the instrument. Even though no notes emerged, he could hear them in his mind. He became so good at this that the sound of the pads clamping made their own music.

Mrs. Coltrane devoted herself to her son, working so that he could practice and helping by not interfering. Her friends would ask, "Why don't you make that big boy go to work?" Aunt Betty would protest against John and his friends doing nothing but practicing, "Make them gigolos go to work. All they do is blow them horns all day!" Sometimes, even Mary would agree with her mother. John wouldn't say a word. His mother would gently answer, "Leave John alone. Let him stick to his music. He'll be alright." He was a soloist with the Joe Webb band, featuring the blues singer, Big Maybelle, when one of his friends-to-be, Calvin Massey, came into town.

Calvin was a trumpet player who at age 17 left home and studies at the Pittsburg Institute of Music, to travel with a band. After being stranded several times, playing in other bands, and hustling white folks when times got lean, he came to Philadelphia looking for his father, whom he had never seen. His parents had separated when he was only six months old.

On one bright summer day Calvin was walking down South Broad St. with all he had, a brown pin-striped suit, camel-hair beret, a trumpet, and five pennies. Suddenly, the leaping sound of an alto saxophone stopped him in his tracks. Astonished he said to himself, "I know Charlie Parker's in New York. Who in the fuck could that be!" He followed the sound, down some dungeon dark steps into a well lit ballroom, where a band was rehearsing. Calvin stood motionless while John finished his solo. The audience applauded wildly, but John only walked quietly back to his seat. The loud applause, contrasted against John's humble acceptance, was too much for Calvin, who had to shout, "God damn, that's a bad motherfucker!" Joe Webb, the bandleader, turned around and noticed the trumpet under Calvin's arm. Webb, thinking of the band trumpet player who was misreading his part, stepped down and asked Calvin to play a piece of music. After playing he was hired in the time it took to walk to the bandstand, and the former trumpet player to step out of his seat. Calvin, now sitting right behind John, couldn't take his eyes off him. "Look at this nigger. I bet this nigger get high playin' like that. Ain't no mother fucker gonna play sober like that!"

After rehearsal he followed him like a puppy following his master, asking questions as John walked ahead.

> "What's your name, man?"

> "John Coltrane."

> "Coltrane? What in the fuck you get a
> name like that? Damn! I know you gonna
> make some money with a name like that —
> Coltrane!"

John didn't wince a smile and as usual was very serious. Calvin persisted.

> "Man you get high? You smoke reefer?"

> "No."

> "You use cocaine?"

> "No."

> "You use a little heroin?"

> "No."

> "You don't do nothin'?"

> "No, I don't do nothin'."

> "Well, how can you play like that?"

Trying to get rid of him, John kept walking ahead. Calvin followed onto the streetcar which he could afford now, since Joe Webb had given him a two dollar advance. Finally he said the one thing that would make John stop — that he had met Bird. John opened up, relaxed, though not completely. Calvin followed into his apartment. They sat and talked — about music, Bird — and John finally felt comfortable around this man, who only a few minutes ago had been a nuisance.

As they talked, Calvin noticed the sparse furnishings, narrow cot, and flimsy partition. John surprised him when he offered to share his apartment, since Calvin had no place to sleep.

> "Well, man, uh, God damn. How we gonna

> do that, man? Man, you ain't got nothin'.
> How we gonna sleep?"

> "Man, we'll take turns . . . "

Calvin interrupted,

> "How we gonna do that? I can't
> sleep with the women! You ain't
> got nothin' but a cot, man."

> "We'll take turns. I can practice
> some while you sleep. Then you can
> practice while I sleep."

> "Well, man, I can't do you nothin'.
> Shit, it's better than walkin' the
> streets all night. Solid! But I'll
> tell you what you do. You sleep in
> the bed and I'll sleep in the chair."

They became good friends as Calvin's body adjusted each night to the unyielding chair. John came to call him "Folks," after Calvin's mother's maiden name. John preferred "Folks," possibly because of its quick "down home" sound, and he was always playing with words.

When the Joe Webb band went on the road it traveled by sleeper bus, in which the seats could be unfolded into beds at night. John and Folks shared one of these beds. As the bus rambled along, a kerosene stove played teasingly from side to side, making everyone afraid it would tip over one night and burn them up. By its menacing light Folks would think how John was so much like Bird, full of warmth, openness, and spirituality. He would say to himself, "I'm sleeping beside a great man someday." When they arrived in Albany, Ga., Folks told John, "Man, I'm going back home. I'm going back to Philly and see if I can find my father. I'm tired of this shit." Joe Webb and Folks had been arguing. John pleaded with him, "Don't go, Folks. Man, don't go now. We're going to New Orleans for three weeks and make some money."

Calvin: "Man, loan me seven dollars. I'm seven dollars
            short on my train fare. I'll give it to you
            when you come home."

John: "Man, you ain't makin' sense to leave the band
            now. The other cats are going to be making

$75.00 a week when they get to New Orleans.
You and I and the other featured guy are going
to be making 90. Man, we gonna make some money,
don't leave now!"

"Naw, I'm going back."

"Okay, here's seven dollars."

This was the first of many times that Folks would borrow money from John.

After Joe Webb, John played with King Kolax. Around 1947 he had an opportunity to play with the well known Eddie "Cleanhead" Vinson, who sang the big hit, "Kidney Stew Blues." Vinson played alto in a coarse, strong blues style.

The only obstacle to John's joining the band was that Vinson wanted a tenor, not an alto saxophonist. John protested mildly that he was an altoist but easily made the change. The switch to tenor may have been welcome since he was dissatisfied with his playing, even though the other musicians felt he was good enough to be a major figure. To him it seemed impossible to keep up with Bird. Bird was playing so much harmonically, melodically — in every way. On tenor Vinson thought he was good, but John felt he had much to learn. Sometimes he would play very little, making it necessary for Vinson to play most of the night. Vinson would ask, "Man, why don't you play?" John answered, "I just want to hear you play." Most times though, John would play all he could, because he enjoyed creating so much. Vinson noticed that John was searching, changing his style frequently.

The change to tenor opened a world of emotions. " . . . When I bought a tenor to go with Eddie Vinson's band a wider area of listening opened up for me. I found I was able to be more varied in my musical interests. On alto Bird had been my whole influence but on tenor I found there was no one man whose ideas were so dominant as Charlie's on alto. Therefore, I drew from all the men I heard during this period. I have listened to almost all the good tenor men, beginning with Lester, and believe me, I've picked up something from all of them, including several who haven't recorded.

"The reason I liked Lester so much was that I could feel that line, that simplicity. My phrasing was very much in Lester's vein at this time.

"I found out about Coleman Hawkins after I learned of Lester. There were a lot of things that Hawkins was doing that I knew I'd have to learn somewhere along the line. I felt the same way about Ben Webster. There were many things Hawk, Ben and Tab Smith were doing in the forties that I didn't understand but I felt emotionally.

"The first time I heard Hawk I was fascinated by his arpeggios and the way he played. I got a copy of his *Body and Soul* and listened real hard to what he was doing. And even though I dug Pres, as I grew musically I appreciated Hawk more and more."[16]

John learned much from Jimmy Oliver, one of the men who had never recorded. Oliver was one of the foremost tenors in Philadelphia. John and his friends would listen to him at the Downbeat club or the Woodbind club, an after hours place, about one-half block from John's apartment. Both were places where musicians would congregate and have jam sessions.

John may have been interested in Jimmy's playing for at least three reasons. One was that Jimmy was influenced by Lester Young and John could hear that same simplicity and phrasing. There was also Jimmy's ability to construct highly creative solos in which florid images resided about his horn. Then there was the mastery he had of the tenor. He could play anything he thought of. John would sit in with him on stage or listen intently from the audience.

Jimmy also liked John's approach to playing and they became good friends, each respecting the other's ability. Once at John's apartment Jimmy told him, " . . . I think there's something at the top of these horns." He was speaking of playing a higher sound on the saxophone, which would later become a characteristic feature of John's playing.

In 1947 John met Miles Davis, then twenty-one years old. Davis had worked with Charlie Parker, Coleman Hawkins and another saxophonist, Benny Carter. John and Miles played a few times at the Audubon Ballroom in New York City. Sonny Rollins, just graduated from high school, was also in the group. John could see that Miles was working on a new concept in music and that he would one day like to play permanently with him.

After four years in Philadelphia John was firmly into a new phase of his life. The presentation of several elements would take him in directions which would have been less likely, had he remained in Highpoint. He made new friends and played with a number of blues-oriented bands around the country. Graduation from music school did not finish his education. There was much to learn from the legacy of Bird, Hawk, Pres, Dizzy and others. Through these men, through playing in blues bands, through gospel, jazz and blues he heard in High Point, he was further informed of the blood line of his people. From these experiences in Philadelphia time continued to weave the tapestry of his life, sewing strands of happiness or destruction.

V

Crystal Daggers

In the Philadelphia of 1948, unique musical forces were flourishing. This fertile environment provided valuable training for young musicians. There was also a prevailing attitude of mutual encouragement. Established musicians such as Bill Baron or Jimmy Oliver mingled freely with the younger ones and willingly offered advice or even regular instruction. Standards were high. To jam with the Philadelphia musicians, you'd better be capable.

It was also possible for a musician to earn a reasonable living in Philadelphia. Not only could he play the music of his own culture but there were jobs playing music of other ethnic groups as well. Clubs to play in were popping up all over. The cocktail lounge format of previous years had been abandoned. Now customers were sold alcohol or food·and listened to music, rather than talking over it. Many of these clubs were Black-owned and in the Black community. The new music associated with Bird and Dizzy was on most radio stations, indicating wide though belated popularity.

The most ardent champions of the new music were the young musicians. Many members of this group were in the band of alto saxophonist, Jimmy Heath. This band included Calvin Massey, Bill Massey, John Drew, and Johnny Coles on trumpets, James Foreman on piano, Specs Wright on drums, Willie Dennis, trombone; Nelson Boyd, bass; Johnny Ace on a variety of instruments; Benny Golson, tenor saxophone; and John Coltrane on alto saxophone. The band made only a few club dates. Most of its time was spent rehearsing and keeping abreast of recent developments in the music. Jimmy Heath did most of the writing for the band but often another band member would bring one of his own compositions to rehearsal. John once did an arrangement of "Lover Man" which had a beautiful counter-melody. The band liked it so much they encouraged him to write more. But John would say that he had little time for writing, and would rather concentrate on playing. When Jimmy and John practiced, John would write sketches of the melodic ideas that he came across while playing. At this time their playing was so similar that they would jokingly ask themselves, "who's imitating whom?" John spoke of this period: "I had met Jimmy Heath, who, besides being a wonderful saxophonist, understood a lot about musical construction. We were very much alike in our feeling, phrasing, and a whole lot of ways. Our musical appetites were the same. We used to practice together, and he would write out some of the things we were interested in. We would take things from records and digest them. In this way we learned about techniques being used by writers and arrangers.

"Another friend and I learned together in Philly — Calvin Massey, a trumpeter and composer — his musical ideas and mine often ran parallel, and we've collaborated quite often. We helped each other advance musically by exchanging knowledge and ideas."[1]

Bill Massey, Calvin "Folks" Massey, and a baritone player named Stewart frequently practiced with John at his apartment. They admired him to the point of being defensive. Folks began calling one local musician "skunk" because he felt that he wouldn't let John solo enough.

John and his friends practiced for hours. They would make frequent trips to the library to read books on music or other subjects. They would also listen to those European composers whose music was rhythmically involved like Bartok or Stravinsky, and Folks would steal the scores.

. One day Folks ran to John's apartment with a stolen copy of Stravinsky's *Firebird Suite*. In reading it they came across many interesting musical concepts, one of which was the use of the double diminished scale.[2] When played, the scale may give a feeling of falling uncontrollably downward. John played the scale backwards, forward, testing numerous variations. He added it to his growing body of ideas.

John and Folks enjoyed themselves listening to Charlie Parker records and Sarah Vaughn or "Sassy" dramatically singing "You're

Blase" and "Time After Time." Folks' mother became so peeved at all the attention he was giving John, that she told her son, "You always got your nose stuck up John Coltrane's asshole." Nevertheless, they continued doing things together like going to Mom's church, listening carefully as the minister rared back, shouting "aaAAA MEN!", then going back home and trying to imitate it by singing a chord. They had fun together, but not by attending parties, dances, baseball games, movies, or other social events. They were too deeply engrossed in music for this.

One reason that Folks, Bill, Stewart and others stayed close to John was his constant warmth and relaxed openness. A story about the Jimmy Heath band shows this.

Howard McGhee, a trumpet player, took over the band because he had a bigger name than Jimmy. This enabled the band to get more lucrative work. They got a job at the Apollo Theater in Harlem but one trumpet player had to stay behind. Folks made all the rehearsals and was eager to get paid for the Harlem job so he could buy a winter coat. He was disappointed when Jimmy picked John Drew. It may have been that Jimmy felt that Drew was a better trumpet player, but Folks felt that Drew couldn't blow his nose, much less a trumpet, and was selected because his father supplied money for the bandstands and uniforms. He cried, went to John, who embraced him saying, "Folks, it'll be alright. You get some money and come to New York 'cause we'll have a whole house to rent and you can eat there. Write me and I'll send you bus fare." Folks felt better but stayed anyway since the others would be playing and he wouldn't.

After the Apollo engagement John received what was probably his first public notice. The brief story appeared, most likely, in the Philadelphia Tribune, in the late 40's.

> Had a long and interesting conversation with North Philly's John (The Train) Coltrain, the also ace of the former Jimmy [sic] · Heath band, which is now being fronted by Howard McGee. Tells me that gig at New York's Apollo was really a gone thing. Said they will lay "dead" awhile, then might take a trip to Detroit.
>
> This week's treat' column is quite short due to the fact that one of my very close friends has passed away, and the same has taken away all the gump in your man. So with that I say next week when "Round Midnight" really dresses up with oceans of news of your favorite music persons, and loads of pictures.
>
> So till next Tues.
>
> Your man, Squire

However, all wasn't progress for John during this time. Thousands of tiny crystal daggers pierced him invisibly, camouflaged by the brightness of day. Around this time John began using drugs. Aunt Betty, who was home more, kept it from his mother. Drug use was prevalent among musicians of this era. In the thirties "gin and weed" were the vices. Now the more debilitating heroin had taken hold. Narcotics were a pervasive part of the musician's environment, and more than one friend or acquaintance would suggest it. Strangely, it could always be found in the Black neighborhood. If a white musician wanted drugs, he would have to ask a Black musician to get it for him.

There would always be someone offering a musician "free trips" the first few times. It would make you feel good, and put you in a state of euphoria. One forgot about the outside pressures and, if you were a musician, you could concentrate on developing your technical skill and hearing the music — at first. Then you concentrated on finding drugs.

Financial conditions were far from ideal. Only a handful of Black innovators received adequate publicity. Through 1950 *Down Beat* had few pictures of Bird and even fewer articles. Monk, Kenny Clarke, Max Roach and many others received meager attention. Only Dizzy Gillespie was well publicized. Writers for *Down Beat* gave grudging acceptance to the new music. Record reviews were usually less than enthusiastic. Studio work in TV and radio, which supported many white musicians well, was scarce for Blacks. You soon learned that talent was not the only qualification for financial success.

Younger musicians emulated the lifestyles of those they admired. The beret, goatee and thick-rimmed glasses of Dizzy Gillespie were in vogue. Some wore crumpled suits thinking it was a new style that Bird had originated. Actually Bird never took time to iron his clothes and often slept in them. They also copied Bird's and other's narcotic addiction. At every opportunity Bird bluntly denounced the use of narcotics though he couldn't save himself. " . . . any musician who says he is playing better either on tea, the needle, or when he's juiced, is a plain straight liar."[4]

John entered a period of depression. He worked in clubs around Philadelphia under a lot of pressure. He wanted people to know through music, what he knew of beauty, excitement and love, so he would play with all sincerity. Instead of audiences or club owners at least listening, they would snarl that it was too "way out." They wanted him to play walking on top of the bar, outside on the sidewalk and HONK. He did it but didn't like to. The first time he almost cried.

He had practiced and studied intensely for hours, more than most musicians. Yet when he went to Greensboro, N.C., and sat in with some musicians, they dreaded to see him come, saying that he couldn't play because they didn't understand what he was doing. John felt it was they who couldn't play. But years of criticism began to erode his confidence. Also it seemed like a dead end street when not even his idols, who were blessed with talent, could get the recognition they deserved. He may have started drugs at the suggestion of a friend. Maybe drugs gave relief to a man who was depressed — temporarily.

Call To Prayer

God is the Most High
I witness that there is none to worship except God
I witness that Muhammed is the Apostle of God
Arise to prayer. Arise to divine service.[5]

Islam was a force which directly opposed the deterioration of the mind and body through either spiritual or physical deterrents. Among musicians the religion began to grow in the mid-forties when Art Blakey, Talib Daoud, Yusef Lateef, Ahmad Jamal, Sahib Shihab and other musicians raised money to bring Moslem teachers of the Ahmediyya movement from Pakistan to the United States to show musicians the way. In the thirties there had been a small group of Moslem musicians, but they did not make as much of an effort to propagate the religion.

Many musicians were searching for a foundation in life. Islam taught that one should keep his body clean and healthy. It elevated the mind from the morass of American oppression and myths about Blacks.

Around 1947 when singer Aliyah Rabia (Dakota Staton) and her husband, drummer Talib Daoud, moved to Philadelphia, the religion began to blossom there. Other groups such as the Moorish-Americans, and Elijah Muhammed's Muslims were also in Philadelphia. But none was as popular among musicians as the Ahmediyya Movement. An advanced piano player, Hassan, was a friend of John's. They would discuss Islam as well as exchange musical ideas. John's exposure to Islam may have played a role in his struggle with drugs.

In Philadelphia, Islam was a positive force, while the Philadelphia police was a negative entity. The police harassed Black people, kicked doors in, early in the morning, presumably in a search for drugs. Then they would tear up the house as badly as any thief. Finding nothing, the attitude was — "It's just another nigger's door." An integrated nightclub audience would be harassed by the police. They would find the slightest excuse to close the establishment down.

Nasseridine, a drummer, loved John. Nasseridine had progressed greatly in the religion, studying it from a theoretical as well as from a spiritual basis. He was advanced musically, spiritually, and intellectually. As he elevated himself in the religion he began to compare the society to what he had learned, and developed a dislike for whites because of the suffering they inflicted upon Black people.

He was a devout Moslem who carried his prayer rug wherever he went, and prayed dutifully five times a day, regardless of where he was. While praying, nothing distracted him. Friends would pass by, and he wouldn't see them, sometimes seeming to look right through them.

One night he stayed up, praying continuously at John's house. The next day on the way to his sister's house he stopped to pray under a tree at 22nd or 25th and Diamond Streets. Two policemen came by and saw him kneeling, nearly motionless. They asked what he was doing. He said nothing and they kept probing. Finally Nasseridine stated, "I would like for you to leave me alone. I'm trying to do what I think is right."

An argument ensued. According to the police, Nasseridine either threatened them with scissors or began throwing rocks. They beat him savagely. He spent four days in the hospital and died on the last day. Nasseridine's loss sent a shudder through the music community. John, who loved Nasseridine, was hurt.

John believed very deeply in the Christian faith as taught in his community in High Point. Christian ideals contrasted strongly with his use of drugs. This conflict between his faith and his actions was prominent in his mind. Islam was another force which John studied and discussed with friends. This contact and involvement with Islam very possibly also pointed up the contradiction between religion and his actions, and added to his general spiritual knowledge. He continued playing with a variety of musicians in a variety of contexts in his climb to . . . .

In 1949 John worked one job with pianist Bud Powell. "It was a dance gig at the Audubon in New York. Sonny Rollins and Art Blakey (drums) were with him. Bud was really playing, so was Sonny. Those guys you can really call great."[6]

In late 1949 John and Jimmy Heath joined Dizzy Gillespie's band as alto saxophonists. When he wasn't performing John practiced tenor while traveling from job to job.

John made his first appearance on records with this band. The recording session took place on November 21, 1949, in New York on the Capitol label. Two other recording sessions took place before John left the group in 1952. The music on these three dates consisted of Latin-American music, originating from Cuba, combined with the African-American concept of the 1940's.

In Pittsburgh, the band was playing an arrangement of "Minor Walk." Dizzy was in front of the band, pleasing the audience with his showmanship, when John charged into a solo. Dizzy snapped around and stood with his mouth hanging open, as if hearing something he had never heard before. That was only one of several nights that John took over.

Jimmy and John would listen to tenor saxophonists like Dexter Gordon, who had a high, exciting tone, and Wardell Gray, whose tone was deeper and who had the ability to unfurl phrases of great strength and creativity. They also admired the wild innovation of fellow band member, Paul Gonsalves. But it was Sonny Stitt who knocked John out. "Sonny's playing sounded like something I would like to do. He sounded like something between Dexter Gordon and Wardell, an outgrowth of both of them. All the time, I thought I had been looking for something and then I heard Sonny and said, 'Damn! There it is! That's it!' "[7] Still, problems mingled with discovery. Narcotics were more of a shackle than a release. Once while on tour with the band John fell unconscious in a hotel room. Jimmy blew desperately into his mouth and revived him. John wanted to stop. His basic personality had not changed. He was still the gentle and sincere man who maintained respect for everyone.

While on the road John, Jimmy, and Specs Wright, the drummer, had no money to buy drugs, so they suffered the agony of withdrawal. The band went to California, where Specs and Jimmy found a pusher and ran back to John.

"C'mon. We found a cat and we gonna cop."

John: "Well, how much is it?"

"Eight dollars."

John: "Man, I think I'm gonna go ahead and cool."

Specs and Jimmy kidded him about being too stingy to cop, or buy more drugs. They laughed, left John, went to the pawn shop, traded their watches, and bought from the pusher.

John struggled with withdrawal symptoms, trying to suppress the desire and pain by playing his instrument. Next he began drinking heavily in an effort to suppress the desire for drugs, reasoning that of the two evils drinking was the lesser. When the band arrived in Canada, Dizzy fired Specs and Jimmy after discovering they were getting high. At the same time John was fired for missing a show after getting drunk. Specs and Jimmy went back to Philadelphia. John asked Dizzy for the job again and stayed with him in a small combo, playing tenor.

This was a time of great inner turmoil for John, not centered, however, around drugs, but around his struggle with the music. "What I didn't know with Diz was that what I had to do was really express myself. I was playing cliches and trying to learn tunes that were hip, so I could play with guys who played them."[8]

After his tenure with this band John returned to Philadelphia. There he played with many bands of variable quality. He and bassist Jymie Merrit played polka music in upstate New York. He took another job with a musician named Lonnie Slappery. John continued in a state of depression. "I just took gigs. You didn't have to play anything. The less you played, the better it was."

"Anytime you play your horn, it helps you. If you get down, you can help yourself even in a rock 'n' roll band. But I din't help myself."[9]

Later in 1952 he joined Earl Bostic's band. Bostic was a popular rhythm and blues alto saxophonist who played in a forceful manner. "– I went with Earl Bostic, who I consider a very gifted musician. He showed me a lot of things on my horn. He has fabulous technical facilities on his instrument and knows many a trick."[10]

"I didn't appreciate guys like Bostic at the time because Bird had swayed me so much. After I'd gotten from his spell I began to appreciate them more."[11]

*   *   *

During this period he was gradually moving away from the influence of Bird. " – When I first heard Bird, I wanted to be identified with him – to be consumed by him. But underneath I really wanted to be myself. You can only play so much of another man."[12]

*   *   *

Mayombe — bombe — mayombe
Mayombe — bombe — mayombe
Olasope — bombe — Olasope

The ancestors walk in the land of dreams
They inhabit trees, rivers, and the whirlwinds
Watching the souls of their children
To whom gifts of life are borne

Abruka!!! Swish! Swish!

*   *   *   *

In a dream Charlie Parker visited John telling him gently that there was no longer a need for the alto saxophone. After receiving Bird's guidance, John felt even more encouraged to practice the tenor exclusively.

Time hovered again over the family. Aunt Betty became seriously ill. John left the Earl Bostic band briefly, which was on the road, to donate blood for her. Soon afterwards she died, never having told his mother of his addiction. Aunt Betty was buried in High Point. The band was performing in nearby Winston-Salem, so many of the band members came with John to the funeral. Afterwards the band returned to work.

John recorded twice with Earl Bostic. Both times he played tenor sax exclusively. The first session took place in Cincinnati on April 7, 1952, and the second in Los Angeles on August 15, 1952. It may have been while with the Bostic band that John was stranded in Los Angeles. Eric Dolphy, a musician who would be more prominent in John's later life, got him money to return to Philadelphia.

Later in 1952 John joined the Gay Crosse band, which combined visual showmanship, good musicianship and humor in its performances. Crosse played tenor and sang in a very rhythmic manner. John made one record with the band in Nashville, in late 1952. He played both tenor and alto sax but the instrument he studied most was the tenor.

Playing in rhythm and blues bands raised John's income. He spent money wisely and cautiously. If he could afford only one pair of pants, he would buy only one, but one of the best quality. When friends too often asked for loans, his subtle sense of humor would emerge. Like a deaf mute he handed them a card saying something like,

I am broke. I have no money.
I need a loan. Would you lend me . . . ?

One day John asked Folks to take a walk with him. As the hue of the neighborhood changed, Folks asked, "Man what you doin' way up here in white folk's neighborhood?" John answered, "I want to show you something, man." They walked on and finally reached a row of impressive brown houses across the street from a green-carpeted park. John pointed to one of the houses and asked, "What do you think of this house?"

Folks: "Man, it's .... Beautiful, man!"

John: "I'm gonna buy this for my mother."

Glad tears from Folks' eyes — he grabbed John and hugged him saying, "Good deal, motherfucker!"

When the gig with Crosse ended, John returned to Philadelphia and joined a rhythm and blues group, Daisy Mae and Hepcats. John enjoyed working in this group, because all the musicians could play well. However, in many of the other groups with which he played, the musicians were not so good, and he would have to perform stunts, which he considered unnaturally derived from the music. He would have to wear uniforms, do dance routines, sing or jump up at certain points in the music. During these early 50's he played short engagements with local groups, among them Bullmoose Jackson's rhythm and blues band. He also spent time with friends.

Jackie was John's girl and Carol was Jimmie Heath's.[13] The four of them would go out together. Roy Haynes, a drummer who had played on a permanent basis with Lester Young and Charlie Parker, would also see Jackie when he came through Philly. He and John would see each other and talk amiably about the women they were both dating.

Around 1954 John began seeing more of his old friend, Folks. They hadn't seen much of each other since 1950 when Folks became part of Billy Holiday's group and John was traveling with Dizzy. When home, they ate, practiced and joked together as before. Folks was married and John had a fiancee who was orthodox Moslem. Her religious name was Naima and her western name, Juanita, which John shortened to Nita or Neet.

When Folks had his first child, a baby girl named India, John came to his house with a red rattle for her. They left the house to celebrate, buying some wine and beer on the way to Nita's house. Folks had a cigarette but no matches, so they stopped at a corner to ask a fellow for one. As soon as they stopped, the police swarmed over them and put them all in jail. The charge was "corner lounging," or in other words, standing on the corner. They were in a hot cell with six other Black men and nervous because they had never been in jail before. One man named Caesar helped break the tension. He was boasting in a loud but imploring voice about what he was going to do. "I'm getting out of here — tonight! I know one thing, my chick's out there. My woman's gonna bring my five-hundred dollars down here."

John spoke in his usual even manner with no expression on his face, "Well, I know right now buddy, all you got is an asshole full of jail."

VI

Crystal Tapestry

Limiting, limited, limitless, limit
Layed laughing lowly
As the grains of life swirled

> Slowly
> Down
> the
> Hourglass
> World

crystal daggers
into
crystal tapestry

Naima

She's as beautiful as the name. Say it again slowly. Na-ee-ma, delicate, soft, complex sounds said so effortlessly. A dark, natural, slender woman, her deep set eyes transfer an inquisitiveness and interest that open you up, to talk about who cares what subject. There is an almost indiscernible nodding of the head when she talks, which is even less noticeable when she listens — and she always listens. You also begin to listen. When is the last time you listened to someone? Try it, and they may in turn listen to you.

She first heard of John when a friend, who was a tenor saxophonist, asked her to go with him to hear John Coltrane. After hearing the name she wondered out loud, "Who is that? What kind of name is that?"

Three years later in 1954 she found out. There was a gathering of friends at bassist Steve Davis' house when John just happened to walk in, in his customary way, wearing a sheer shirt, with no undershirt and no socks on. One of the girls teased, "You don't have any socks on yet?" Everyone looked down at his feet and cracked up. To Naima he was so funny, walking in all bold and everything, with his clothing all loose.

Naima's first impression was that of a friendly, likable, boyish, plump man, flopping around in his soft shoes, who radiated something uplifting as he talked — like having a wide field suddenly open before you and being swept into it happily.

John and Naima had to go the same way home, so they walked together unaware of time and talking about everything — people, religion, family, music. John told her he was shy and, "I can't talk to a lot of people."

Naima answered, "You're not shy to me. You talk plenty."

It was a hot, humid night in July, so they walked to the park to cool off. The park was even more uncomfortable. They left the park and even though home for them was only ten to fifteen blocks away they spent the whole night walking and talking. John spoke so fondly of his family, especially cousin Mary and his mother, that one of the first things Naima wanted to do was to meet them. This was the greatest gesture he could make toward her, greater than an expensive present or a fabulous night on the town, because he valued the warm relationship with his family so highly, and she was a kindred spirit.

When Nita met John's mother and cousin Mary she was immediately struck by their family pride. She noticed how well he treated his mother and reasoned that a man who treats his mother well would also be good to his wife. The fact that she was 26 when they met (John was 27 going on 28) gave her the advantage of having experienced the faults of other men. She contrasted them with John and quickly appreciated the kindness and depth that she saw in him. They could talk for hours together, naturally, effortlessly, about any subject. Once she showed him an advertisement for hairstyles. The models were white with straight hair. Nita asked which one he liked, and he answered, "I don't like white women."

She explained, "I wasn't asking about the women. I asked about the hairstyles."

On another occasion he asked what she thought of a musician who also wanted to be a Christian. This question revealed his conflict between the attitudes in High Point, where jazz was seen as something opposed to religion, and his desire to play music. Nita answered that she saw no conflict between being a Christian and the music because the music was of a different nature than the bars it had to be played in.

He talked about his problem with drugs saying how drugs helped him get over the nervousness he felt whenever beginning a new engagement. He explained that he was struggling to stop the habit and told of his discouragement with trying to make a living as a musician, playing music that was genuine and sincere.

In the same year that he met Naima John joined his childhood idol, the alto saxophonist Johnny Hodges. While with this band he learned more of musicians from previous generations. The music was well up to his standards of sincerity. "We played honest music in this band. It was my education to the older generation.[1] I really enjoyed that job. I liked every tune in the book. Nothing was superficial. It all had meaning and it all swung. And the confidence with which Rabbit (Hodges' nickname) plays! I wish I could play with the confidence he does. But besides enjoying my stay with Johnny musically, I also enjoyed it because I was getting first hand information about things that happened way before my time. Take Art Tatum for instance. When I was coming up the musicians I ran around with were listening to Bud Powell, and I didn't listen too much to Tatum. That is, until one night I happened to run into him in Cleveland. There were Art and Slam Stewart, and Oscar Peterson, and Ray Brown at a private session in some lady's attic. They played from 2:30 in the morning to 8:30 — just whatever they felt like playing. I've never heard so much music. Yes, there's a lot to learn from the past."[2]

On August 5th, 1954, in Los Angeles, he played tenor saxophone with the Hodges band in a recording session. Others on the date were: Hodges, alto sax; Harold Baker, trumpet; Lawrence Brown, trombone;

Cal Cobbs, piano; John Williams, bass; and Louis Bellson, drums. Song titles were: *Burgundy Walk, Sunny Side of the Street, Sweet as Bear Meat, Used to Be Duke, All of Me*, and *Skokiaan*.

In *Down Beat* magazine Nat Hentoff reviewed *Burgundy Walk*. Giving it a rating of four of a possible five stars he wrote:

> "An easy-rocking two-sided blues with generous choruses from the Rabbit, Harold (Shorty) Baker, and Lawrence Brown, all held together by overly familiar but rollingly moving ensemble riffs. Also on hand are tenor Johnny Coltrane, pianist Cal Cobbs, bassist John Williams, and as a special added starter, Louis Bellson on drums. A good time was had by all."[3]

After working with Hodges a total of six or seven months, John returned to Philadelphia, where he worked brief engagements with a variety of local bands. Again he had to face the gimmicks that some groups required. However, something of benefit may have derived from one gig he disliked. This job was with an organ player. John would improvise from the higher intervals of chords that the organ played. This was the only way he was able to obtain pleasure from the music and remain compatible with the scream of the organ. This adjustment may have been a step toward the high sound he developed on his horn. Other contributing factors may have been his prior experience on the higher pitched alto saxophone, hearing Dexter Gordon whose tone was high, and listening to the comments of Jimmy Oliver on the possibilities within the high register. John may have developed the tone independently of these influences. Basically, there was an innate quality which made him naturally seek or "hear" a high sound.

In the early and middle fifties there were numerous clubs for musicians to perform in, who played in the tradition of Charlie Parker. Many of these clubs stretched along Colombia Avenue: among them were Spider Kelly's, Zanzibar, the Web, Downbeat, Cafe Society, and the Crystal Bar. Around 52nd St. and Market there were clubs such as The Red Rooster or 421. Smaller clubs that usually had music only three days a week and were situated on a corner were called "corner bars."

In this wide variety of clubs the foremost local musicians stood tall — John Coltrane, Jimmy Oliver, Clifford Brown, Red Garland, Richie Powell, Bill Barron, James Golden, Jymie Merritt, among many others. Bill Barron and Jimmy Oliver were the primary sources of the "Philadelphia Sound" which was a certain way of playing saxophone.

This manner of playing probably contributed to John's style.

At the Woodbind club John met Odean Pope, a 16-year-old tenor saxophonist who was seeking a musical direction. Odean soon learned that John would rarely initiate a conversation, but when asked questions, a fountain of words would flow. John spoke to him of his involvement with changes, and methods of constructing a solo. He told Odean that two of his favorite songs were *Come Rain or Come Shine* and *Lush Life*. He explained to Odean that he liked to sing through his instrument and that it was valuable to listen to good singers like Billy Eckstine or Sarah Vaughn. If one could duplicate their phrasing, emotional effects, and human quality, or just think of singing while playing, it would be easier to move an audience. The relationship which John felt between his playing and the human voice parallels the similar insights of Lester Young, the blues musicians, and indeed, goes back to the first masters of African music.

Though already highly original and much praised by the musicians John continued searching. He was constantly studying music books, one of which was the *International Thesaurus of Scales and Melodic Patterns* by Nicolas Slonimsky. This book contained numerous ways of arranging sequences of notes with different rhythms, mixtures of sequences, and many variations. He experimented with improvising on the unusual intervals of a chord. He had an analytical mind which would take concepts such as one of the sequences or scales in the Thesaurus and play it several different ways. While the search continued John faced grave frustrations. More than once he left the bandstand crying, after trying desperately to reach what he wanted to hear. Drinking plagued his life. Sometimes other musicians would have to help him to the stage. Once he was so drunk that he appeared on stage with his shirt on backwards. But no matter how drunk he was he could always play with great fervor. In spite of John's dissatisfaction with his own playing he was in constant demand by many groups, both local and from out of town. He preferred to free-lance so that he could have more time for study.

He worked with a conga player named Bill Carney. This job was satisfying creatively for the musicians but for audiences John commented, "We were too musical for certain rooms."[4] He worked with other groups such as that of organist Shirley Scott.

Within John there existed the constant contradiction between his genius and the chains which kept that genius from its full expression. He was a powerfully built man who didn't project aggressiveness as did other men his size. His outward appearance was always calm. His problems he kept to himself and rarely discussed them even with his closest friends. His ups and his downs stemmed solely from his music, not from being sick from alcohol or drugs. He studied and practiced constantly, searching for something. His desire was to please people and make them happy through music, but not through the conventional routes. The vision he saw would give greater happiness and more deeply felt emotions than any of the conventional forms alone could produce. By this time he had been informed of his heritage in music and appreciated the contributions of his predecessors. He and Naima drew closer together.

But 1955 was marred by the death of Charlie Parker who still had not received the recognition he deserved. Wardell Gray also died that year in Las Vegas, under suspicious circumstances. These men were more than distant idols with whom the musicians had little personal contact. Many had played with them in jam sessions, and lent them their horns if necessary. Wardell and Bird were only five and six years older respectively than John. Even those who had little personal contact felt the loss. Musicians didn't have to know each other to communicate. They can love each other without saying a word — except through their instruments.

Late in 1955 John joined Jimmy Smith for a two-week engagement at Spider Kelly's. He was crazy about working with Smith. "Wow, I'd wake up in the middle of the night and hear that organ! Those chords screaming at me."[5]

After one performance, someone from the audience commented on his high tone. "You sound like another notch on that organ."

Smith asked John to join him on a permanent basis. Working with him would have provided a steady income since Smith had a long list of bookings. But at the same time, a drummer from Philadelphia, "Philly" Joe Jones had recommended John to Miles Davis, who was organizing a new band. Philly Joe called John to tell him that Miles wanted him to join the group. He decided to go with Miles, but always careful in making decisions, he weighed and balanced the advantages of both opportunities he now had. In this balancing process he would often ask the opinions of his friends. He told Neet, "Miles Davis asked me to go with him," and asked for her thoughts. Nita, who felt that John actually had already made up his mind, said that the organ was more dominating and that John would have a better opportunity to get his message out with Miles. He called Odean Pope and asked him to substitute for him, during the last week of the engagement with Jimmy Smith, which Odean did.

The following day, Philly Joe called John to make a date with the band in Baltimore the next day. Never before had they played together, but on opening night a musical telepathy prevailed that fused each member with the whole. This was an important week for another reason. Naima came to Baltimore on the weekend. She and John were married there in a simple ceremony on October 3, 1955. After the Baltimore engagement, the group went to Detroit. Nita and John's new step-daughter Saida, nicknamed Tony, stayed in Philadelphia where they moved in with John's mother and cousin Mary.

The Miles Davis Quintet was on its way to becoming one of the most influential groups of the 50's. Its members were Miles on trumpet, John on tenor, "Philly" Joe Jones, drums (at times substituted by Arthur Taylor), Red Garland on piano and Paul Chambers, only 19 years old, on bass. Some listeners observed the closeness of this band's birth to Bird's death. They considered the Miles Davis Quintet to be the new standard bearer of the music.

There was no rigid format for the group. It functioned instead through the medium of each other's feelings. During the group's existence there were few rehearsals. Most of the learning was done on the bandstand. If a piece were performed exceptionally well, Miles would say, "Okay, that was good. Now you play it just like that tomorrow." Rather than restrict the musicians, Miles encouraged them to explore. John learned much from him. Still very self-critical, he spoke of his attitude on joining the group. "I began trying to add to what I was playing because of Miles' group. Being there, I just couldn't be satisfied any longer with what I was doing. The standards were so high, and I felt I wasn't really contributing like I should."[7] This contrasted with the opinions of other members of the group who had much admiration for his contribution.

The first recording session of the group took place on October 27, 1955. The album was entitled, "The New Miles Davis Quintet" and had the selections: *Stablemates, How Am I to Know?, Just Squeeze Me, Miles' Theme (The Theme), S'posin'*, all on the Prestige label. Two other tunes recorded that day were on Columbia, *Budo* and *Ah-leu-cha*. After this album John recorded prolifically. His compositions also began appearing more frequently on recordings.

Next, with pianist Elmo Hope as leader, John recorded on May 7th, 1956. Personnel were: John Coltrane (tenor sax), Elmo Hope (piano);

Donald Bird (trumpet); Hank Mobley (tenor sax); Paul Chambers (bass); and Philly Joe Jones (drums). Selections, all on the Prestige label, were: *Avalon, On It, Polka dots and Moonbeams*, and,

Weejah

Force, Force, Force, Uhh!!
Horn awakens shocks soul inward to itself
and sweeps it uhh!! each stage higher
by jolts, jolts uhh!! spit out spit out
Five notes in the time of one, one note like it
oughta be Five. EeeeeeFabalabudabah singed
Quiet is shattered, inverted whirlwinds twist your
essence to gripped Fury Drop to your knees

Part of Coltrane solo

About two weeks later on May 24, 1956, John was in New York City riding to a record date with the members of the Miles Davis rhythm section. Sonny Rollins, the leader on the date, wanted to use Philly Joe, Red Garland, and Paul Chambers. John fell asleep in the parked car while they were in the recording studio. Shortly, someone awoke him and asked if he wanted to play on one selection with Sonny. To this John readily agreed. This was how the title song for the album, *Tenor Madness*, came about in which John and Sonny exchanged solos that were filled with ideas. Many listeners considered it a "battle of the tenors" and felt that John had gotten the upper hand over Sonny, who was the most renowned tenor at the time.

The first album with Miles Davis, *New Miles Davis Quintet* was reviewed in the May 16, 1956, issue of *Down Beat* magazine. *Budo* and *Ah-leu-cha* were the only tunes recorded that day, that were not on the album which was released to the public. Hentoff gave the record a rating of four instead of the maximum five stars solely because of his dislike for John's contribution. The other members of the band received rave reviews,

Miles Davis

" . . . in wonderfully cohesive form here, blowing with characteristically personal, eggshell tone, muted on the standards, open on the originals."

Red Garland

" . . . plays some of his best choruses on record here."

Paul Chambers

" . . . lays down support that could carry an army band."

Philly Joe Jones
" . . . pulsatingly crisp as usual . . . "

John
"Coltrane as Ira Gitler notes accurately, . . . is a mixture of Dexter Gordon, Sonny Rollins, and Sonny Stitt. But so far there's very little Coltrane. His general lack of individuality lowers the rating."[8]

Hentoff's statement represented much of the contemporary critical opinion. However, being in the Miles Davis group gave John wide exposure. Many musicians were struck by his harmonic and rhythmic conception. He improvised on unusual intervals of chords, ended his solos in a unique manner, and had a piercing, jolting sound that raised the level of excitement. The exposure was valuable because some musicians and many audiences were not accustomed to such a different approach to music. When individuals first heard this approach they would often reject it. But after repeated hearings they would become almost obsessed with his music. In these early stages there was severe criticism. Many said he wasn't playing anything, or that he played too many notes. In Philadelphia they would say that he was "scribbling" meaning – he was just guessing and didn't really know what he was doing. Then there were those who understood his message right away, and Coltrane for them became one of the most exciting musicians in the country.

Miles would often play only a couple of choruses and leave the bandstand for an hour or more. This gave John even more exposure and he was musically strong enough to lead the group.

As great as the group's impact was, work was sporadic. There were periods of steady work and periods of working one week and being inactive the next three weeks. Out-of-town engagements were often difficult to make when snows were deep. Once John and Paul Chambers, who traveled together, were stranded in Canada, when Miles and Red Garland didn't show up.

Within the band itself all was not well. Most of the band members had a lax attitude towards the group and were dissipating. This caused them to be frequently late or absent, and many engagements were missed. The owner of a major record company had been urged by musicians to sign John. He went to the Cafe Bohemia in New York, but was disappointed when he saw John leaning on the piano, and decided not to give him the contract.

At another time, outside the Cafe Bohemia, a 15-year-old tuba player, Ray Drapper, had come to see the Miles Davis Quintet. He was impressed by everything he saw that night, and made no distinction between the good and the harmful. Since he was under-age for a nightclub, some members of the quintet stashed him in a secluded corner. John came to the bandstand and looked like anything but a musician who was about to play before a packed audience. His horn had rubber bands on it. He looked disheveled, with his shirt collar dirty, buttons missing from his shirt, and his suit dirty and wrinkled. He seemed locked in a struggle, playing only snatches of phrases and spitting out jumbles of notes. There would be long pauses of silence followed by brief spurts of more notes. Miles appeared angry with him.

Ray went downstairs to the basement to talk with the musicians. John was sitting down, sick and uncommunicative. Two members of the quintet ran out to find him some drugs, after which he was a different person, talking and looking much better.

When the band went to St. Louis, Paul Chambers and John stayed in the same hotel room. Having run out of money, they climbed out the window with their belongings to avoid paying. When John returned to Philadelphia, he found that Naima and Saida had moved to New York.

John and Nita had been discussing the move for some time. For John it would be easier to make contacts in New York than in Philadelphia. He tried making New York contacts by asking those he had met there to call him collect. Few calls came. Calls from Philadelphia musicians were numerous. He was popular in that city. However, his friends Jimmy Oliver and Calvin Massey, who had been encouraging him to move to New York, were correct in pointing out that it was there where the record companies, publicity, and important jobs were. Naima also had reasons for gravitating toward New York. When John would make prolonged road trips with the Quintet she would visit Paul Chamber's wife, Annie, in New York. She came to like the city, and decided to move there while John and Paul were in St. Louis.

When John arrived, he questioned the action but did not object. He then broke the bad news to her that he no longer had a job because Miles had disbanded the group. John was optimistic that they could survive in New York regardless, but still had not made up his mind that it was the best thing to do.

It was June, 1956. John was no longer using drugs. He felt that he had conquered the habit physically and mentally. They stayed in one hotel briefly, then moved to another, the Marie Antoinette. There they had only one room, with a sink and a restroom down the hall. In New

York he made contacts easily. Sometimes while just standing outside the musician's union he would meet someone with a job for him. He was always elated about these record dates and would come home telling Nita all about it. But the pay received as a sideman on a record date, about $40 to $80, was not enough to support a family in New York City, or anywhere else for that matter. Unfortunately, in the same hotel there happened to be a "friend" who started him on drugs again. Each time he felt he had stopped for good there had always been such "friends." He was shaken by the fact that he was using drugs again, since this time he had felt strongly that he had overcome. Discouraged, he wanted to quit music, and made an application to the New York Post Office.

But Naima could see that he didn't want to quit. She challenged the decision to get a post office job, "A Post Office job?" John answered, "Yeah, cause things are bad."

In November of the same year the family returned to Philadelphia. Also in November two more reviews of records John had been on appeared in *Down Beat*. The Paul Chambers record with John's composition *John Paul Jones* was given three and one-half stars out of five, by Ralph Gleason.

> "The other tracks all feature Drew's funky deep piano soloing, excellent rhythm from Philly Joe Jones and Chambers and an occasional solo from John Coltrane on tenor. Coltrane sounds best on *Visitations* where his tone and attack are not so freakish. The best side for me was Coltrane's original, *John Paul Jones*, a great swinger and on which Chambers' solo is a gas."[9]

In the same November 14th issue, Nat Hentoff reviewed the Elmo Hope album with *Weejah*, giving it three stars.

> "The two tenors are apostles of the hard-swing, hard-toned approach. The more rewarding of the two appears to be Coltrane who is with the Miles Davis band, and who has improved considerably in the last year. Coltrane has an expansive (albeit hard) breadth of tone and attack, whereas Mobley by contrast rather muffles. Both, however, have yet to obtain a personal conception that is sufficiently arresting as to be immediately self-identifying."[10]

In the December 12th issue Hentoff reviewed *Tenor Madness*.

> "It's this long number that is least effective in the album because of

Coltrane, who appears to be pressing and lacks Sonny's compactness of impact."

After complimenting everyone else on the date, Hentoff ended his article with,

"The *Madness* track mars what would have been an interestingly balanced all-Rollins LP."[11]

Concurrent with the appearance of this criticism, John was continually asked to play on record dates. September 10th the Quintet recorded for Columbia. In this session John took a memorable solo on *Round Midnight*.

Another album under Paul Chambers' name was recorded on September 21, 1956. John had two originals *Just For Love* and one for his wife, *Nita*. In *Nita* at least two characteristics appeared which would be more extensively developed in later compositions. One was the use of a device termed pedal point, which gives the effect of a constantly repeated sound or pulse. The other was the elegant simplicity in the structure of the composition. There was an equal distance between each of the chords. Each chord was separated by an interval or distance called a fourth.

On October 26th the Quintet recorded again on Prestige. The following month pianist and composer Tadd Dameron had John on another Prestige album. One of the compositions was *On A Misty Night* on which John, in the first few notes of his solo, was able to capture the fuzzy coldness of tiny drops of water.

He was appearing on many albums but was personally discouraged with himself. One reason for his continued depression was the fact that he had been with name bands but still received little acceptance and recognition. He received another shock when Miles Davis regrouped and didn't ask him to return. Sonny Rollins was hired instead. Nita tried to bolster his spirits. "Miles Davis' isn't the only group. Get your own group."

One afternoon in army fatigue pants with big pockets, and a short-sleeved shirt with open collar, John went to hear Folks play with his band at the Red Rooster, on 52nd Street. Folks played trumpet, McCoy Tyner was on piano, Clarence "C" Sharpe was on alto saxophone, Jimmy Garrison played bass and Al "Tutti" Heath was on drums. Folks introduced John to McCoy who immediately liked John's pleasant, smiling manner.

Folks also introduced him to the club owner who asked John to play there the following week. John needed a rhythm section, so it was arranged that McCoy, Jimmy Garrison, and "Tutti" Heath would play with him. He also asked a trumpet player, Johnnie Splawn to join. At this time John had stopped using drugs but was drinking heavily. During this week he was confronted with a crucial decision.

The beginning of the week went badly. He wasn't playing with the proficiency of which he was capable. Still McCoy could hear something of value in the high expressive tone and the profound manner in which John approached chords. He knew that there was something unique that was caged in. Wednesday, as John left the bandstand for intermission, Reggie Workman, a young bass player, stated bluntly to him that his music would be much clearer if he kept his body clean, and asked how long he was going to try to play music without cleansing his body. Reggie challenged him with, "You're John Coltrane!" and stated that he was disappointed to see him juicing and so high that he "couldn't get his stuff out."

At the beginning of Reggie's statement John looked down at him, surprised that someone would speak to him in this manner. Then he paused and began to listen carefully. They then sat at a table with Nita and discussed the concepts Reggie had confronted him with. John told him that he agreed with what he said and understood.

The next day, Thursday, the music flowed. He had stopped drinking. On Friday, the music soared, but the effects of alcohol withdrawal began to hamper him. He was up on the stage playing when finally he could no longer find the keys on the saxophone. Abruptly he walked off. Naima, who was sitting at a table asked, "What's the matter?" John answered, "I just can't make it." They left and went home. The musicians who had accompanied him were shocked. They feared that one of them had made a mistake which John found intolerable.

He was very ill at home and unable to finish the engagement. For three days he was tense and quiet, responding only briefly to conversation. Troubled thoughts pressed upon his mind, while outwardly he was completely disengaged. He told Neet that his thoughts were jumbled. Whenever he spoke, the first portion of the sentence would be clear, but the remaining words would only tumble over one another.

Three days passed and he had only partially improved. By this time Nita feared that he would have a nervous breakdown and wanted to get a doctor. But Mary and his mother felt it best to just let him be and to maintain the daily routine as closely as possible, to which Nita agreed. He found strength in God and prayed, cried and asked God to help him. Throughout much of the day he would pray. Folks would come by every day, and Johnny Coles, periodically, to discuss music, music, music. This helped to divert John's mind from his illness. He continued to develop strength until one morning, about two weeks after the ordeal began, he awoke bright and happy in Final Freedom.

"I got it licked! I don't have a desire for liquor anymore. I've got to call my friend Eric and tell him!"

Nita, not knowing that he and Eric had been friends since John was stranded in California, suggested that instead of calling all the way to California why not wait until Eric came to New York? John called anyway, and Eric was ecstatic, "I knew you could do it, man!"

About three days later he awoke and suddenly sat up. Noticing his quietness, his wife asked what the trouble was. He answered, "Neet, I had a dream. I heard this beautiful droning sound. It was so beautiful."

Nita asked what the sound was like, but he couldn't explain it. He went to the piano in an attempt to recreate it. But it was not within the piano's capabilities. This was the beginning of a long search for that sound.

VII

God's Touch

Demons no longer sapped his energy. He could now create freely. He felt that God had touched him and that he had experienced a spiritual awakening. Searching more intensely than before for the "life side of music," he began trying a new approach to chords. "I decided I didn't want to play the way I had been playing anymore. I wanted to unlimit myself some way. I had been playing straight along the chord — I wanted to play on the outside of the chord. In 1957 I was hearing some musicians playing what I wanted to play. It was being done, but I didn't know how to do it. So I decided to find out!"[1]

It is difficult to know exactly what he meant by "outside the chord." He may have meant improvising from chords related to but different from those of a composition. Or he may have meant the extension of phrases in such a way that the end of a phrase would not be determined by the end of the time allotted to a chord. This latter possibility would produce a continuous flow of music.

During this period John and Odean Pope would see each other often in the various Philadelphia clubs. He told Odean that he had asked the Creator to enable him to reach out into the audience and hug them, as he opened his arms wide in an embracing gesture. He felt that through music much could be done if it had the right qualities and goals. He wanted to be able to strengthen people through music. John was very happy. He was writing, researching, and practicing with results that pleased him. To reach his goals he instituted a program of strict discipline with a schedule in which a predetermined amount of time was devoted to specific categories of study. For example, one hour was spent on long tones, one for listening to other musicians, two on chords, two on other aspects of theory. He would emphasize that minimum times should be set in the schedule and, furthermore, that nothing, not even visiting friends, should interrupt. He also told Odean of the value of a tape recorder in practicing. It enabled him to select the one of numerous ways of playing an idea that was closest to what he was trying to reach. With all the progress he was making he was still open to ideas or suggestions. He would inspire younger musicians such as Odean to continue working on a concept, if they really believed in it, no matter what it was. Whenever they presented him an idea with which he disagreed, he wouldn't be able to completely hide his feelings, but always encouraged them to go on, the only requirement being that they believe in it.

Other Philadelphia musicians visited him, such as Hassan, the pianist, with whom he discussed Islam and exchanged musical knowledge, and John Glenn, a tenor saxophonist, who would fix horns for other musicians. Glenn had developed a technique of playing two or three notes simultaneously on the saxophone, and showed John how to do it. John rapidly began practicing the technique to acquire a mastery himself.

John, Folks, and Johnny Coles would still practice together

frequently, going over different chord progressions. John was very involved with a particular progression that would later be used in a number of musical contexts. One day he excitedly told Folks, "Man, I gotta tell you somethin'! Man, I had this dream last night that scared the shit outta me!"

Folks: "Yea, man?"

John: "I dreamt about Bird. I woke up in a sweat."

Folks: "What was the dream?"

John: "Man, I dreamt that Bird came to me and said, 'Keep, keep on those progressions cause that's the right thing to do'."

Folks, now also excited, shouted, "That's it. Do it!"

These progressions in their final development took the form of a formula which would be used to add more chords to music in which there were few. By using this formula he could obtain more color and variety in his improvisation, using a scheme that could easily be remembered on the bandstand or used when sitting down to compose.[2]

In the evenings McCoy Tyner, then only 17, was a frequent visitor at the Coltranes. John would explain to McCoy many of his musical concepts as well as his discovery of the progressions, on which Charlie Parker had told him to continue working.

This was not the only time that John found music in his dreams. Once he was lying on the couch again with his head facing the back while Nita worked in the kitchen. Suddenly he awoke and jumped up to the piano. Nita wondered what had happened but thought it best not to say anything. After finishing John told her, "I'm glad you didn't speak to me because I heard something so beautiful in this dream, and I wanted to catch it before it went away."

She asked, "How did it go?"

"I got part of it."

John was commuting frequently between New York and Philadelphia, recording just as prolifically as he had since 1955. For Prestige on March 22, 1957 he appeared on an album entitled "Interplay For Two Trumpets and Two Tenors" with Webster Young and Idrees Sulieman on trumpets, himself and Bobby Jaspar on tenor saxophones; Mal Waldron, piano; Kenny Burrell, guitar; Paul Chambers, bass; and Arthur Taylor, on drums. On this recording, as well as many others during the fifties, his solos produced a rising spiritual quality of his music. The next business step was for him to obtain a contract and record under his own name. However, the recording industry was not nearly all that was to be desired.

Recording opportunities under contract were scarce and often resulted in compromise. Musicians were often told by a company representative to play whatever was selling at the time. Many musicians refused to record under such circumstances. The economic aspects were less encouraging than the artistic ones. Advances on record sales were very small, usually about three hundred dollars, out of which the leader of the group would sometimes be required to pay the sidemen on a recording session. Sidemen received a meager forty to eighty dollars per record.

Percentage of royalties on record sales were pitifully low, usually 3% but as low as 2% for the uninformed. One was doing well to get 5%. A musician found it difficult to meet living expenses, even on a record that sold well. This was not only because of the low royalty percentages but also because the record company reserved the right to delay distribution of the record for months, or years. There were other insidious practices. Sometimes the cost of the recording session would be charged against the musician's royalty account. Thus, if a record didn't sell well, a musician could end up owing the company money. It was common practice that the musician's compositions would automatically be published by the company. Therefore, any revenue received from playing the record on the air would go to the company, not the artist. An artist could also be cheated out of a portion of his royalties by the company's selling the record abroad where it was easier to disguise the actual number sold. Regardless of the restrictions sometimes, not always, placed upon creativity, and the always exploitative state of the business, a musician relied on record companies to be heard. Hopefully, he would build an audience and reach a better bargaining position. This was the predatory nature of the business when John was offered a contract by Prestige records.

His bargaining position was poor. Prestige was signing many musicians at the time, at rock-bottom prices. There is evidence that Prestige was not very interested in John and that it was only at the urging of another musician, possibly Red Garland, who was a big seller for the company, that he was offered the contract. John asked his friend, Folks, for advice. Folks told him to sign, but with a one-year option to avoid being bound to the company. Probably in late March, 1957 he signed with the option and a $300.00 advance on each album. The fact that John's recordings from this period were labeled with Prestige as the publishing company indicates that his compositions were owned by Prestige. After signing he came home and told Nita, "It's no money. But it's a start."

On one of John's frequent trips to New York, he and Thelonious Monk, the pianist-composer, visited the apartment of the Baroness. The Baroness was a member of the affluent Rothschild family. She possessed a true appreciation and love for music and would come to the aid of musicians whenever misfortune befell them. After a gratifying nightclub performance, the musicians would sometimes want to continue playing. At the Baroness' apartment they could play through the night and have breakfast together the next morning.

While at her apartment John played *Monk's Mood*, one of Monk's compositions. Monk liked his treatment of the piece so well he asked John that day to join his group. When John returned to Philadelphia he told Nita, "Monk wants me to play with him. I don't know if I can do it, but I'm going to try." Being confident of his capabilities, she encouraged him to accept.

On April 12th, 1957, Monk recorded an album originally intended to be composed entirely of solo piano. However, Monk insisted to Orin Keepnews, head of Riverside records, that *Monk's Mood* be included with John accompanying him. Four days later John came from Philadelphia specifically to make the session with Monk. They did four tunes, *Nutty, Trinkle Trinkle, Ruby My Dear,* and *Monk's Mood.* The first three were planned for another album. Immediately after *Monk's Mood* was taped, Keepnews, overwhelmed by John's solo, rushed out of the studio and asked, "What's your recording situation?"

John answered, "I signed with Prestige three weeks ago."

Keepnews: "John, I'm really awful sorry that I didn't get to know you or hear you earlier than this."

John: "No, I wish I had known myself earlier."

April 18th John was a sideman on an album with Kenny Burrell on guitar and Idrees Sulieman on trumpet. April 19th he was a sideman with pianist Mal Waldron and Arthur Taylor on drums. April 20th he recorded again as a sideman with Cecil Payne on baritone sax and Doug Watkins on drums. On this session he contributed one of his compositions, *Mary's Blues*, titled after his cousin, Mary. Completely ignoring the negative criticism John had been receiving, the musicians were eager to have him play with them. The musicians always ignored the critics in forming their opinions of other musicians.

In the April 18th, 1957 issue of *Down Beat* Nat Hentoff reviewed "Tenor Conclave and Mating Call." The "Conclave" album was given four and one-half stars, and the comment,

" . . . Coltrane who has been improving rapidly never has struck me as impressively as he does here."[3]

But "Mating Call" he gave three and one-half stars, writing:

"All six [tunes] are Dameron originals and are, in a sense, the prime virtue of the data . . . [sic]

"Although Coltrane receives most of the solo time, Dameron is heard on each number, and his playing is functionally conceived, harmonically sensitive, and personal . . . Simmons and Jones provide steady anchoring.

"Coltrane, who has become increasingly known as a result of his work with the Miles Davis Quintet, continues to improve, and this record contains some of his best work. As Ira Gitler points up in the informed notes, Coltrane comes in part out of Sonny Stitt and Dexter Gordon, as well as Sonny Rollins. (His fourth favorite is Stan Getz.) Like many disciples of the first three, Coltrane's tone is often strident at the edges and rarely appears able to sustain a legato softness, as Getz can.

"Coltrane has a feeling for variegated moods, but his tone doesn't yet display enough range and control of coloration when he expresses gentler, more complex feelings.

"There is an express power in Coltrane, an anapolegetic projection of spontaneous emotion. And as Ira Gitler says, he is a 'searcher' with often arresting conception.

"Another horn − a gentler trumpeter, say − would have helped complement the not always attractive Coltrane sound and also would have illuminated the originals more fully in what would have been more substantial ensemble passages. But it's an album worth absorbing nonetheless."[4]

Hentoff's statement reveals at least three common failings of critics of Black music and possibly music of any culture. First, there is the arrogance which blinds him to the fact that he has not mastered the saxophone, and therefore is incompetent to make statements like "Coltrane . . . continues to improve." Secondly, he confuses inability with honest differences, writing " . . . Coltrane's tone is often strident at the edges and rarely appears *able* to sustain a legato softness as Getz can." Hentoff seems not to have considered the possibility that each musician may have a particular sound because he likes it, not because he *can't* produce a particular sound. Thirdly, there is bias. Hentoff would like to hear a certain type of "softness" in the record. This is a value judgment which indicates shallow thinking, not unique to Hentoff. He states that "gentler" sounds are more complex and that "power" in Coltrane's playing as "spontaneous emotion" is less complex. Who can say that power is simpler than gentleness? Hentoff seems to have one standard to which he would like every musician to adhere.

In the May 16th issue of *Down Beat*, Ralph Gleason echoed Hentoff's opinion of John's tone in a review of a Miles Davis Quintet album, "Round About Midnight."

> "The break at the end of Davis' statement in *All of You* is as close to a wail as he produces on this album and yet it is a very moving thing. His solos build beautifully to logical climaxes, and Coltrane, who customarily enters after Miles, seems here to have more of the melding of Pres and Hawkins and less of the bad tone which has been his lot up to now."[5]

Gleason's qualifications on Miles' wailing, " . . . as close to a wail as he produces on this album and yet it is a very moving thing," and Hentoff's predilection for a certain type of "softness," bring to mind Barrelhouse Dan writing in 1940 against the use of prominent bass and drums. Each of these objections is against a distinctive aspect of Black music — wails, dynamism and deep sounds with drums. This continuity suggests that a cultural bias is at the foundation of these objections. Another continuity can be found, probably based on what people are accustomed to hearing, in the initial objections to the tone of innovators. Lester Young was condemned for his lighter tone which followed the previously established heavy sound of Coleman Hawkins. Charlie Parker was criticized with the same words, "bad tone," for his sound. John, also, in these early years received loud objections to his sound. Critics would like his tone on some tunes and abhor it on others. This was because he changed his sound to fit various moods. On one composition his tone might be mellow. On another it might be clear and high as if to clean the air and replace impurities with excitement. Audiences' opinions were still divided, ranging from absolute acceptance and pleasure to absolute rejection.

During his stays in New York John would visit Monk. "I'd go by his house and get him out of bed. He'd get up and go over to the piano and start playing. He'd play one of his tunes and he'd look at me. So I'd get my horn out and start trying to find what he was playing. We'd go over and over the thing until we had most of it worked out. If there were any parts that I had a lot of difficulty with he'd get his portfolio out and show me the thing written out. He would rather a guy would learn without reading because you feel it better and quicker that way. Sometimes we'd get just one tune a day.

"When I met him I started hanging around with him because I liked his kind of music. We'd already recorded one song together, *Monk's Mood*. I liked it so well I told him I wanted to learn it, so he invited me around."[6]

On May 30th John moved to New York, leaving Nita and Toni in Philadelphia, to join him later. John stayed at the Alvin Hotel on 52nd Street in Manhattan. May 31st he recorded his first album under his own name. It was titled *The First Train*, and had Johnny Splawn on trumpet; Sahib Shihab, baritone saxophone; Red Garland, piano; Paul Chambers, bass; and Al "Tutti" Heath,[7] on drums. Two of the six selections were John's compositions, *Straight Street* and *Chronic Blues*. Another composition, *Bakai*, was written by Folks. "Bakai" is the Arabic word for "cry," which Folks used as the title in memory of Emmet Till, the 14-year-old boy who was murdered by white men in 1955. Other selections were *Time Was, I Hear A Rhapsody, While My Lady Sleeps* and *Violets For Your Furs*. The last tune was suggested by the head of Prestige, Bob Weinstock. John accepted it because he thought it was beautiful. Weinstock soon realized that when it came to music there was no way to get him to play something he didn't want to. *Straight Street* begins with the baritone, trumpet, and tenor saxophone playing the theme. This theme is in the tradition of Charlie Parker and others in its phrasing, which may resemble the phrasing of the Yoruba language. If written syllables are applied to each distinct sound on the record, the similarity to language can be seen. The sound is deep and resonant.

> Oscoobadobahdeeebaaaa
> Oscoobadobadeebabadobadebadeeee
>   babadee babadeee bababaaap
> Scabadobadabadaaaaa
> Scabadobadabadaaahh
>   Yaaaa bada baaap
>
> Ya da ba waah
> Ya da ba waaah
> Ya da ba waaah
> Ya da ba da waah
> Ya da ba waah
> Waa - da - ba - dwa yaaaa baaaa baaaa daaaa

On a soaring solo John enters with the high tone opening, brief moments of speech, roughness, tenderness — continuous ideas flow, each seemingly begotten of those that came before.

John chose another tune on the record, *While My Lady Sleeps*, because when the hour became late in a nightclub where he was playing, he would look up and see his lady, Nita, asleep.

Wispy strange slow
entertwinings of heated passion
the sounds breathe you
   breathe
   more deeply
     far
       away
        feeling
         a
        SHOUT
        a
      child's cry the trumpet
      joins John
        who disappears
         returns
        bearing a gift
         three notes
           three jewels
        Ruby, Sapphire, and Pearl

In mid-June Monk, with John on saxophone, Shadow Wilson on drums and Wilbur Ware on bass, opened at a converted bar in the Bowery section of New York, The Five Spot. As news of the music that was being made got around, lines began to form outside the club. Monk's debut there firmly established The Five Spot as a prominent nightclub. After soloing Monk had the habit of getting up and dancing around the club to a rhythmic sense that was all his own, and which appeared prominently in his music. The problem was that traditionally the pianist had the important function, when he wasn't soloing, of playing chords of a tune, thereby acting as a map for others in the group. In an interview John was asked how it felt to play while Monk danced. "I felt sort of lonesome, but I would count on the bass player. And with a guy like Wilbur Ware, he's so inventive. He doesn't always play the obvious. He plays the other way sometimes. If you didn't know the tune you wouldn't be able to find it. He's superimposing things, building the tension so that when he comes back to it you feel everything suck in. I knew the changes so we would manage to come out together. It's lots of fun playing that way. Sometimes he would be playing a different set of altered changes from those that I'd be playing and neither of us would be playing the changes to the tune. We would reach a certain spot and if we got there together we'd be lucky, and then Monk would come back in to save everybody. A lot of people used to ask us how we remembered all that stuff, but we weren't remembering so much. Just the basic changes and everybody tried anything they wanted to. Monk's always doing something back there that sounds so mysterious, but it's not [mysterious] at all when you know what he's doing. Just like simple truths. He might take a minor chord and leave the third out. Yet when he plays the thing it will be in just the right place and voiced the right way to have a minor feel, but it's still not a minor chord. I learned a lot with him. If you work with a guy that watches the finer points, it kind of helps you to do the same. In music it's the little things that count. Like the way you build a house. You get all the little important things together and the whole thing will stand up. You goof them and you got nothing."[8]

Monk's inclination to do what he felt at any moment meant that John had to be watchful. "I always had to be alert with Monk, because if you didn't keep aware all the time of what was going on you'd suddenly feel as if you'd stepped into an empty elevator shaft."[9]

By being with Monk, John learned much. "Working with Monk brought me close to a musical architect of the highest order. I felt I learned from him in every way — through the senses, theoretically, technically. I would talk to Monk about musical problems, and he would sit at the piano and show me the answers just by playing them. I could watch him play and find out the things I wanted to know. Also, I could see a lot of things that I didn't know about at all.

"Monk was one of the first to show me how to make two or three notes at one time on the tenor. John Glenn, a tenor man in Philly, also showed me how to do this. He can play a triad and move by false fingering and adjusting your lip. If everything goes right, you can get triads. Monk just looked at my horn and 'felt' the mechanics.

"I think Monk is one of the true greats of all time. He's a real musical thinker — there's not many like him. I feel myself fortunate to have had the opportunity to work with him. If a guy needs a little spark, a boost, he can just be around Monk, and Monk will give it to him."[10]

On August 10th Naima and Saida, "Toni," joined John at the Alvin Hotel in New York. On August 23rd they moved to a small, sparsely furnished apartment in Manhattan near Central Park West. For a considerable time there were only a mattress for the three of them and a T.V., which John bought for Saida to make the move to a new city easier. The only other pieces were a refrigerator and a stove that came with the apartment. His day consisted mostly of getting up early to breakfast, drinking fruit and vegetable juices, lifting his weights, practicing his horn and thinking. He had developed an interest in health foods during his stay in New York. By the time he finished practicing it would be time to go to work at The Five Spot.

During intermission he would either go into a back room to practice or sit at a table with a worried look on his face, thinking of how he could improve his music. He would frequently try different reeds, whittle them down — trying to reach for something.

As far as the audience was concerned, the heights had already been reached. The lines kept forming and the group stayed at The Five Spot through most of the remaining year.

Archie Shepp, a tenor saxophonist from Philadelphia, then only twenty years old, came to The Five Spot every night. He had been receiving deep musical messages from John, as he had from Ben Webster, Sonny Rollins, Jimmy Heath, and other musicians of his heritage. Shepp was in New York on a work term from Goddard College, where he was studying play-writing. He introduced himself, "Hey, John, man. How you doin'. I'm from Philly," as Cats from Philly always introduced themselves. They talked briefly and John gave him his address with an invitation to come by.

Shepp came by — *early* — the next morning. He didn't realize that he had only shaken the man's hand at five a.m. and that playing all night consumed so much energy. John was sweetly asleep. Nita answered the door graciously, welcoming him, and went to the bedroom to wake John. He came out in his T-shirt. They talked for a minute and John picked up his horn, playing a cycle of fourths to teach Shepp. Shepp had his alto saxophone with him and played for John, who advised, "Shepp, don't let your hands go so far from off the keys. Keep your hands close to the keys, that way you can play faster."

Soon Johnny Coles, the trumpet player with whom John had played in Jimmy Heath's band in Philadelphia, dropped by. They took a walk down Central Park West, where tranquil nature and the clumsy city meet. John told Shepp that Miles and Monk had taught him much about harmony. He also told him of his experiments with the formula for adding chords, and of various ways to play chord progressions. It was a musical day. Each concept opened a world of branching concepts for Shepp, giving him much to practice when he returned to Goddard.

One night at The Five Spot, another saxophonist, Rocky Boyd, came to give John a message. Rocky had been sent by Miles, who was playing in another New York Club. Miles told him, "See that big fat girl up there? Go to The Five Spot and tell John that girl's looking for him." Her name was Margaret.[11] Her parents had hosted John and other members of the Miles Davis Quintet when they played in Boston's Storyville. She was only 13 or 14 years old, but her measurements were probably the reverse of her age, and she had a crush on John, running away from home to see him. Rocky rushed to The Five Spot and conveyed the message. John hid in the kitchen and told Rocky, "Tell her you haven't seen me." After Rocky spoke to Margaret, Miles gave him her parents' phone number, and they came to New York and took her back home.

Ray Drapper, the young tuba player who had seen John sick two years ago in the basement of the Bohemia, had moved to an apartment on 106th Street. He was overjoyed when Red Garland, who lived in the same building, told him that John had an apartment only a few blocks away. Ray was only 17 years old and attending the High School of Performing Arts. He was probably the youngest musician with a Prestige contract. He was displeased, however, with the way the company viewed the fact that his instrument was a tuba. To them it was a freak, a bastard horn. Ray felt that if he could get John to record with him he would be treated more seriously. The next day he paid him a visit.

Toni opened the door. Ray was struck by the Spartan appearance of the room, and even more surprised when he saw the change in John, who told him of his spiritual awakening like a call to the ministry, and of being touched by God.

Ray would visit every afternoon. John showed him how to score his compositions and taught him the importance of breathing properly while playing an instrument. John was practicing, intensely as before, scales with numerous variations, intervals, harmonies, the upper register of his horn, playing two or three notes at once, and what he termed a 3-on-1 chord approach. He explained what he meant by this. "I could stack up chords — say, on a C-seventh, I sometimes superimposed an E-flat-seventh, up to an F-sharp-seventh, down to an F. That way I could play three chords on one."[1] [2]

While developing this approach, John was listening to an advanced European harpist named Salzeda. He owned a record of Salzeda's, "Transcriptions For Two Harps." For a period of a few months he listened constantly to Salzeda's recordings in his usual position on the couch, and went to sleep at night by them. Later, he bought records of other harpists, but Salzeda was his favorite. The music of the harp is sweeping and continuous like waves of the ocean. The music he created from the 3-on-1 chord approach, as well as other devices, was similarly fluid. Scales formed the body of this sweeping whirling fabric. These were played incredibly fast, with an unpredictable variety of accentuations, phrasings, and intonations. Wave after barrage after wave of notes woven . . .

The gap between his art and critics' perception of it was narrowing. His audience was steadily growing. Many of them were excited by the emotional content of his music. An indication of his gradual acceptance was given by the International Critics Poll in *Down Beat* August 22nd, 1957. John was voted second, behind Sonny Rollins, in the new star category. Critics from the non-English speaking countries may have been responsible for his high placement in this poll.

On days-off from The Five Spot engagement John would sometimes make gigs in Washington, D.C. He had no steady band, but would gather musicians whenever a job came up. At one of his performances he met a group from Liberia which was close to the Liberian ambassador to the United States. He enjoyed this group of people so much that he wrote the composition, *Liberia*.

On a night off John called Folks, who was living in Brooklyn, and told him that he wanted to see him. They took a long ride in John's first car, which he had bought while with Monk. He would drive it everywhere, even to a store only a block away. They rode to New Jersey without John saying a word. To break the ice, Folks interrupted the silence, "What you want to see me about, man?"

Very bluntly John answered, "Do you think I should get a band?"

Folks: "Hell, yeah! And when you get it, get all them saxophones lined up like that rich white boy. That rich white boy Charlie Barnet. Play the tenor. Play the soprano, and for God's sake go back to the alto. Play the flute. Blow all them motherfuckers, man. That'd be a gimmick, and you'd make a lot of money, John."

John, hesitating, "But I ain't got no personality like you. You know, I'm shy and shit."

Folks: "Yeah, but you can play. That's the difference. I can't play. I got to have personality to get across. You can wail. I can't wail. You ain't got to have no personality. All you got to do is blow that horn."

John thought this over carefully. In the meantime he recorded again on September 15th with Blue Note records, by "courtesy" of Prestige. On this date he had with him, Lee Morgan, trumpet; Curtis Fuller, trombone; Kenny Drew, piano; Paul Chambers, bass; and Philly Joe Jones, drums. Three of the five selections, *Locomotion, Blue Train* and *Lazy Bird* were written before he came to New York permanently. At the recording session he was told at the last minute that another selection was needed to complete the album. John then wrote a composition which he aptly titled, *Moment's Notice.* In this composition he utilized the pedal point device which he had employed before in *Nita.* The theme of *Moment's Notice* is a happy and arresting statement. *Blue Train* is an eerie blues on which John wails with fire and a high degree of inventiveness. There is a sound throughout his playing that lifts your perception of feelings and of your surroundings.

In John's beautiful rendition of another selection on this album, *I'm Old Fashioned*, an extremely important device is revealed. Within a portion of his solo he plays with shifting accents, alternating delicately, his sound with that of the piano. A feeling of floating slowly upward is created. This same device of shifting accents is used frequently in John's later music, in high energy pieces, as sort of a signal to move the band as one unified mass in stepwise manner, to a higher level.

Toward the end of the year Monk became tired of working and disbanded his group in late December. Orin Keepnews, head of Riverside records had tried to record the group live at The Five Spot, but was unsuccessful, because of the great rivalry which existed between Prestige, which had John under contract, and his company which had contracted Monk. Keepnews asked Weinstock, head of Prestige for permission to record John. Weinstock agreed on condition that Monk be allowed to play on a Prestige record with John as leader. Keepnews reluctantly agreed.

Monk allegedly refused. He had been with Prestige before signing with Riverside and felt so bitter that he didn't want to record with them under any circumstances. While with Prestige, Monk was at a low point in his career. His cabaret card had been cancelled, and he was not allowed to play in any nightclub in New York. He felt that Prestige dealt with him unfairly during this period. When he left the company, he allegedly owed *them* money. Therefore, much of the historic music of this period was never recorded.

Miles Davis asked John to rejoin his group. John accepted and the group played in Chicago during the holiday. As 1957 ended, further signs of John's increasing popularity with the public appeared. The first enthusiastic review of John's playing in *Down Beat* appeared in the December 26th issue. Dom Ceruli wrote the review of *Monk's Music*.

> "It's a tribute to Monk that within this intensely personal music, a soloist like Coltrane can develop a singularly personal style of his own, while fitting into the frame of Monk's reference. Trane's work on *Epistrophy*, for example, is about as fine as I've heard from him on record. In person, his playing is constantly tense and searching, always a thrilling experience."[13]

Also for the first time John placed in *Down Beat*'s regular tenor saxophone category in addition to the new star category. John was 11th in the regular saxophone category. Sonny Rollins was second and Stan Getz was first.

Nineteen fifty-seven was a year of transition for John. His spirit finally broke the glass enclosure that had mentally and physically incarcerated him. Even during his period of depression he had maintained his religious beliefs. But now his actions were at one with his faith, thereby creating an immense positive force. Through music he was free to convey strength to people, making them better able to sustain the trials and tribulations of life. While gaining impetus from his spiritual awakening and through communication received from his predecessor Charlie Parker, numerous technical developments began to appear in John's music.

Already a heavy practicer, he instituted an even stricter program to develop his concepts. His search for a "sweeping sound," his listening to the harp, revealed his interest in producing continuous music. Some of the concepts he was in the process of developing were formulas for adding more chords to a composition, the ability to play two, or three tones at once, and the 3-on-1 chord approach. Scales played rapidly and with numerous variations were an increasingly important component of his music. One scale led to another and another and another, making the vertical approach to music also a horizontal one.

Musically, and in general, he was wide open and continued to learn from Monk and Miles, as well as from many who were not well known, and even those less competent than himself.

One characteristic of Monk's music was wide intervals from one note in the melody to another or from one chord to another. This may have encouraged John to investigate intervals more fully. The use of wide intervals is a characteristic feature of Black music. Singers, for example, sing a low note, then all of a sudden jump high into what is called "falsetto."

Much was revealed in John's ballad renditions, in which he utilized fast-moving, rich ornamentation against a slow tempo, a heartfelt feeling, and a naturalness that could cause a listener to breathe in a more natural manner, with full even breaths.

Whether the music was at a slow or fast tempo, there was always passion in his playing. At fast tempos, there were zeal and towering strength of soldiers of the Zulu warrior Shaka and of Mohammed's horse riders who would die for their religion, and of the barefoot soldiers of Toussaint who smashed the best forces of Napoleon.

The coming impact of Coltrane could be seen by considering the opposition to his music. In the tradition of previous innovators, there were heated objections to his tone, or sound. Such objections seem to have presaged each musical revolt of Black music in western society. Indeed, other rumblings of revolt were being heard in the recordings of musicians like Ornette Coleman, Sun Ra, and Cecil Taylor released during this year. Several conceptual streams of musicians began migrating to New York because of the greater opportunities for recording, performing, and publicity. The business part of the music, however, was overwhelmingly exploitative, and though opportunities appeared colorful, there was only a wall of frustration at the end of the rainbow. These elements and others, made up the swirl of circumstances that John and his small family moved into, in 1957.

74

VIII

Breaking Babylon's Walls

Returning to the Miles Davis group in late December, 1957, John found changes in the personnel as well as the music. The group was now a sextet with Julian "Cannonball" Adderley on alto saxophone, "Philly" Joe Jones or Jimmy Cobb on drums, Wynton Kelly or Bill Evans on piano, Paul Chambers on bass, Miles on trumpet and John on tenor saxophone. The musical changes involved Miles' use of chords. John explained, "On returning . . . I found Miles in the midst of another stage of his musical development. There was one time in his past which he devoted to multi-chorded structures. He was interested in chords for their own sake. But now it seemed that he was moving in the opposite direction to the use of *fewer and fewer chord changes* in songs. He used tunes with free-flowing lines and chordal direction. This approach allowed the soloist the choice of playing chordally or melodically."[1] (author's italics)

The changes in Miles' music can be seen by comparing *Oleo*, in which there are many chords, to *So What*, which has a sparsity of chords and is also based on the Dorian Mode. Miles' use of different modes encouraged John to go further into this concept in his own writing. However, he continued his original interest in multi-chorded structures, while at the same time investigating Miles' idea of having only a few chords in a composition. "Miles' music gave me an opportunity to see both sides of the question. It was simple and direct enough to superimpose chords − to stack them up − if you wanted, and if you wanted to play melodically you could. I had mixed emotions about it. Sometimes I'd follow Miles' lead and 'play lyrically'; other times I'd say, 'That's the end of it, and play the other way.' "[2]

When John played the "other way" he would use his 3-on-1 chord approach along with other devices for superimposing or stacking up chords. An example of this can be seen, as he has said, in going from a C-seventh chord to F.

In "stacking-up" or "superimposing" chords he would move in equal steps from C-seventh to F. Sometimes these steps were minor thirds. This would result in two more chords being added and greater possibilities for improvising in the context of chords as a guideline.

When John followed "Miles' lead" and played lyrically he would not add more chords but would use, for example, the C-seventh and F-seventh, and improvise on the melody. John was exposed to at least two important concepts on rejoining Miles — the use of fewer chords and the further exploration of modes in composing.

Just as Bird and other innovators had a particular rhythmic feeling, one aspect of John's playing was its unusual rhythmic effects, accompanied by barrage after wave after barrage of overpowering notes. He often played in meters that differed from the basic pulse, creating two pulses, or would enter with a shock effect in unusual places in the music. He gives an idea of the way in which he combined profound analysis with emotion. "I found there were a certain number of chord progressions to play in a given time, and sometimes what I played didn't work out in eighth notes, sixteenth notes, or triplets. I had to put the notes in uneven groups like fives and sevens in order to get them all in. I thought in groups of notes, not of one note at a time. I tried to place these groups on the accents and *emphasize the strong beats* — maybe on 2 here and 4 over at the end. I would set up the line and *drop groups of notes* — a long line with accents dropped as I moved along. Sometimes what I was doing clashed harmonically with the piano — especially if the pianist wasn't familiar with what I was doing — so a lot of times I just strolled with bass and drums."[3] (author's italics)

Another characteristic of John's playing was explained by Miles when speaking of the objections he received. "I always liked Coltrane.

When he was with me the first time, people used to tell me to fire him. They said he wasn't playing anything. They used to tell me to get rid of Philly Joe Jones. I know what I want though. I also don't understand this talk of Coltrane being difficult to understand. What he does, for example, is to play five notes of a chord and then keep changing it around, trying to see how many different ways it can sound. It's like explaining something five different ways. And that sound of his is connected with what he's doing with chords to any given time."[4] Their personal relationship was as close as their musical understanding. John called him "the teacher" and Miles would tease him about being overweight. Miles sold him some of his exercise equipment, with punching bag, boxing gloves, and bars. On the bandstand Miles would occasionally ask, "Why you play so long, man?" John would answer, "It took that long to get it all in," which Miles accepted. He never interfered with the personal musical ideas of his sidemen.

Miles had the habit of leaving the stage after finishing his solo. Many in the audience would interpret this as a display of arrogance. But often what he was doing was sitting by Nita in the audience and enjoying the music of his sidemen. By becoming a part of the audience instead of staying on the bandstand, Miles would get a better idea of what the audience was receiving. Sometimes the music would get through to a listener either the way in which it was intended or in ways that depended on who was listening. Once while touring the south, a white boy walked up to John, "Mr. Coltrane, I don't like your music. It sounds like nigger hate music to me." Surprised, John had no words with which to answer.

John was still considering a group of his own, taking his customary long length of time in making important decisions. During the weeks when the Sextet wasn't working he would travel to various cities picking up musicians wherever he went. When in Philadelphia he played at The House of Jazz, where McCoy Tyner had a house trio. McCoy's familiarity with John's concepts and emotions increased through playing with him. John and Nita went to McCoy's house and asked if he would join a group if one were formed. McCoy's answer was a solid "yes." However, it would be some time before John finally left Miles. John told another saxophonist, Wayne Shorter, of his desire to go on his own.

Just before Wayne left the army, they met in New York's Birdland. Discussing the similarities in their playing, John told him, "You like to play up in that high register. That's something I like to do, [get] up in there and then go all over the horn." He invited Wayne to his apartment.

When he came by, John just continued practicing. He walked from room to room blowing his horn, occasionally getting something to munch on and interspersing the practice with talk, often speaking of reaching for things. Through the day many musicians walked in, stayed awhile, then left, not insulted, but understanding that he was simply working and would not be stopped. Still he and Nita maintained an atmosphere in the household that, regardless of what they were doing, others were always free to come by, stay, leave, play records or do as they pleased.

The conversation between him and Wayne drifted to the critics and the *Down Beat* reader's poll. In this poll the magazine's readers were asked to send in a vote for whomever they thought was the best musician in a particular category. They both agreed that even though they didn't like what the critics wrote or even the existence of a poll, a musician couldn't worry about the poll if he wanted to remain creative. Both felt that those readers who weren't interested in the technical aspects of the music could relate to the poll in the same manner one related to a sports competition. For these people it was exciting to vote and see who would be on top each year. They concluded that the main problem with the poll was that certain musicians who were not innovators were getting top places. They were simply those who capitalized from previous developments. In the late afternoon or evening they would practice together, exchanging places at the piano or saxophone. Another practice partner appeared by way of a practical joke.

One day John received an unusual piece of mail. Someone, with an uncanny ear had sent him a copy of his solo on *Blue Trane* – note for note and with exact time values. Accompanying the music was the message, "Does this look familiar?" Amazed that someone could copy this intricate solo, he waited eagerly for its author to call. The sender was Zita Carno, a pianist who played mostly European music, but was also familiar with African-American music. She had sent similar surprises to other musicians without calling them. But this time she became curious and called John.

When they spoke he told her how happy he was to hear from her because he wanted to meet this person who wrote out his solos so precisely. Zita became a frequent visitor, often sitting at the piano and playing chords on which John improvised.

Nineteen fifty-eight in the recording studio was busy, as it had been
for John since joining Miles in 1955. On February 7th the album
"Soultrane" was recorded. Arthur Taylor was on drums. Paul Chambers
played bass and Red Garland was on piano. Six tunes were on the
album: *Russian Lullaby, Theme for Ernie, You Say You Care, Good
Bait,* and *I Want to Talk About You.* The last tune was written by Billy
Eckstine, who sang with force and had a wide interpretive range. He
was one of John's favorite singers.

I WANT TO TALK ABOUT YOU

High	Spiralling	arms	ribbons
note	ribbons	wider	softly
lifts	of	than	broadly
into	grape	wider	expansively
a	note	receiving	softly
cloud	breaks	all	falling
of	drop	giving	the
warm	to	all	wind
embraces	one	glass	the
surrounds	knee	walls	breath
you	surging	no	oooh
with	LOVE	more	
hugs	SHOUT	gentle	
and	John	warmth	
caresses	opens	suspended	

On another one of this year's record dates John played with a big
band led by pianist-composer George Russell. Russell was assigned by
the record company to write music that expressed his feelings about
New York. Poet Jon Hendricks wrote poems for the date in which he
spoke out against the social ills of New York and America in general.
For this date, Russell assembled a band composed of a mixture of
studio musicians and musicians who made public appearances. He
wanted John to solo on an arrangement of the show tune, *Manhattan.*
The arrangement was nothing more than the standard chord changes
with a few embellishments, but when John received the music from

Russell he looked at it and walked off into a corner.

Russell and some of the musicians understood what John was doing. But some of the others didn't. The representative from the record company, the A&R man, didn't understand either. He was thinking about how much the date would cost the company. The longer it took to record, the more the musicians had to be paid.

As time skipped along one of the studio musicians let it be known how HE felt about the delay, saying to the others, "Jesus Christ, he's fuckin' up the whole date. He doesn't know what he's doing. He doesn't know his changes!"

It was an hour before John returned to the band. Russell and some of the other musicians knew that John "knew his changes" better than anyone else in the room. He could have improvised on the changes in the usual way but had his own way of approaching chord patterns. In order for him to utilize this method, he had to study the chords. When the solo was played there was no question that the hour was time well harnessed.

However, John was unhappy about this recording date. It could be that he felt he could have played even better. He may have felt that he was being put into a commercial context with the presence of the studio musicians and being asked to play show tunes like *Manhattan*. Or he could have sensed the displeasure of the A&R man and some of the musicians.

Critics continued to wallow in their customary ignorance, engaging in the ludicrous practice of grading art for a large number of people, their readers. Some used the A to F system, some used the five to zero star system, and others simply placed their stamp of "good" or "bad" on a work of art. It was like a teacher, who didn't know as much as a student, grading that student. In the January, 1958, issue of *Metronome*, a British "jazz" magazine, John's first album, the *First Train*, met with an unenthusiastic response.

> The sound John Coltrane gets on tenor has true Mid-east qualities. That East centers not so much in New York as in the Moroccan belt. It is an extremely hard sound, something like what we're used to hearing from primitive Arabian instruments. This quality gives all of John's soloing a strained emotional sound, a hard reedy sound that at times seems closer to the oboe than the tenor. This reediness is not oboe-like in range, of course, but in sound texture.
>
> The album has good pacing both in tempos and in the choice of material although as usual with musicians centered around the hard-bop core, there is a predominance of tunes with that sometimes

monotonous minor feeling, structure and sound. – Jack CODA: From
John Coltrane's first album as leader, we surmise that he's used his head
in choosing material, tempos and men; that he plays with a great deal of
both sincerity and intensity although with a certain lack of
imagination.[5]

An even more caustic opinion was given on the album "Interplay for
2 Trumpets and 2 Tenors" in the February *Metronome*.

> This is an embarrassing album to review. How do you say just about
> everyone on the date plays out of tune; that nothing except the ballad
> gets off the ground, and not seem cruel. But that's actually what
> happens. The out-of-tuneness is a real handicap and annoyance to the
> listener. There's a real lack of competence in the musicianship, too.
> Technically and emotionally, there's little projection and a great many
> goofs. The soloists seem never to unlimber. Everything is extremely
> stiff. Mal Waldron wrote all the tunes on this date. His ballad, *Eyes*, is a
> gaunt, moon-washed thing. The best track of the album. – Jack CODA:
> Just one of them things.[6]

In the United States Don Gold writing in the January 23rd issue of
Down Beat, on "The First Train," repeated a common line of critics of
the time – that the written music was only an excuse for improvisation.
Gold also did not like John's tone in his interpretation of the ballad
While My Lady Sleeps. The critic was probably more accustomed to the
usual subdued tones, and widely-spaced feeling that were most
frequently employed in ballad interpretations. He may not have been
accustomed to, or inherently receptive to, the passionate feeling that
John rendered.

> Coltrane, who has worked with Dizzy, Miles, and Monk, makes his
> debut as a leader on this LP, if anyone can be identified as a "leader"
> on such a date. At any rate he has most of the blowing room.
> His tone is hard; his conception is bluntly surging. There is little
> subtlety in his playing, but there is strength and confidence. He is a
> hard-punching tenor man. This approach tends to diminish the
> effectiveness of his ballad interpretations, which seem to differ from his
> up-tempo races only in terms of a difference in tempo.
> The charts are excuses for blowing, except for Cal Massey's moody
> *Bakai*, which in its minor explorations, makes sense. The blowing, then,
> determines the value of the set. Although Coltrane plays with a good
> deal of authority, I do not feel that his work on this specific LP is
> excitingly impressive, but listeners who dig blowing sessions and tenor
> men of the hard-charging school may find value in this set.[7]

The April 3rd issue of *Down Beat* had a review of "Interplay for 2 Trumpets and 2 Tenors," by John Tynan. This review, in its praise for the musicians, was in direct contradiction to the scathing opinion in *Metronome*. Giving the record four stars, Tynan wrote,

> Coltrane reveals himself as an impassioned, compulsive musical personality in the various tracks. In his exchanges of eights with Jaspar, in *Anatomy*, he sometimes squawks like an outraged hen. Always, however, his is hard-hitting, (sic) plunging conception and as Ira Gitler notes, he is " . . . a cruising, long-lined, digging-in swinger."
> Spirited blowing by some of the younger lights, "Interplay" is worth a place in any contemporary library.[8]

In spite of the favorable Tynan review, unfavorable criticism persisted. Don Gold, reviewing the Miles Davis Album, "Relaxin' ", recorded in 1956, wrote in the May 15th, 1958, *Down Beat*.

> "There is a hesitancy and lack of melodic content in Coltrane's playing at times that hampers his effectiveness for me and lowers the rating of the LP. This is particularly true on the first two tracks, on which his solos seem to me to be rather aimless and somewhat strident. However, he is quite fluent on *Oleo* and *Book*. His efforts throughout the LP lack a consistent quality."[9]

Gold gave the record four stars instead of five, repeating Hentoff's practice of withholding a star because of his dislike for John's contribution.

Dom Ceruli, who had given John his first favorable review in *Down Beat*, continued to receive the music well. Writing a review of "Traneing In," in *Down Beat*, Ceruli praised John for his tone in ballad interpretations — the same quality that Don Gold condemned him for in the ballad *While My Lady Sleeps*. Ceruli gave the record four stars and coined the phrase that became well-known among Coltrane listeners, " . . . the only thing you can expect in his playing is the unexpected."

On July 3rd, 1958, the Miles Davis sextet performed at the Newport Jazz Festival. A very dumb-assed review appeared in August 7th *Down Beat* on the music they made. The term "angry young tenor" may have begun with this review.

> "Unfortunately the group did not perform effectively. Although Miles continues to play with delicacy and infinite grace, his group's solidarity

is hampered by the angry tenor of Coltrane. Backing himself into rhythmic corners on flurries of notes, Coltrane sounded like the personification of motion-without-progress in jazz. What is equally important, Coltrane's playing apparently has influenced Adderley. The latter's playing indicated less concern for melodic structure than he has illustrated in the past . . .

With the exception of Miles' vital contribution, then, the group proved more confusing to listeners than educational. After a needed intermission the Dave Brubeck Quartet appeared."[10]

Through the remainder of the year most critics continued with disapproving articles. In December, however, Ceruli wrote another favorable review, of "Soultrane," which had been recorded in February, 1958.

In this very, very good LP, John Coltrane gives a picture of himself which is true in several dimensions. This set, first of all, is one I consider representative of what Coltrane is doing today with the Miles Davis group. That I consider him one of the few most exciting tenor-playing individuals in jazz today has no bearing on the rating, but I do use the word "individuals" in its fullest connotations. Coltrane has been, and is here, playing in a highly personal manner. What he is doing has been described variously as sheets of sound or ribbons of sound or, by some less interested ears, as a haphazard running of as many notes as possible. I find a logic in his playing. And although he does sometimes fail to get his flow underway, the times that it does happen are among the most tingling in modern jazz. What I do admire in him is that he is always going for something beyond him, and that he never falls back on easy or accepted ways of doing what he wants to do.

On this set, Coltrane also has some passages of extremely lyrical playing, particularly on the ballads, *Talk* and *Care*. He blows straight-forward and with warmth.

Backing is first rate and Garland's solo spots are fine. By all means hear this one.[11]

Later in December, a perceptive article appeared in what was probably a Cleveland newspaper. With the article was a list of the top twenty "Jazz" albums of the year. Three albums under John's name were on the list. Two others on which he was a sideman with Red Garland and Miles Davis were also among the twenty. An admirer sent the article to John, writing on it that "Soultrane" had been among the top ten in that area for four weeks.

The sounds that flow from John Coltrane's tenor are accomplished as they are by any other sax player in a technical sense by the use of the hands and mouth. The fact that he has risen above most of his contemporaries is due to a number of reasons. The most important being that he has within him a dedicated desire to be a great musician. Not great in the eyes of the public, but great in his own feelings.

This is not a result of a super-ego for John is one of the most humbly shy persons we have ever met. It is however the result of his desire for perfection. [sic] It is musicians such as he who are responsible for the public's new acceptance of jazz on a level with other arts. [sic] The fact that after more than ten years of professional playing critics and fans all over the world of Jazz are now recognizing him as a gifted tenor voice seems to make little or no impression on him. To be sure he's grateful, but he's more concerned with improving his music.

Coltrane was born some 32 years ago in Hamlet, North Carolina. His father was a tailor by profession, but a violinist at heart. His mother had aspiration of being a concert singer, but John's grandfather, a Methodist minister, didn't approve. [sic] Today she is still singing in the church choir in Philadelphia. With such a background it makes it easier to understand why music is a part of him.

A few years ago John almost gave up music. As he puts it: "I really have much to be thankful for. My father died when I was around twelve. My mother made many sacrifices to enable me to study music. She never married again. Some years ago I went into a period of depression and almost gave up. I thank God for enabling me to pull out of it. My wife Nita was a great help to me, also. She and daughter, Toni, have made my life far happier."

Actually the new Coltrane emerged after a brief period with The Thelonious Monk Combo. Coltrane who joined Miles in 1955 and remained with him until illness forced Miles to disband, joined Monk shortly after. Of this period he says, "This was a most impressive period for me. Monk is an exceptional musician. The time I spent with him was most stimulating."

Although he has drawn his influences for styles from Dexter Gordon and Sonny Stitt, he has been basically influenced by Monk and Davis, especially in his chord structure and musical thinking. Today he is back with Miles exerting a freedom of experimentation that is not hampered, but encouraged by Miles.

Coltrane's influence on other saxophonists is being heard today in more and more of his contemporaries. It is almost safe to say that when he has blown his last note he will be recognized as one of the great jazz influences of our time.[12]

His popularity among the public was growing rapidly. Among critics, there were also some indications of rising acceptance. Their opinions began to diverge in 1958, with John being condemned and praised for the same reasons, and with the appearance of the first substantial notices of favorable opinions. In the International Critics Poll he held second place in the New Star category, behind Benny Golson. He placed fifth in the regular saxophone category, with Sonny Rollins second and Stan Getz first. Critic Ira Gitler, on hearing the continuous way his playing moved, coined the term, "sheets of sound." In an interview by Gitler, appearing in the October 16th *Down Beat*, John said what he felt about the term "angry young tenor" and touched upon other issues. At this time he responded humbly to the critics. Not only was he his most severe critic but also his most objective. However, the statements of the critics may have influenced his thinking. In spite of attempts to ignore them, his response in the late 50's was to feel that he was at fault by not playing as well as he should. He responded similarly in other situations, such as in a disagreement with a friend. His first question would be "What did I do wrong?" The Gitler article began with his response to the phrase "angry young tenor."

"If it is interpreted as angry, it is taken wrong. The only one I'm angry at is myself when I don't make what I'm trying to play."

The article went on to his 3-on-1 chord approach, revealing how uncompromising he was even about his own ideas. "Now it is not a thing of beauty and the only way it could be justified is if it becomes that. If I can't work it through, I will drop it."

Details of playing were discussed. "I have more work to do on my tone and articulation. I must study more general technique and smooth out some harmonic kinks. Sometimes while playing, I discover two ideas, and instead of working on one I work on two simultaneously and lose the continuity."

His advice to other musicians was, "Keep listening. Never become so self-important that you can't listen to other players. Live cleanly . . . Do right . . . You can improve as a player by improving as a person. It's a duty we owe to ourselves."

The interview ended with a brief statement of his goals. " . . . Music is the means of expression with strong emotional content. Jazz used to be happy and joyous. I'd like to play happy and joyous."[13]

IX

Giant Steps

Late 1958 or very early 1959 John left Prestige. Orin Keepnews, head of Riverside records, who had been eager to sign him two years earlier, was one of the first to approach him. But negotiations with Riverside reached an impasse. John's position was that he should get a one-thousand-dollar advance per album, which few "jazz" artists were getting. He also felt that he should make four or five albums a year. Keepnews agreed to the thousand dollars but felt that only three albums a year should be made stating that John couldn't come up with enough fresh material, in a year's time, to produce five albums of value.

Concurrently negotiations were progressing with Atlantic records. Harold Lovette, who was Miles' attorney, also took on John's legal affairs. John stayed close to Lovette, consulting him for even the most minute legal transactions, such as buying a car or any matter in which money was involved. Lovette introduced him to Nehusi Ertegun, head of Atlantic records. They agreed to $7,000 each year or year-and-a-half. Another important step was taken by the establishment of a publishing company under John's name. The company was titled "Jowcol" for John William Coltrane. Through the publishing company he received benefits from radio stations which paid each time one of his records was played on the air. This also gave him control over how his music was used. Lovette became John's manager and arranged to have Shaw Artists' Corporation, which had handled Miles' group, also book John, with Jack Wittamore as his agent. The first album with Atlantic was recorded on January 15th, 1959, with vibraphonist Milt Jackson as co-leader.

Still living in his mind was a group of his own. Monday nights in New

York nightclubs are nights when the regular group is off and the clubs either close, hold jam sessions, or feature special shows. One such night in early 1959, John gathered a group of musicians: Wayne Shorter, tenor saxophone; Freddie Hubbard, trumpet; George Tucker on bass; Tommy Flannagan and Cedar Walton alternating on piano, and Elvin Jones on drums. Music! Wo! raised audience to hallelujah excitement. After this night John was definite about leaving Miles. He called Nita and surprised her with the news. She advised him saying, yes, it was true that he had developed a large following, but it would be better to wait until after Miles made the European tour. This would give him time to think about the kind of band and the music he wanted. One thing was fixed in his mind though. That was the drumming of Elvin Jones. Jone's art was still developing. Few musicians, even other drummers, heard any of his praiseworthy features. Instead Elvin was the target of ridicule. To other musicians, except for John, he was, at best, unorthodox and, at worst, just plain comical. The time would come when those who once laughed would become Elvin's imitators.

Music completely possessed John. He would work intensely for periods of two to four weeks, followed by a two-week period of relative rest. April of this year he was working, thinking, day and night. At the dinner table the saxophone would still be on his neck, coming off only when he took a shower. Late at night, instead of going directly to bed, he would sit on its edge thinking, with the horn still strapped to his neck. Finally, in this position, he would fall asleep. Naima would have to remove the horn and put him to bed. She never knew at what time he awoke because he would always rise first and start practicing. Once he awoke with the horn in his mouth. Some days he would work straight through for twenty-four hours without food or sleep, stopping only when he was physically unable to continue. Too exhausted to play, he would talk about music.

Much composing was done during this period. Many of the ideas that were begun in Philadelphia reached fruition, as well as his execution of them on his instrument. Very prominent were the progressions that Charlie Parker had told him to keep working on. In May John's efforts were recorded on an album entitled "Giant Steps", which was an awesome rendition of the work with which he had been involved. The album was awesome in the technical proficiency shown, the tight mathematical logic behind the compositions, the utilization of ideas such as ostinato, pedal point, the extensive use of minor thirds instead of the traditional fourth or half-step, maintaining a blues feeling using chords that were not typical of the blues, the power and beauty of the music, and the love shown toward his family and friends.

The title composition, *Giant Steps*, derived its name either from its bass line or from the relationship of its chords. In John's words, " . . . the bass line is kind of a loping one. It goes from minor thirds to fourths, kind of a lop-sided pattern in contrast to moving strictly in fourths or in half-steps."[1]

Another image may have been involved with his arriving at the name, *Giant Steps*. By the time the record was released John and his family had moved into a house in Queens. Between the last step, on the front of the house, and the street was a long distance, compared to the previous steps. He confided in Folks that this long step was what brought the title to mind.

An example of the logic in *Giant Steps* is the section written for the bass. Each note is related to the chord accompanying it, as well as to the other notes in the bass clef.

Cousin Mary was named after the cousin with whom he grew up in High Point, who was like a sister to him. "She's a very earthy, folksy, swinging person. The figure is riff-like and although the changes are not conventional blues progressions, I tried to retain the flavor of the blues."[2]

On the original worksheet that he used in writing the composition, another title is scratched out which may have been written before the title *Cousin Mary*. The title was *Old New Blues*, probably because, as he said, the chords were not those of a conventional blues. Minor thirds and fourths were used in this composition instead of the typical blues pattern of I IV V I.

[3]

Countdown is an extremely logical composition in which his formula for superimposing chords is used to make something new out of Miles Davis' composition *Tune Up*. The structure is like a perfect matrix and utilizes a constantly repeated relationship between chords.[4]

On the recording, Arthur Taylor on drums begins alone, tapping and booming at kindling speed. His solo ends with a boom on which John joins with fiery ideas blowing long, long phrases, at an incredible, then

more incredible rate. Tommy Flannagan, on the piano, jumps in,
playing only the chords; then the bass, Paul Chambers, joins.

Forms	rasping	spaces	
garble	Fires	tempo	
out	Bottom	slows	
like	drops	John	meaning
sounds	out	soars	
From	pressure	in	
a	rises	a	
holy	an	valley	
roller's	explo –	of	
mouth	no!	grandeur	
speaking	the	and	
in	field	majesty	
a	opens	ending	
thousand	into	on	countdown?
tongues	wider	the	
tipped	and	C	
by	wider	chord	

Spiral brings to mind the image of a spiral, a feeling of turning,
descending and ascending. Within and around the spiral you may see all
kinds of living changing shapes.

Syeeda's Song Flute gets its name from his step-daughter Saida, who
was only nine at the time. The title shows his tendency to play with
words, changing the spelling of Saida to Syeeda, and writing Song Flute
instead of Flute Song. This composition resulted from a melody that
Saida played on a small wind instrument, and John's work at the piano:
"When I ran across it on the piano, it reminded me of her because it
sounded like a happy child's song."[5]

The album was like a portrait of family and friends. Another
composition was for his wife and titled after her, *Naima*. He spoke of
the technical aspects of the composition. "The tune is built on
suspended chords over an E-flat pedal tone on the outside. On the

inside — the channel — the chords are suspended over a B-flat pedal tone."[6]

This is an exceedingly beautiful composition, giving a feeling of being carried from one cloud to the next ascending one, or of touching different stones on a necklace staircase. It doesn't end when you expect it to, but continues on a suspended phrase as if he wanted to touch each of her fingers at once and separately at the same time.

Mr. P.C. was for bassist, Paul Chambers, whom John described as, " . . . one of the greatest bass players in jazz. His playing is beyond what I could say about it. The bass is such an important instrument, and has much to do with how a group and a soloist can best function that I feel very fortunate to have had him on this date and to have been able to work with him in Miles' band so long."[7]

The composition was a blues, based on a minor scale. This practice of playing a blues in a minor scale would be used extensively in later music, giving it a distinctive, earthy yet exotic sound. Throughout the album a waiL wail wAil waIl Wail turned and bent.

The Miles Davis Sextet continued its travels around the country as one of the most influential groups of the Fifties. Below is an article from the *Oakland Tribune*, June 4, 1959, written by Russ Wilson, which indicates the impact of the group.

> If the Miles Davis Sextet is not in the forefront of the 1959 jazz polls, this listener will be very much surprised.
>
> After hearing the group several nights during its San Francisco debut, an engagement at the Blackhawk which still has a couple of weeks to go, I am convinced that the combo is not only outstanding in its own right but furthermore is the best that Davis yet has come up with. This judgment is based on a number of factors. First of all, you have a group of excellent musicians . . . John Coltrane ranks no worse than second to Sonny Rollins as the guiding light among tenor saxophonists . . . Davis who is the musical director of the group has woven it into a remarkably cohesive unit which reflects his sensitivity, feeling for dynamics, melodic stress, and use of space. The rapport is especially noticeable, of course, in ensembles but it goes far beyond that.
>
> The group's repertoire includes several new originals by Davis, one a still-untitled blues that starts and ends in three-quarter time; another that employs an Afro-Cuban beat. There also are such standards as *Autumn Leaves, Billy Boy,* and *Two Bass Hit.* Each selection runs to some length, since Davis permits his sidemen plenty of solo room.
>
> Miles himself seems to be blowing forcefully more often than has been the case in the past, a quality which I believe enhances his overall performance, but his delicate, moody horn still is his forte . . . Coltrane . . . has progressed since his last appearance here with

Miles in 1957. He can get a beautiful tone (though at the moment this is somewhat hampered by the fact he had to get an eight-tooth upper front bridge in Chicago a few weeks ago), he keeps his dazzling runs under control, he has a great feeling for the blues, and his ballads are expressive.[8]

On June 14th another article appeared in the *Oakland Tribune* on the possible departure of John from the group.

John Coltrane is considering leaving the Miles Davis Sextet to form his own quartet.

"There's nothing definite yet," he said the other evening at the Blackhawk, where the Davis combo today starts the last week of its engagement, "but I have been seriously thinking of it." Coltrane has informed Miles of this, and should the parting come, it will be amicable. Davis understands Coltrane's viewpoint and will not stand in his way.

Should Coltrane depart from the group, his replacement probably will be James "Little Bird" Heath, a brother of bassist Percy Heath. Jimmy, who has worked with Davis previously, has just returned to the music scene.

Coltrane, who has played with Dizzy Gillespie and Thelonious Monk, has been with Davis since 1955 except for a couple of brief instances when Trane headed a quartet. In the last year or so he has come to be regarded as one of the most exciting and influential tenor saxophonists in jazz, a factor that figures in his thinking.[9]

While playing at the Boston club, Storyville, the young tenor saxophonist, Rocky Boyd, sat in with the group. Afterwards he and John went to Chinatown for supper. John told him he was looking for a cheaper place to stay. He didn't want to pay the high fee at the hotel where he had been staying. Rocky showed him a rooming house on Claremont Park Street near the railroad tracks, into which John happily moved.

Soon after seeing each other in Boston they met again in New York. Rocky had no place to stay and no money. He was looking for nightclub engagements and recording opportunities; but the business side of the music was not as open as he must have first envisioned. He was constantly being frustrated by recording studios telling him to come back at a certain time, and then on returning being told either that he could not record or must come again. John invited him to stay with his family in their small apartment.

At home John was always busy practicing his horn, playing the piano, writing, going to the music store. There were also household matters, bills to pay, getting things fixed. At times he would be up all night working on music. Other nights he would return from the nightclub and sit up talking. And sometimes he would be silent, sitting or lying on the couch, thinking.

John was practicing harp music on his horn during this time, transposing instantaneously and playing the long 16th-note arpeggios and various rhythmic patterns characteristic of the harp. Practice still continued up to the time for him to work, where, instead of relaxing during intermission, with a drink, he would go directly into a backroom to practice more.

The critics' opinions were slow in changing. The results of the critics' poll appeared in the August 6th *Down Beat*. John was voted 6th out of 6 places in the regular tenor saxophonist category, receiving only 4 votes of a total 97 cast. In the New Star category he was second again behind Benny Golson. But a division was becoming apparent between the critics, the musicians and audiences. Saxophonists, young and old, were incorporating various elements of his art. Audiences were becoming more excited by his approach, which they could not comprehend earlier. The albums "Blue Train" and "Soultrane" were among the "Jazz Best Sellers." The growing dichotomy between the critics and audiences is evident in an article from the August 6th 1959 issue of *Down Beat*, in which the critic's opinion differs widely from that of the audience.

> The character of the Sextet's engagement — for a reputed $2,500 a week — threw into razor-sharp focus the question of night club entertainment vs. untrammeled expression by jazz artists of varying maturity . . . Miles would informally open a number, blowing down into the mike, oblivious of the audience. Coltrane would follow, strolling out of the backstage shadows, to blow long and searchingly . . . Coltrane communicated a sense of inhibition (sometimes even frustration) with his calculated understatement and contrived dissonance. On the whole, the tenor man's contributions suggested superficially stimulating, lonely and rather pathetic self-seeking. Is this truly the dilemma of the contemporary jazz artist? One hesitates to believe so. For all the showcasing of the frequently brilliant soloists, one yearned to hear ensemble performance . . .
>
> Predictably, the audience — which packed the Seville opening night — expressed appreciation with much palm-beating.[10]

The critic repeats the theme that an artist should remain on the bandstand, while the others in the group are playing. No such objection is heard when the conductor of an orchestra turns his back to the audience, and conducts, thinking only of the music. The critic also thought that horns should play ensemble more, instead of soloing. This is only a preference in what passes as an objective article. At the end of the article the critic does admit that the audience enjoyed the performance.

In the October and November issues of *Jazz Review*, an article appeared which was unusual in that it offered information rather than the usual ignorance on the music. Zita Carno was the author.

> . . . Benny Golson, and to a lesser extent, Hank Mobley and Junior Cook, have been most strongly affected. Especially interesting is Golson because until recently he sounded like a cross between Lucky Thompson and Coleman Hawkins, with other elements thrown in. Such a complete switch as this is as clear an indication as any of Coltrane's influence. Cannonball Adderley is by now classic proof that you can't play with Coltrane without being influenced by him. Even Miles Davis and Horace Silver have picked up a few things from him and have been working around with them.
>
> Just what is he doing to have such an effect? A lot of people may be moved to think of Charlie Parker as the widespread influence. Everyone tried to imitate him as much as possible, to sound as nearly a carbon copy of him as they could — which was only natural when you consider that he revolutionized jazz.
>
> But what Coltrane has been doing is to get the ones he has influenced into the "hard" groove and then stimulate them to think for themselves . . . Coltrane's style is many-faceted. There are many things to watch for in his playing, and the fact that he is constantly experimenting, always working out something new — on and off the stand — leads to the conclusion that no matter how well you may think you know what he's doing, he will always surprise you.
>
> To begin my discussion . . . I would like to elaborate a bit . . . concerning the failure of listeners to find anything "familiar" — any cliches — in his solos.
>
> He does have a few pet phrases that he will use in his solos. But you could hardly refer to them as cliches. They are his own, and he never even plays them exactly the same way twice . . . I would like to discuss a most controversial aspect of Coltrane's playing: his technique. It is an excellent one — one of the finest. His command of the instrument is almost unbelievable. Tempos don't faze him in the least; his control enables him to handle a very slow ballad without having to resort to the double-timing so common among hard blowers, and for him there is no such thing as too fast a tempo. His playing is very clean and accurate, and he almost never misses a note.
>
> His range is something to marvel at: a full three octaves upward from the lowest note obtainable on the horn (concert A-flat) . . . what sets

Coltrane apart from the rest of them is the equality of strength in all registers which he has been able to obtain through long, hard practice. That tone of his . . . has been . . . a subject of debate. A result of the particular combination of mouthpiece and reed he uses plus an extremely tight embouchure, it is an incredibly powerful, resonant and sharply penetrating sound with a spine-chilling quality . . . Those listeners who say he plays out of tune have been deceived by that sharp edge in his sound . . . he plays in tune. There is far more to Coltrane's style than "hard drive." Hard drive is only one aspect . . . and even that is an entirely different kind from that of, say, Sonny Rollins. Coltrane seems to have the power to pull listeners right out of their chairs. I have noticed this terrific impact on the various rhythm sections he has played with; he pulls them right along with him and makes them cook, too . . . Say Miles Davis is the first soloist. Notice that the rhythm section doesn't push. They are relaxed behind him. Now Coltrane takes over, and immediately something happens to the group: the rhythm section tightens up and plays harder. The bass becomes stronger and more forceful, as does the ride-cymbal beat; even the piano comps differently. They can't help it – Coltrane is driving them ahead . . .

Coltrane's harmonic conception is perhaps the most puzzling aspect of his style, inasmuch as it is so advanced. For one thing, he really knows what to do with the changes of the tunes he plays. This is apparent not only in his playing, but also – as we shall see – in his writing . . . He is very subtle, often deceptive – but he's always right there.

An excellent insight into these harmonic devices of his can be found in that weird phenomenon which has been variously referred to as "sheets of sound," "ribbons of sound," "a gosh-awful lot of notes" and other things. These are very long phrases played at such an extremely rapid tempo that the notes he plays cease to be mere notes and fuse into a continuous flow of pure sound. Sometimes they do not come off the way he wants them to, and that is when the cry of "just scales" arises. That may be, but I dare anyone to play scales like this, with that irregular, often a-rhythmic phrasing, those variations of dynamics, and that fantastic sense of timing. But more often they work out the way he wants them to, and then one hears things. There is an unbelievable emotional impact to them, plus a fantastic residual harmonic effect which often is so pronounced that in many instances the piano wouldn't be missed if it weren't playing.

Coltrane's sense of form is another source of wonderment. He has very few equals at building up a solo, especially on a blues – and building up a solo on a blues is not easy . . . [11]

Part II

That is Coltrane the instrumentalist – powerful, sensitive, ahead, and always experimenting. Now I'd like to talk a bit about Coltrane the jazz

composer and arranger, inasmuch as it may throw still further light on
certain other aspects of his conception . . . for one thing, his melodic
lines — blues or not — are all very powerful, direct and straightforward,
with strong emotional impact . . .

His approach to arranging is just as different as everything else he
does. Very often what he does amounts to an almost complete
reharmonization or reconstruction of a tune or part of it . . . the only
thing to expect from John Coltrane is the unexpected.[12]

This was one of the best, if not the best, analyses of his music. By
1959, however, he had progressed beyond the material that the article
dealt with. Still, the characteristics Miss Carno discussed were basic to
his expression.

next stop jupiter

next stop jupiter

jupiter   jupiter   jupiter   jupiter   jupiter

The Potential

Beyond other things and other worlds
are the things that seem not to be
And yet are.
How impossible is the impossible.
Yet the impossible is a thought.
And every thought is real
An idea, a flash of potent fire
A seed that can bring to be
The reality of itself.
Beyond other thoughts and other worlds
Are the potentials . . .
That hidden circumstance
And pretentious chance
Cannot control.[13]

Late 1959, John met Sun Ra who speaks of angels and higher beings
as naturally as if we were to speak of the rain or leaves dropping from
the trees. The poem and other words above are his concepts and give an
idea of the content, the energy of Sun Ra's music. A partial account of
his stay on this planet reveals a fuller understanding of this energy.

When only seven years old he "knew everything there was to know about folks on this planet." His mother brought his sister a piano for her birthday. At school, he had learned the names of the notes. Knowing only this, he read a book of hymns and played one of his grandmother's favorites for her. Watching him play was a violinist friend of the family who asked the small child, "How'd you do that? You weren't really reading that. You haven't had no training." Ra insisted that he was reading. The next day the violinist brought some European music and Ra surprised him by playing it. Each day he would bring new pieces of music finding it hard to believe that Ra could play it for him.

Feeling that he needed to know more, Ra asked his sister to teach him. But she rebuffed him with, "You can't learn to play no music." Angered by this, he stole a book from her house (she had recently married) and kept it for a week, after which he could play anything in it. From this book he also was able to deduce the total scheme or structure of music. But he didn't want to become an artist. Having read in school of their lives, it seemed that they always had hardships, died young and suffered. He led a band in high school, but thinking of what he had read, he decided to forget music, go to college, and become a teacher.

On registration day at Alabama A and M, in Huntsville, the entire band he had in high school showed up. The school had no facilities for a band, but the school president and registrar were both musicians and saw to it that band facilities were rapidly obtained, as well as scholarships for everyone in the band. Sun Ra, against his original intentions, was back into music.

Alabama A and M was all Black, and had an excellent program for training teachers. Ra had high grades and could have easily moved into the high financial stratum of Black society that being a teacher automatically moved you into. But the Creator intervened, telling him to study the music, leave Huntsville, leave his family and all associations to go to a place he knew nothing about – Chicago. He went there, most likely, in the early Fifties. Sun Ra commented on this decision in his typically Black southern way of speaking. "In a sense I gave up my life. Most men give up their life and die. But anybody can do that. He ain't got nothin' to worry about. But if you give up your life and you're still livin' and you see all the world passin' you by – all kind of persons getting famous, making money and you're told by the Creator, 'Don't have nothin' to do with that. Stand your ground.' You have all kinds of difficulties that other folks don't have. But that's a test."

In Chicago he worked with many of the local musicians. The word was that Sun Ra was strange, but many musicians appreciated him and always saw to it that he had a place to work. When Fletcher Henderson hired Ra for his band, the horn players protested. They said he was playing "strange" and that they couldn't get their improvisation moving well with him playing.

Ra's playing had developed to such a point that it no longer sounded like a piano but was more like one of the electronic instruments of this present era. Tired of their objections, he left the band. Fletcher, who understood what Ra was doing, didn't hire another piano player for three or four days. The horn players became so tired of playing without a piano they asked for Ra's return.

At another point in the early 50's, Ra had a seven-piece band that he led at the Grand Terrace in Chicago. For part of the show, the band had to play for a line of chorus girls.

Ra had seen a cartoon in the newspaper which involved the sun and thought it would be a good joke to play on the chorus girls; so he cut it out and put it on the club bulletin board. The girls went to their dressing room and made negative comments about him and his cartoon. Ra was downstairs playing while the girls were upstairs preparing to come on stage. While they criticized and laughed, a voice from nowhere filled the room, "Yes, he has that down there. And what he's talkin' about is true. And besides that, he's gonna do everything he say he's gonna do. And nothing will stop him."

One of the girls ran down, asking "Did Sun Ra come upstairs?" A fellow named Don told her that he had not been anywhere else but downstairs, playing the piano for a considerable time, and that he still was playing. She told the other girls, and they became frightened. The next night the producer of the show went to the dressing room and sprinkled a powder to keep away whatever it was that had spoken.

After leaving the Grand Terrace, Ra formed another band. This band, however, was of a unique nature. Ra told the musicians that the band was not going to make money now. Instead, they should rehearse for five years to develop a new music. He told them that they all should play in other groups to make money, but their own band was for experimentation.

Ra speaks of his reason for starting the band. "[There are] many different musicians all over the planet who are experimenting, particularly the white musicians who are trying to do something to change their race over another way, 'cause they knew something was going to happen to them if they don't change . . . In the Black race, it hasn't been like that. Musicians weren't planning nothing for their people as far as change is concerned. I had dedicated a so-called lifetime to doin' exactly that 'cause I knew we was gonna need it."

For a considerable time, they rehearsed every day for six hours. At these rehearsals, Ra's enormous creative energy would become evident. He was always anxious to rehearse and would present endless ideas. He might come to a rehearsal with two or three compositions and leave with three or four more. In the middle Fifties, he bought one of the first electronic pianos made and was one of the first, if not the first, to play it publicly.

Ra spoke of his writing for the band, saying that he "tailor makes" musical parts for each member of his band " . . . according to his vibrations, capabilities and potentials." "Can't nobody else in the world play it. It's just like a suit made for you. It might fit somebody else who looks like you but it'll fit you [better] because it's made for you."

When one listener at a rehearsal told Ra that the world should hear the music, he answered, "We're not concerned with the world. Other music has been started over in dope dens. This music is started another way. It's started from an intellectual point of view and a spiritual point of view. It's being developed without any white person sponsoring it. It's another kind of music. I want it like this to purify our own music. We have to do it this way."

But the listener persisted, "Now Birdland, you-all oughta be around there. Why don't you go around there and play?"

Ra: "I don't want to play around there. Cadillac Bob's not interested in this kind of music."

Listener: "If I got you all a job there would you play?"

Ra was forced to answer, "Yes," because the band members had previously expressed a desire to play together in public rather than always playing in different groups. The listener returned,

"Cadillac Bob wants to hear the band — now!"

When they arrived at Birdland, Ra still wanted to discourage Cadillac Bob, and picked the farthest out piece for their audition. While they played, Cadillac Bob got up, walked around, wondered, then demanded,

"Play that one again."

They repeated the piece and Bob shouted,

"You hired."

The band played there for two years.

In following years, they played in other local clubs. The advancement of the music continued with Sun Ra as the band's spiritual and musical leader. "My music comes from the Creator of the universe. Everything I ever played I played for him. All the while during those years, the early years, when I was at this piano anything I played, I played it for the Creator of the universe. I get right now at home, I play this. I don't have nothin' else to offer you [the Creator] but the music. You got everything else. Everything I create I'm offering it to you. And that's what I did . . . That's the way I praise the Man. I don't really need to pray. We're companions and friends. I just play these compositions for my friends . . .

"One time I had a series I called *Music from the Private Library of the Creator of the Universe.* There've been cases where I've tried to record it. It wouldn't record 'cause it was his property. And some things he don't want nobody else to hear it. That's it. So he kept it for himself, which I understand that. It wasn't for the world . . . It was really like forbidden territory for them."

Ra's spiritual and musical guidance inspired the men in his band to develop new ways of playing their instruments. The horn players would play notes that were usually considered "out of tune," and honks and screeches that were not considered "music."

Lester Young, many years before the formation of Sun Ra's band, had played many of these honks and screams and influenced Pat Patrick, the baritone saxophonist for the band. Another influence on Pat was Chicago saxophonist, Vaughn Freeman, who had played with Sun Ra earlier. While practicing his instrument, Pat found that the saxophone easily lent itself to these sounds called "overtones," and began to explore them.

One night while at Chicago's Sutherland Lounge, Pat heard the Miles Davis Sextet. For him, John was "magnificent," playing the things Pat had heard on the instrument in the back of his head. John's ideas were so "right," resolving, emerging, building up to the same logical conclusion he would have envisioned. His playing "seemed to fulfill so much."

Pat introduced himself and told how impressed he was. He noticed the humble manner in which John accepted his compliment. Next Pat mentioned Sun Ra and arranged for them to meet. Before they parted John gave Pat the aluminum pitcher in which he mixed his fruit and vegetable juices.

Ra had been doing much research on the origins and condition of Black people and had made some profound discoveries. These discoveries were printed on sheets of paper and passed on to Black people. Pat felt that John could benefit from this knowledge and gave him one of the sheets, entitled *Solaristic Precepts*:

To those who seek true wisdom, the bible should be considered as the Code (Cod) word instead of the Good Word or God Word. If you regard the bible as the "Code Word," you will be able to gain its hidden secrets. The hidden secrets of the bible are revealed visibly in its outer manifestations. The fabulous ramifications of the vibrations of sound in the outer sense which is the center and middle of the solaristic Eternal Thought can easily result in the creation of a Phi Beta sequence of life, which is twofold. The Divisions of Two: First Two: The sequence of life is the thorough consideration of the patterns of the past because coming events cast their shadow before, therefore the keys to wisdom are revealed in the unfolding of Hebraic SHD - ology in the life-giving form and the principles of ancient Sinology plus the sealed and hidden books of the angels of God, namely the Teutonic race of angels which are the visible host of the Eternal God according to the earth grammatical conception but according to our conception for every angel who is for US because you are either for US or against US. Us IS, US ARE, US BE, US AM (RE AM). Second 2: The sequence of life is sound diminished to its smallest point, the we of the Time to Live which is not recorded in the bible and therefore is in opposition to those who do not have a sine and since they are without the proper certification as those who are sine-conscious they are not aware of the diminished part of the Kingdom, as it is written "only the Few are eligible."

It is lamentable that NOT many people will understand this treatise which could well be a treaty via the Akhneaton version of sound (tone), if the many were not bound to the Christ-covenant which states that only the Few are eligible for life so in order not to antagonize the Kirk, only those who have shall get. The decree is that those who have knowledge shall understand our words which are a passport to Life.

Secrets Keys To Biblical Interpretation Leading To True Eternal Being —

The Number 9

1	10	19	28	37	46	55	64	73	82	91
2	11	20	29	38	47	56	65	74	83	92
3	12	21	30	39	48	57	66	75	84	93
4	13	22	31	40	49	58	67	76	85	94
5	14	23	32	41	50	59	68	77	86	95
6	15	24	33	42	51	60	69	78	87	96
7	16	25	34	43	52	61	70	79	88	97
8	17	26	35	44	53	62	71	80	89	98
9	18	27	36	45	54	63	72	81	90	99

Akhnaton
"Ra"

Warning: This treatise is only for Thinking "Beings" who are able to conceive of the negative reminiscences of Space - Time, as is expressed in Is, Are, Be and reconcepted "AM" which to the initiate is $---$, a symbol of Not or Non: Of course the idea is The Time To Live because if you are, you be, you is and Re $-$ Am is more appropriate than I AM (which according to the bible is A Dead Dog).

AKHNATON
"Ra"   [14]

Soon Sun Ra and John met for about four hours, during which Ra explained his music and played tapes for him. John told him that he had become dissatisfied playing with Miles because he had many things he wanted to do and didn't know where it would fit in with the sextet. They both agreed that it would be beneficial to play together. Ra was recorded by Saturn Records, headed by a brother named Abraham. But John had signed with Atlantic. Whenever John was in Chicago, they would see each other and Ra would give him more of his literature.

Toward the end of the year John was making gigs under his own name, when the Miles Davis sextet was off. At the Bohemian Caverns in Washington, D.C., he made one job with pianist Albert Dailey. During this engagement, two important requirements for a group of his own were apparent. One was that John's pianist could not play multi-noted choruses while he soloed. Rather, the pianist would have to play only the chords and play sparsely in order to function as a platform from which John could soar. The drummer would have to be constantly contributing ideas, playing more than was customary at the time.

John told Dailey that he felt that they had a good rapport and asked him to come to New York. When Dailey answered that he had a family to think about and wasn't ready to move to New York, John offered to make arrangements for his family. But Dailey still declined, feeling that the situation had to be more definite for him to take the chance with his family. It was on returning from this or another job in Washington that chance, time's cousin, presented John with a gift. "Three of us were driving back from a date in Washington in 1959. Two of us were on the front seat and the other guy, a sax player, in the back. He was being very quiet. At Baltimore we made a rest stop, then got back in the car, and 30 minutes later realized that the guy in the back wasn't there. We hoped he had some money with him and drove on. I took his horn and suitcase to my apartment in New York. I opened the case and found a soprano sax. I started fooling around with it and was fascinated. That's how I discovered the instrument."[15]

In studying the new horn, his investigation of the past bore fruit. Sidney Bechet was a phenomenal soprano saxophonist and clarinetist of the 1920's and '30's, who played with thrashing abandon, excitement, and a full, warm, wavering sound. John had at least one of his records entitled *Sidney Bechet, the grand master of the soprano saxophone and clarinet.*

In late 1959, another musical force was about to erupt. Coleman was a self-taught alto saxophonist and composer, who, as a natural outgrowth of the way in which he heard music, arrived at a different basis for improvisation.[16] He called his theory the Har-Melodic theory of music; one of its conclusions is the elimination of chords as a basis for improvisation. Knowledge of his life gives a better understanding of his contribution.

Ornette was born in Fort Worth, Texas, March 19, 1930. When only seven, his father died. His mother, a seamstress, did her best to make beginnings meet. Ornette remembers hearing music everywhere, "I used to go in the neighborhood and hear guys playing Kazoos, and various kinds of odd instruments, combs, for example. But I really didn't get into any kind of music myself until my first year of high school."[17]

He begged his mother for a horn, but she couldn't afford it. Finally, she broke down, on condition that he get a job and help with family expenses. He agreed. "One night she woke me up and told me to look under the bed, and there was an alto saxophone. I never touched a horn before."[1][7] He soon began playing in rhythm and blues bands in Fort Worth. He would sit at home, listen to the latest R & B record, go to a club and try to stand up to one of the older saxophonists. When he couldn't stand next to them he usually got no help, but was sent back home to listen to his record some more. One musician whom Ornette admired, Red Connors, did help by teaching him the value of reading music and introducing him to types of music other than rhythm and blues. This other type was the "modern" or "progressive" music of the time, played by men like Charlie Parker, trumpeter Fats Navarro, drummer Max Roach, or bassist Charles Mingus. The first Charlie Parker composition he heard was *Now Is The Time*, which he thought was the rhythm and blues tune called the *Hucklebuck*. Actually the *Hucklebuck* was based on *Now Is The Time*. Ornette reasoned that since *The Hucklebuck* and *Now Is The Time* were the same composition, then "modern" music and R & B must be related. In spite of this realization, there was the fact that he wanted to do more with music than the places where rhythm and blues was played would tolerate.

After traveling with a number of unfulfilling bands, he joined an R & B group headed by Clarence Samuels. In Baton Rouge, the band was playing in a tough dancehall. Ornette suddenly decided to play more, adding his own ideas and those of the "progressive" music in the middle of his blues solo. This was not appreciated. He only succeeded in stopping the dance and upsetting some of the meanest dudes at the dance.

During intermission a girl told Ornette that someone outside wanted to see him. He took his horn in its case and walked out. Outside he found himself on a hill in the darkness. At least three men surrounded him, and he could feel, before they touched him, that they were going to beat him up. His first thought was to protect his horn, so he bent over and wrapped his arms around it. They unfolded him and slung the horn brutally down the hill; then proceeded to just whip his ass.

Afterwards he went to the police, who told him if he didn't leave town by sun-up they would kill him. Fortunately, he was able to take refuge in a friend's house.

Soon he would learn that even musicians who played "progressive" music could be just as hostile as the public to his ideas. When trying to jam with other musicians, they would often walk off the bandstand. They would say that he couldn't play, because they had never heard a concept quite like his. They thought that he couldn't play changes.

What they didn't understand was that he was playing the changes, but as *he heard* them, not as he read them. When the pianist played a chord with variations he would play according to the way the chord sounded, not what it would be if it were not varied. This insistence on playing what he, Ornette, heard formed the seed of an important theory of music.

After much financial hardship, and the sadness of rejection and isolation from most musicians, he gradually met others who were also experimenting in streams complementary to his. These musicians became strong supporters. Among this group were drummer Billy Higgins, bassist Charlie Haden and trumpeter Don Cherry. This was the quartet that he took with him to New York to play at The Five Spot. The traditional piano in the quartet was not necessary because the piano was no longer needed to play chords as a guide for the group. His theory is very complex and has many ramifications. Part of it is explained in his directions to his bassist, "Forget about the changes in key and just play within the range of the idea. If I'm in the high register just play within that range that fits that register and just play the bass, that's all. All you've got to do is play the bass."[18]

Haden expressed his difficulty with this concept, to which Ornette answered, "Well, just learn."

Ornette explained how his advice was taken. "So after a while of playing with me it just became the natural thing for him to do. All that matters in the function of the bass is either the top or the bottom or the middle, that's all the bass player has to play for me. It doesn't mean because you put an F-seventh down for the bass player he's going to choose the best notes in the F-seventh to express what you're doing. But if he's allowed to use any note that he hears to express that F-seventh, then that note's going to be right because he hears it, not because he read it off the page."[18]

Ornette's concept of music developed from the way in which he heard chords on the piano, which eventually developed to the elimination of the need for chords as a map or guideline. Instead, the music was held together by the shape of the idea, whatever it may be, that excited the group at the moment.

Ornette's debut at The Five Spot caused a wide variety of reactions. George Hoeffer of *Down Beat* wrote, "Some walked in and out before they could finish a drink, some sat mesmerized by the sound, others talked incessantly to their neighbors . . . " Comments also varied: "He'll change the entire course of jazz." "He's a genius." "He swings like hell." "I'm going home to listen to my Benny Goodman trios and quartets." "He's out, real far out." "I like him, but I don't have any idea of what he's doing."[19]

A new presence had struck the music scene, causing the same confusion that had occurred with past innovators.

Another assault on the chordal basis of music was made by George Russell, who had John on his record date for *New York, New York* in 1958.

This assault came in the form of a book which Russell wrote and entitled, *The Lydian Chromatic Concept of Tonal Organization.* Russell commented on this theory, "The jazz musician, to some degree, has had to learn traditional music theory only to break many of its rules in practice. Other theories have come along, but the jazz musician has made fractional use, if any, of them. Perhaps because they weren't a natural evolvement from the chord basis that underlies jazz and all traditional western music.

"A theory of any kind demands obedience at first in order to master it. However, a really useful theory doesn't enslave one without making the period of servitude interesting and worthwhile and without eventually freeing its subscribers through its own built-in liberation apparatus.

The theory which forces you to rebel against its concepts in order to find freedom is obviously not fulfilling the needs required of it."[20]

Russell felt that western theory was only a rationalization of the way western music behaves. He also felt that the "jazz musician is in an excellent position because he has really had to go into chords more than others," and that this intensive exploration of chords led to the expansion of chords and ultimate liberation from their restrictions. In his theory, Russell merely "codified the normal tendencies of jazz musicians" and took these tendencies to their final conclusion.

One day Ornette and John visited Russell, who explained his theory, saying it allowed you to play any interval to get to any point, any note. John, however, did not give an indication of readily accepting this idea. It seemed that he wanted a scheme that took him to definite points by a definite formula. Russell sent him a copy of his book.

As 1959 ended, John's popularity had increased significantly, among the public if not the critics. In the *Down Beat* Readers' Poll, John placed third in the established saxophonist category, with Getz and Rollins first and second respectively. Two years earlier he had been only eleventh. Financial advancement was reflected by the family moving into a house in St. Albans, Queens. His rise in popularity did not come about by sacrificing his goals. Rather he developed his voice, his art, even further.

In November, 1959, he recorded another album, entitled "Coltrane Jazz." Some of his compositions on the album were *Fifth House, Harmonique,* and *Like Sonny.* The Title, "Fifth House," comes from astrology, in which planetary bodies reside in twelve houses. The fifth house is the house of love, creativity, children and things of a similar nature. The title also comes from the fact that the chords of the composition are partially based on the chords of the popular song *What Is This Thing Called Love?* These two facts combined to form the title. *Like Sonny* refers to the tenor saxophonist, Sonny Rollins, whom John and Naima *had* to see whenever he was playing in New York. John would select a seat directly in front of the bandstand so that he wouldn't miss a thing. One night Sonny played a figure that doubled John over into laughing pleasure. He and Nita went home, and John picked up his horn to play what he had heard. Out of this musical figure came the composition *Like Sonny. Harmonique* is a piece in which John extensively uses his ability to play three notes at once. Once in a club he played an entire ballad in tritones, in other words, playing three notes at once instead of only one at a time.

For John the music had broad dimensions inescapably bound with a search for new feelings, a knowledge of himself, understanding his existence and place in the universe, and a desire to be close to God. These strivings stemmed from a kind and intense spirit. His religious background and innate tendencies led him to the study of Eastern religion, Islam, Hindu, and Yoga, about which he read many books. Throughout his life he had constantly been reading, but much of the reading on religion began after he borrowed a book which pianist Bill Evans had, *On and By Khrishnamurthi.* After finishing it, he asked Naima for her thoughts on the book; she answered by asking what his thoughts were. He simply said that he would "like to look more deeply into that."

He assimilated and interrelated knowledge voraciously, reading books on nearabout every subject. His library grew with books on other cultures, math, art and artists such as Van Gogh, music theory, physics, biology, African history, spirituals, among others. He was engaged in an accelerated accumulation of knowledge and understanding, almost as if he had to rush to finish something before the . . .

His record library also increased to include music from all over

Africa, Afghanistan, Russia, France, Early England, Greece, the American Indians, India, Arabia, as well as all types of African-American music. His search continued for the drone he heard after finally dominating the habits that were preventing him from reaching his potential. He found a sound close to the drone in Indian music. Still, it was not exactly what he had heard that night.

In many of his dreams he would hear music or feel something which he did not want to forget. He wouldn't want to be disturbed some mornings on awaking and would lie motionless in bed, his eyes closed, for about 30 minutes. Naima understood and would not disturb him. Afterwards they would talk about what he had heard. For her, being with John, with the records from all over the world, his broad interests in practically everything, and his dreams, was like taking a trip without really having gone anyplace.

Once when he was with the Miles Davis Sextet at the Apollo Theater in Harlem, he got down on his knees, throwing off the fire of his improvisation. On another occasion at the Apollo, he just played; closed his eyes and continued over the twenty-minute time limit the Apollo set for each group. The lights were blinking. Curtains were going back and forth. The station manager shouted to Miles, "Go get him, man! Go get him! We runnin' over the show! Stop him!" but John kept on playing. That's how much he was in love with creating.

E-flat was his favorite key for ballads; he would amuse himself by playing two notes in all the keys. He enjoyed going to art museums, especially when there were exhibits of abstract art. In his backyard he had a telescope, through which he would gaze upon the heavens. Movies didn't interest him except when Saida wanted to go, or something special was playing.

His laughter was still natural and his speech hadn't adopted the er's and er ah's that some Black people took on when they moved up north — trying to speak "proper." He still liked the raisins he carried in his pocket when a child, but now he would also buy stacks of boxes of butter rum lifesavers and eat them when at the nightclub; offer them to his friends. Once he was involved in a minor car accident. At the police station, the policeman claimed that he had whiskey on his breath. John denied this, saying that if anything it was the butter rum lifesavers he was eating, and showed them to the policeman, after which everyone had a big laugh.

He loved to eat and his diet, as well as that of the family, would vary from strict health foods for a while to an unlimited variety. He would get a taste for one particular food at any time of the day or night, and would drive long distances to get it. There was a chicken giblet place in Boston, that for him and Naima was a must whenever they were there. He liked to go to dairy restaurants. In Manhattan there was a Pakistani restaurant where he and other musicians who played with him would go. Sometimes Naima would prepare a big dinner. John would come home and say "Let's go eat" this or that. The dinner then would be packed away in the refrigerator, and they would eat wherever John had a yearning. One day Nita and Tony cleared a long shelf in the kitchen. John had a taste for watermelon and the next day the entire shelf was filled with them. He often drank fruit juices, and when he felt he had gained too much weight, he would go on week-long crash diets of fruit juices and nuts.

He still didn't wear socks and hadn't worn underwear since he was eighteen. He disliked anything that was restricting, from music to the clothes he wore. Once he was asked about utilizing Schonberg's 12-tone system in his improvisation. His answer was, "Damn the rules; it's the feeling that counts. You play all twelve notes in your solo anyway." Around the house he would flop around in old soft shoes with the back of his shirt halfway out in a comfortable carefree manner. When in Philadelphia, he once bought some new stylish shoes, but they were uncomfortable, and he wore them only long enough to show his mother.

At home he liked harmony and peacefulness. He had much respect for many musicians known and not well known. Often he would compliment them so sincerely that it would be embarassing to someone who was with him. Some thought he was henpecked because he was so quiet and often asked Naima's opinion on various things. But early in their marriage, she learned that if he saw the sense in something he would pursue it to its conclusion. But if he didn't see any sense in it, it was a waste of time to push him, because he was "like a brick wall ten feet high, ten feet wide, ten feet long, and ten feet into the ground." He "was the strength" in their house. Many who met him felt he was an "angel" or a "saint." Freddie Hubbard felt "kind" when around him. He would often talk to people, trying to uplift them, and when they finished conversing with him, they would feel better. He felt very keenly about the injustices that his people had to suffer and, although, as he said, he was not one to get up "on a soapbox," he always felt that he wanted to do something to help. When it came to the psychological damage or brainwashing that had been dealt upon his people, he would joke with friends, saying that, if someone built a Black housing project where the rent was only a dollar a month, some Blacks wouldn't move into it unless it was integrated. He was also disturbed by the gang warfare in which Chicago Black youth were fighting and killing one another. He was concerned to the extent that he wanted desperately to do something about it.

Many spirits were finding each other in the latter part of 1959, in preparation for the next decade. The Black protest movement was probing the iron curtain of racism. A new consciousness was evolving, containing elements of the resounding eloquence of Martin Luther King, the hard rhythmic words of Malcolm X, the stern red courage of Patrice Emery Lumumba, the theories of Ornette Coleman, the energy of Sun Ra and the strength, compassion, and all-embracing love of John Coltrane.

X

The Search

By early 1960, momentum for John to leave the Miles Davis Sextet had grown immensely. *Giant Steps* was widely acclaimed as an artistic as well as a technical milestone in music.

> For several years now, John Coltrane has been one of the most influential tenor saxophonists in modern jazz. With his latest album, "Giant Steps," (Atlantic) he definitely becomes the No. 1 man in his field. Backed only by a rhythm section, and playing only his own compositions, Coltrane is as clearly revealed as a redwood in a pasture. He meets the inspection admirably as he displays his emotional intensity, his lyricism, his technical command of his horn, and his beautiful sense of form. The ballad, *Naima*, is a delightful demonstration of Coltrane's ability to make moving use of few notes. At the opposite extreme is *Countdown*, in which the racing solo

suggests the path which Ornette Coleman is following. Coltrane's solo on *Spiral*, which uses a descending chromatic line, is intense yet not fierce. Space forbids going into other details, but it should be said that this is definitely an important jazz album.[1]

Oakland Tribune, 1960

Also during this time, the Sextet went on its European tour. Upon returning, John gave Miles a two-week notice of his departure. He bought his first soprano saxophone in February. Later Joe and Iggy Termini, co-owners of The Five Spot, offered him twenty weeks at their new club, the Jazz Gallery, and promised him the same salary paid by Miles. Although this was a small amount of money for a leader, John accepted. He realized that the value of the Terminis' offer was the extended length of time he would have to play continuously with his own group. This would enable him to clarify the musical elements necessary to produce the feeling he sought.

Rather than twenty weeks John took only nine. He was a free agent, and everyone — listeners, musicians, critics, recording companies — waited impatiently to hear the music that would result. Among musicians, the word was out that John was looking for sidemen. Pianist Steve Kuhn called him, saying, "I imagine you don't know who I am. I feel as though I can contribute to your music, and I would be very happy to play with you."

John was reluctant to respond definitely. He knew nothing of Kuhn. But a week later when Kuhn called again, he was receptive, possibly after having obtained a personal reference. They set up a meeting at a rehearsal studio. After playing together for a while, John told him that he would call him back to let him know of his decision. He called two days later and asked if $135.00 a week would be enough. Steve readily accepted.

Sonny Rollins and John were discussing various musicians at this time. Rollins suggested a drummer, Pete La Rocca, who had played with him. For bassist John chose Steve Davis from Philadelphia, in whose house he had met Naima. The quartet was now assembled. May, 1960, was the premiere.

It was a warm day in the Village, where there was always an air of festivity, which was enhanced by the event that was going to take place. The Jazz Gallery was a large club. As you walked in the door, you first saw a horseshoe bar beyond which there was a large audience area with tables and chairs. There were also chairs along the side and in the balcony. At the end of your walk you came to the bandstand. A feeling of expectation and curiosity thrived. In this audience were players of African-American music, European music, actors, writers, Beatniks, staunch "jazz" fans and just plain folks. Cecil Taylor was in the balcony. Monk was down front waiting for it. Time created a gap between the full house of waiting people and the quartet which had not yet appeared.

Finally they came on stage. John's usual nervousness on beginning a job was probably heightened now by the fact that this was *his* band, *his* premiere. But a huge smile lighted his face, giving the impression that he was very happy, happy to be doing exactly what he was doing at this moment.

Music lashed into the air, and on the first tune both the crowd and the group seemed restless. They began the second tune, and John hit something. The music had a brightness – a buoyancy. It was mostly in a blues vein, raw and genuine. John kept getting deeper and heavier into the music, moving the crowd to a frenzy. Suddenly they stood up in a powerful mass, shouting "Col-trane! Col-trane!" At that point a big, bronze, baldheaded man, who had on no shoes, no shirt, no pants – only a loin cloth – ran up to the side of the stage, arched his body upward and shouted, "Col-trane! Col-trane! Col-trane!" Right behind him followed Monk, who did his dance to the music. John pointed his horn upward, striving for the highest heights. However, Pete La Rocca, behind him, had gotten carried away in the excitement. John had to stop playing and tell him to settle down. This stirred a string of laughter through the audience. Throughout the performance, excitement danced within the Gallery. The night ended. The premiere – an overwhelming success. Emotions broke their barriers. When he walked down the aisle after the performance, people reached out and kissed his hand.

An article appeared in the *New York Daily News* telling of the music being made at the Gallery.

> Run, do not walk or otherwise loiter on your way down to the Jazz Gallery. The reason is John Coltrane, a tenor saxophonist who has the future coming out of his horn.
> This musician is phenomenal. Few jazzmen possess such a thorough knowledge of their instrument plus the combined imagination and feeling to translate that knowledge into great music. Coltrane is not just a player. He is a composer, practicing his craft every moment he is on the stand. He creates huge patterns of interwoven themes united in a beautifully-knit whole. The sounds he produces are often weird, like

they shouldn't be coming out of that horn at all, but somehow he makes them seem natural. It's as if these notes were hiding inside all along, just waiting for someone to appear and release them.

Every now and then, however, Coltrane lays the tenor aside and works on that rare bird of jazz, the soprano saxophone. The story here is the same. Tremendous. If I were a budding soprano saxophonist and heard Coltrane, I'd send my horn to the Salvation Army. Who can follow the boss?

Though Coltrane completely dominates the stage, he has sturdy backing from pianist Steve Kuhn, bassist Steve Davis and drummer Pete La Rocca. Kuhn is especially resourceful and Davis sounds fine. La Rocca, too, performs well, though his occasional histrionics could probably get him a card in Actors' Equity.[2]

John asked Folks his opinion of the group.

"Shit wasn't right."

He told John that the rhythm section seemed to be competing rather than supporting him and, " . . . as soon as you get rid of that white boy on piano . . . " the group would improve. He also said that the bassist was not giving him what he needed. John asked him the names of musicians Folks had used years ago in Philadelphia. Folks answered, "That's who to get. One of 'ems name is McCoy Tyner."

John had been thinking of McCoy all along. But at this time, McCoy was with the Jazztet at the Village Vanguard. McCoy had to take jobs with other bands because he was unable to wait the two years it had taken John to finally go on his own. However, McCoy felt it was his right to be in John's group, especially since he was so familiar with the concepts and feelings involved. During intermission McCoy would run over to the Gallery to hear John's group.

It was also John's feeling that McCoy should work with him. But he was hesitant to interfere with the Jazztet, which had a reputation of being a tightly-knit band. Naima was the catalyst. Finally he asked McCoy, saying "It's up to you, man."

Even though the weight of the decision was placed on McCoy, he gave an affirmative answer. Now John had to ask Kuhn to leave. "Steve, I think I'm going to have to give you a notice."

Kuhn, upset by this asked, "John, can you tell me what it is you want me to do, or don't want me to do?"

John answered, evenly, "No, I can't tell you how to play. I have a great deal of respect for what you do. But it's not what I want to hear."

Two weeks after the Gallery engagement began, McCoy was in the pianist's seat. A different concept was now brought to the instrument.

Instead of prodding and improvising heavily while John soloed, as Kuhn used to do, McCoy provided a platform from which John could flash upward. After John's solo, McCoy would add his own explorations, showing a masterful technique, imagination, and a percussive effect in the sharp way in which he struck his chords. One unique aspect of his playing was the facility of his left hand, which kept a rhythmic chordal sound constantly in the music. McCoy expressed his feeling on the relationship of the soloist to the rest of the group. "A rhythm section is supposed to support and inspire a soloist, and it is a very sensitive thing ... Sometimes when John is soloing I lay out completely. Something important is involved here, I think. The pianist tends to play chords that the soloist knows are coming up anyway. Normally, all the pianist does is try to give him a little extra push in the accompaniment and possibly to suggest some new ideas. When the piano isn't there, the soloist can concentrate purely on what he has in mind with fewer limitations or boundaries. Otherwise, what the pianist plays can attract his attention away from his original thought. So it is all a manner of giving the soloist more freedom to explore harmonically."[3]

About McCoy, John said he liked his " . . . fine sense of form, and the fresh sound he gets on the piano, by the way he voices his chords. McCoy has a beautiful lyric concept that is essential to complement the rest of us." "I've known him for some time and I've always felt I wanted to play with him. Our ideas meet and blend. Working with McCoy is like putting on a nice fitting glove."[4]

Each week a different group was featured with John's: Art Blakey's, Chico Hamilton's, Stan Getz' — among others. Getz was ecstatic as he heard John play. Both public and critics now accepted the music. Even though he was secure financially and had reached an artistic plateau, he continued to search, study and reshape his concepts.

This activity can be seen by these samples from one of his work books, which shows scales from different parts of the world. These samples are on the following page.

His study of Eastern music, Miles' influence in using uncommon modes, his own study of modes, his inner spirit, and Chance, Time's half-brother, led him to another area of music.

One night a regular customer at the Gallery brought in a pile of sheet music and showed it to John. He made special reference to *My Favorite Things* saying, "I think you'll like this tune."

No one realized that this tune would open up even greater success and a new area of exploration. John made only a few rearrangements of

5
Japanese
Pentatonic
Egyptian
Balinese
Persian
Persian

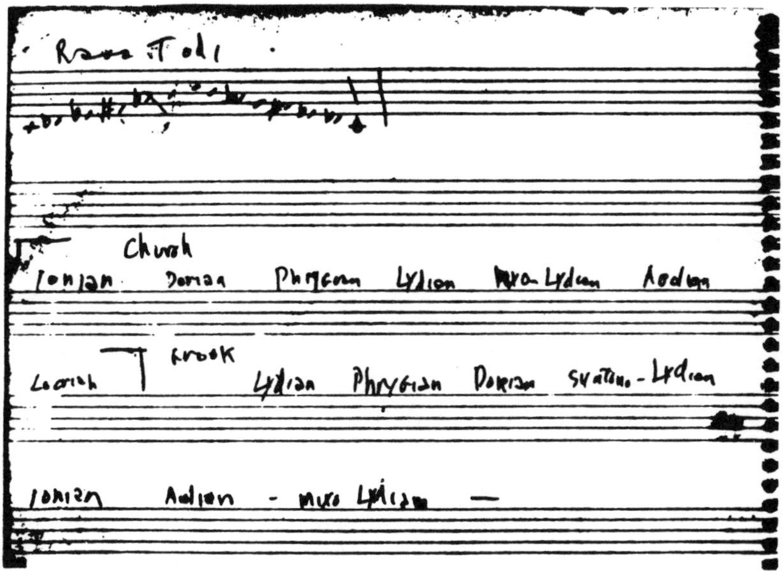
Raga Todi
Church
Ionian Dorian Phrygian Lydian Mixo-Lydian Aeolian
Locrian
Greek
Lydian Phrygian Dorian
Ionian Aeolian - Mixo Lydian —

the song. But these few changes were of crucial importance. At the 17th bar on the chord of E minor, seven bars were added. Farther along in the song at the 35th bar, 23 bars were added on the chord of E major. This apportionment of so much time to one chord resembled Indian music in which numerous improvisations are molded over one chord.

It was also significant that the song had sections based on a minor, in addition to the standard major mode. This minor section enabled John to produce the Eastern flavor in his solos that he loved so well. He played the song with a soprano saxophone that spoke a lilting scream or breathed a soothing stream. Intertwined with this sound was the steady bass pulsation, the jiggling rhythm of the drums, and the hum of the piano, all over a magical waltz tempo. The song hypnotized, producing a beautiful garden of graceful ivy and gushing fountains, whose waters burned a refreshing coolness. After the development of *My Favorite Things* came other compositions with fewer and fewer chords. These contrasted with the multichorded structures of compositions like *Countdown* or *Giant Steps*. The Indian sitar player Ravi Shankar came to the Gallery. He, John and McCoy spoke of doing an album together. But the album was never made.

Part of the agreement with Termini was that the nine weeks at the Gallery could be distributed as John wished. At about the seventh week the group went to Small's Paradise in Harlem. There, much of the group's repertoire was blues played with original improvisatory ideas, to which some of the club's patrons were not accustomed. Once during the first few days, a couple of people booed. But later, the audience response was much improved. John said of cold audiences: "A cold audience will make you fear that you're not pleasing them. It can kind of put a damper on your spirits. You learn that you've got to override this. If you give up and let them dampen your spirits, you can't play. You might as well give up. You've got to bear down and give them all you've got."[6]

After Small's the group returned to the Gallery to finish two more weeks. One night John and his friend Eric Dolphy went to The Five Spot and sat in with Ornette's rhythm section, which consisted of Jimmy Garrison on bass and Charles Moffet on drums. When they started to play, Garrison and Moffet exerted only a mediocre effort. Ornette, who was off the bandstand, considered this a lack of respect and shouted, "What do you motherfuckers think you're doing?" As if coming to attention when the commanding officer orders, Garrison and

Moffet tightened up and began reaching for the moon, just as they did when playing with Ornette.

Afterward John asked Ornette about his method of improvising without using chords as a guideline. Ornette invited him and Eric to his apartment in the East Village. There, Ornette explained his theory and wrote out charts for them, showing the relationships of their instruments to keys, chords and other elements of music under his Har-Melodic theory of music. John was so excited about Ornette that for two weeks at home, he spoke of him continually.

After the Gallery engagement, the group toured the country. Conversation was sparse on these long road trips. This was because driving tired everyone out and John, when he wasn't driving, would sleep. He was not very talkative anyway. When conversation did occur, John would say that if he could sing he would rather do that than play an instrument. Then he might jokingly sing *O Solo Mio* as the others laughed. Conversation took another turn when McCoy joined the group. It turned to religion.

McCoy was a devoted and faithful Moslem. He entered the religion when he was seventeen, the year that he first met John and Naima, as well as his wife Aisha, whom Naima had known since she was a small child. Aisha encouraged McCoy to enter the faith. He changed his name to Sulieman Saud. Uniquely, Saud was a man whose personal beliefs were in complete agreement with his personal practices, regarding family, friends, acquaintances and the Creator. John considered him "an anchor" that gave strength. For him Saud was a spiritual as well as a musical influence. Saud's statement reveals a small portion of his strength: "We talk a lot about freedom in jazz, but there are underlying disciplines too. When you have the discipline of religion, as I have, I think you can meet the demands of music and function better. There are a lot of pressures on musicians' lives, and it is easy to understand why some fall by the wayside. But you have to strengthen yourself to meet these pressures. You can't wait for them all to be removed from your environment.

"There are reasons for the pressures and problems. People will usually think of God at a time of tragedy but not when everything is running smoothly. But most musicians believe in God, because most of them are very sensitive individuals."[7]

Before leaving New York, John told Naima that Pete La Rocca wasn't playing quite what he wanted. She suggested that John tell him what he would like for La Rocca to play. But John refused, saying that he had respect for a person's individual concept and didn't want to interfere with it. La Rocca also was somewhat dissatisfied with the group, though at the same time he enjoyed playing with it. He felt that the many-chord progressions in the music were keeping the group from being a tightly functioning unit. He also felt music in a way different from John. He preferred Miles Davis' music of the late 50's, with its wide spaces and surrealistic sounds. After traveling to Detroit, Chicago and Pittsburgh, the group arrived in Philadelphia. There, with a mutual lack of animosity, La Rocca was replaced by Billy Higgins who had just previously been with Ornette. But the multi-rhythms of Elvin Jones' drums still echoed in John's mind.

Travel was hard for John's as well as other Black groups. They went by car to each city as far as California. It seemed that they would always arrive at their destination just in time to go directly from the car to the club. In Chicago the group had an engagement at the Sutherland Lounge. Roland Kirk, a blind saxophonist who could play three horns at the same time, knocked on John's hotel door.

Oh no!, was John's jocular greeting. Ornette Coleman and Don Cherry came by later. They looked over Japanese and European jazz magazines while John and Roland played and discussed the creation of two notes simultaneously on the horn. After finishing this discussion John turned his attention to Ornette with whom he spoke about music.

The problem was to contact Elvin. Naima tried unsuccessfully to set up a meeting. In Philadelphia, Elvin went to hear Miles, who told him that John was in California and looking for him. Elvin left his phone number and address with Miles. Finally, while off on a Monday night in San Francisco, John took a plane to New York to search for him. He walked into Birdland asking for Elvin. He was not there and no one had seen him. Later that night, they finally met, and John asked him to join the group. Elvin was committed to another band at the moment but said that he would meet John at the next city they played in, which was Denver. There Elvin joined. For the remainder of the tour he and Billy Higgins alternated between sets. By the time they worked their way back to New York, Elvin was the only drummer.

When a critic mentioned that some musicians had said that Elvin was too deep for them to play with, John laughed and answered, "Sometimes I can't play with him." At another time he said: "I especially like his ability to mix and jiggle rhythm. He's always aware of everything else that's happening. I guess you could say he has the ability to be in three places at the same time."[8] This was the primary factor in John's love for Elvin's playing.

A powerful component was now added to the music. Elvin could keep two or more rhythms going at the same time, making it seem that more than one drummer was playing, and bathing the soloist in an electrifying sheath of time. He could add to the emotional quality of the music with creative rhythmic and melodic ideas on the drum. At the emotional highpoints, he would emphasize the turns of feeling with boom, RRRoom, RrRoooom Wham! His playing was deep and strong and added to the intensity of the group.

This intensity was steadily increasing as the fabric of the music was being woven together. John was playing faster and faster against anything until his total sound became a wail. He maintained his use of intricate tones followed by searing long tones and human-like hollers. Sometimes he would sound like some mothers down south, who, instead of shouting their children's names, would put their hands to their mouths and howl a "Whooo" which the children recognized.

Indications of John's rising popularity appeared in the press. The results of the International Critics Poll in the August 8, 1960, issue of *Down Beat* showed John in second place in the tenor saxophone category behind Coleman Hawkins. The September 29th issue of the magazine had an extensive article entitled *Coltrane on Coltrane* which was written by John in collaboration with critic Don DeMichael. Below are some excerpts from this article. Some of these excerpts are found only in the rough draft. He spoke of his 3-on-1 chord approach.

"I haven't completely abandoned this approach, but it wasn't broad enough. I'm trying to play these progressions in a more flexible manner now."[9]

He wrote of his group and the soprano saxophone. Pete La Rocca is mentioned here as the drummer since the article was written while he was in the band, but published after Elvin joined.

"Last February, I bought a soprano saxophone. I like the sound of it, but I'm not playing with the body, the bigness of tone, that I want yet. I haven't had too much trouble playing it in tune, but I've had a lot of trouble getting a good quality of tone in the upper register. It comes out sort of puny sometimes. I've had to adopt a different approach than the one I use for tenor, but it helps me get away — lets me take another look at improvisation. It's like having another hand. I'm using it with my present group, McCoy Tyner, piano; Steve Davis, bass; and Pete La Rocca, drums. The quartet is coming along nicely. We know basically what we're trying for and we leave room for individual development. Individual contributions are put in night by night."

He commented again on the term, "Angry Young Tenor Men": "When I first heard the phrase, I didn't know what the writers were talking about. My playing isn't angry. It's strictly a musical venture with me. All I want to do is produce a lot of music. It shouldn't sound that way. That's why I always thought it meant we were trying to play something different from the patterns we had been bound to. I decided I didn't want to play the same way I had been playing anymore."[10]

He was asked about announcing the men in his group, and the tunes they were going to play, which he rarely did in performance. "Announcements help. There may not be much need for Miles to do it, since everybody who comes to hear him knows the tunes from his records anyway, and in his case it's probably right not to make announcements. But for a group like mine that does tunes that haven't been recorded, it's probably necessary to make announcements. I haven't done so recently, but in the future I will."[1 1]

Afterwards, however, he never kept this promise. The quartet just played music.

The article also touched upon Ornette Coleman in response to the question, "Do you think Coleman's music is the direction in which jazz is headed?"

"Jazz is made by the men who make it. Coleman is definitely one direction — there it is and there he is. Others will follow in it."[1 2]

Next he was asked about Coleman's dispensing with the bar line in his composing. "I haven't experimented too much with time. Most of my experimentation has been in an harmonic form, so far. I kind of put time and rhythms aside. Ornette has certainly given us something to think about though."[1 3]

He went on to write of his goals. "One of my aims is to build as good a repertoire as I can for a band. What size I couldn't say, but it'll probably be a quartet or quintet. I want to get the material first. Right now, I'm on a material search.

"From a technical viewpoint, I have certain things I'd like to present in my solos. To do this I have to get the right material. It has to swing, and it has to be varied. (I'm inclined to not be too varied.) I want to cover as many forms of music that I can put into a jazz context and play on my instruments. I like Eastern music; Yusef Lateef has been using this in his playing for some time. And Ornette Coleman sometimes plays music with a Spanish content. In these approaches there's something I can draw on and use in the way I like to play.

"I've been writing some things for the quartet — if you call lines and sketches writing. I'd like to write more after I learn more — after I've found out what kind of material I can present best. Then I'll better know what kind of writing is best for me.

"I've been devoting quite a bit of time to harmonic studies on my own, in libraries and places like that. I've found you've got to look back at the old things and see them in a new light. I'm not finished with these studies because I haven't assimilated everything into my playing. I want to progress, but I don't want to go so far out that I can't see what others are doing.

"I want to broaden my outlook in order to come out with a fuller means of expression. I want to be more flexible where rhythm is concerned. I feel I must study rhythm some more. I haven't experimented too much with time. Most of my experimenting has been in an harmonic form. I kind of put time and rhythms to one side in the past.

"But I've got to keep experimenting. I feel that I'm just beginning. I have part of what I'm looking for in my grasp, but not all."[14]

The rough draft ended with this statement: "I'm very happy devoting all my time to music, and I'm glad to be one of the many who are striving for fuller development as musicians. I look to the future optimistically and wish for all of us happy and productive lives."[15]

On the back of the rough draft he wrote his change of the last sentence, which appeared in the final copy.

Considering the great
heritage in music that we have,
the greats of past & present &
future, I'm certain I have
every reason to face the future
optimistically.

In the October 10th issue of *Down Beat*, the results of the readers' poll were printed. For the first time John was voted first in the regular saxophone category, with Stan Getz second. A Japanese poll was conducted this year which put John in second place behind Sonny Rollins. One admirer wrote this letter —

Saturday
October 29, 1960

Dear Mr. John Coltrane "Saxophonist Extraordinary"

Please accept my heart felt thanks for an original, exciting, moving and unparalleled experience in modern jazz. Sincerely, I shall never forget your fabulous display of musical maturity and genius.

I read somewhere that no one ever bothered to say thank you to the great Lester Young. Well, sir, I surely do not want to be guilty of committing this neglect against an equally beautiful individual, John Coltrane.

Your exhilarating music thoroughly convinces me that the news I have heard about town is absolutely true: "JOHN COLTRANE IS THE GREATEST OF THE LIVING SAXOPHONISTS."

Jazz enthusiasts in my home town rave over you. You would be amazed to know how many intelligent young people are deeply interested in your splendid work. In fact, my section of Jersey appropriately could be called "Coltraneville."

For over twenty years I've had an avid interest in jazz. In complete truth, I sincerely believe that I witnessed musical history Saturday night at the Half Note.

Your music is a rare jewel of inspiration. The raw emotion and incredible ideas contained therein had me laughing with unbridled exuberance, and in true admiration.

Your indescribable love for music is a touching thing to hear and witness. Your knowledge of chords is stupendous, and your perpetually fresh talent without doubt will become a lasting, living legend. The whole truth of the matter is that any genuinely new sounds in modern music MUST come from the bountiful, free-flowing horn of John Coltrane.

Up on the bandstand with your marvelously cohesive group, you are the epitome of competence — what a truly magnificent sight to behold! Believe me, it is a most impressive scene.

Everyone comments upon how modestly you wear your hard-earned crown of honor. PLEASE do take care and avoid all the pitfalls. You have so very, very, very much to say! PLEASE take your time and say it all note by note, chord by chord. Lecture us thoroughly with your beautiful music. I assure you that we possess immense interest. We are listening constantly. Our appreciation of you and your extraordinary music is as limitless as the far horizons. Heartily we acclaim your bold explorations, your brilliant pioneering.

May God Almighty bless you and your novel work — for surely such a beautiful art has a place in the overall scheme of life.

May God preserve your awesome talent.

May God preserve your sincere and natural friendliness.

May God preserve your fairness, integrity, calm deportment and clean way of life.

If you consider this to be a letter of encouragement, you are one hundred percent correct. I hope that the great sincerity of this letter will be as explicit as the tremendous soul contained in your music. I pray that you always will be such a sterling personality and musician.

Finally, sir, thank you for pausing to converse with me during the intermission. Someday, I will proudly tell my children that: "I had the rare honor of talking with the universally respected and admired John Coltrane, THE GREATEST SAXOPHONIST OF ALL TIME."

Respectfully and sincerely yours

(sgd.)

P.S. Profuse congratulations to you for your unequalled[17] recording of "Traneing in."

Another admirer, from Senegal, wrote on a postcard:

Excuse my bad English

L'AFRIQUE EN COULEURS NATURELLES
120 - Toilettes de jour de fete

Dear Mrs. Coltrane,

I have met your husband during my trip in America last summer. I am an African and was studying in Paris and I was invited by the U.S. Government to visit your country. In Detroit I met Trane who is for me the greatest present musician, maybe because he is to me very near from the Senegalise music. I met him again in San Francisco and there he asked me to send you some card from New York, but when I arrived in that town I was so busy that I could do nothing. I don't know if your husband is back home from his tour but I ask you to tell to him that now I am in my country and that I haven't forgotten the African music records he asked me when I saw him. I should be very glad to know you when I was in New York, but I don't loose hope to know you one of these days.

Good luck to Trane and lot of wishes to you and all the family.

PAPA IBRA TALL
B.P. 1775
DAKAR, Senegal
W.A.   [18]

October, 1960, John took the quartet into the recording studio to tape twelve original compositions and six compositions by others. The originals were: *Village Blues, Blues to Elvin, Blues to Bechet, Blues to You, Mr. Day, Mr. Knight, Mr. Syms, Central Park West, Satellite,*

Liberia, and *Equinox.* The other selections were: *Everytime We Say Goodbye, But Not For Me, The Night Has A Thousand Eyes, Summertime,* and *My Favorite Things.*

The selections by other composers were given a new feeling by being redone harmonically. *Body and Soul,* for example, an old song sung by Billie Holiday, had many chords added to it. Traditionally, the song made one feel sad, bringing forth the tragedy in Billie Holiday's life.

> Purple tears drop from father moon
> Upon the sophisticated lady Billie Holiday
> The more she gave
> The less received
> The more deceived
> Her sorrow we grieve
> Protectively the moon crescents about her weary corpse
> Shielding her from those she loved
> Who gave only misery and despair in harsh return.

But John wanted to create happy music — to uplift people. By adding the chords and the faster tempo, along with the joyous spirit the group put into it, the ring of unhappiness that had surrounded this song for so long was dissolved. A resonant heart-warming effect was created when the bass played at the same time the piano struck each chord.

A variety of moods were represented by these fifteen selections, from the moving tranquility of *Central Park West* to the preaching in *Liberia* and the explosiveness of *Summertime.* Many technical features of his music were put on record. There was his use of substitute chords in changing the harmonic structure of an old song or in creating a new one. There was the steady pulsation of the bass, either of one note, or a constantly repeated phrase. There was intricate and beautiful improvisation with all types of articulation, phrasing, and ideas. There was a deep respect for the blues, which he played in his own way. And as always, each song had a meaning behind it. Mr. Syms was a hairdresser for many musicians' wives. *Equinox* is a moving blues in which the note D-flat is at the center of the melody — equally distant from the lowest and the highest note in the melody. Speculation leads to the idea that D-flat represented the equinox. D-flat also has another ramification. It is considered by many Black musicians to be the "funkiest" key.

In the November 10th *Down Beat*, the group received a very favorable write-up on its performance at the Monterrey Jazz Festival.

The unusual excitement the group communicated was also noted. Financially the group was a success. John's income was now $55,000 to $60,000 a year and for each performance he could now demand from $2,750.00 to $3,000.00.

Near the end of the year, a change was made in the bassist's position. Reggie Workman, who had spoken frankly to John on that crucial day at the Red Rooster, had moved from Philadelphia to New York. There he played with musicians like Jackie McLean, GiGi Gryce, and others. One week he was playing at a New York club with Roy Haynes and Eric Dolphy. John, who was playing the Village Gate, came by to hear them, and later asked Reggie to join him. John said of his playing: "Reggie Workman has a rich imagination and he has a good sense of going it alone. That's important in this band. Most times, the other musicians set their own parts. Reggie, for example, is very adept at creating his own bass line. In this band, nobody can lean on anyone else. Each of us has to have a firm sense of where he's going."[1][9]

The year 1960 carried only a whisper of what was to come. The tempo and temper of the Black struggle for freedom quickened when a group of Black college students refused to leave their seats after being denied service at a lunch counter. The idea caught on like a match in a petroleum field, leading to a rash of similar protests across the country.

On both sides, Black and white emotions would reach the flash point, engulfing the nation in a tumultuous decade of protest and bestial retaliation. The "liberals" would also show their true colors — squealing cries of "reverse racism" as many articles in *Down Beat* magazine did. The same term had been used in the 1800's, when Blacks first strove to form their own unions in the face of outright exclusion from the work force.

Black awareness of their hostile environment, and a willingness to change it, would rise rapidly like a mighty fist during the decade. Around this movement, a higher consciousness would arise which would involve colors of fraternity, fervor, love, beauty, strength, and religion. This consciousness was striving to be free of the low American cultural state as well as the perverted value system. Into this consciousness many musicians known and unknown would add their own colors. In a sense, the music, which was always one step ahead of the people, led the way to the higher level of consciousness that Blacks were seeking. Winding downward, slowly turning, spilling into the grape juice rivers of fragrances — colors — softly — the whispers blow into the sound of . . . . .

XI

The Soul Sings — and Hurts

The quartet had few rehearsals. Instead they would discuss their concepts of life, which included music, or listen to African or other types of records at John's house. Each man on his instrument would develop his own voice and bring back into the group the radiance of his unique aura. The molding force of this energy was John. He moved the music by the way he played and composed, while at the same time the group interacted and projected as a total wave. John would give few specific instructions to the others. They might discuss the feeling he wanted on a composition. With McCoy and Reggie he might go over some facets of the technical structure of the music. Usually it would not be necessary for Elvin to go over the modes, chords, or other aspects. It was assumed that his contribution would fit well within the emotional logic of what was being played. McCoy Tyner expresses the prevailing attitude in the group:

"It's important . . . for a group to be composed of men — real, true men who will accept their responsibilities. I am proud to be part of an organization where each one is dedicated to the whole, and I really enjoy it.

"People sometimes say our music is experimental, but all I can say is that every time you sit down to play, it should be an experience. There are no barriers in our rhythm section. Everyone plays his personal concept, and nobody tells anyone else what to do. It is surprisingly spontaneous, and there's a lot of give and take, for we all listen carefully to one another. From playing together, you get to know one another so well musically that you can anticipate. We have an overall different approach, and that is responsible for our original style. As compared with a lot of other groups, we feel differently about music. With us, whatever comes out – that's it, at that moment! We definitely believe in the value of the spontaneous."[1]

The energy the total group projected would reach into audiences making them musicians also, in a sense. People moved differently to the music. Instead of rocking with their whole bodies backward and forward they would often tap their feet quickly, move their bodies through wide long turns, clink glasses together rapidly, or beat pencils on table tops, as if playing an instrument. However, the music was still going through its continual process of change.

Early in 1961, John revealed some of the changes he was contemplating as well as some of his observations on his music. "I like to play long . . . the only thing is, I feel that there might be a need now to have more musical statements going on in the band. I might need another horn you know. I ran across a funny thing. We went into the Apollo and the guy said, 'You're playin' too long, you got to play twenty minutes.' Now, sometimes we get up and play a solo maybe thirty, or at least twenty, minutes. Well at the Apollo we ended up playing three songs in twenty minutes! I played all the highlights of the solos that I had been playing in hours, in that length of time. So I think about it. What have I been doing all this time? It's made me think, if I'm going to take an hour to say something I can say in ten minutes, maybe I'd better say it in ten minutes! And then have another horn there and get something else.

"I've been soloing for years and that's about all, I feel a need to learn more about production of music and expression and how to do things musically, so I feel a need for another horn for that reason. I could really go on just playing like I am now, I enjoy it playing that long. It seems like it does me a lot of good to play until I don't feel like playing any more, though I've found out I don't say that much more! At the Apollo, *My Favorite Things*, which runs 13 minutes, we played that about seven minutes long. Cut it right in half.

"On *My Favorite Things* my solo has been following a general path. I don't want it to be that way because the free part in there, I wanted it to be just something where we could improvise on just the minor chord and the major chord, but it seems like it gets harder and harder to really find something different on it. I've got several landmarks that I know I'm going to get to, so I try to play something in between that's different and keep hoping I hear something different on it. But it usually goes almost the same way every night. I think that the 3/4 has something to do with this particular thing. I find that it's much easier for me to change and be different in a solo on 4/4 tunes because I can play some tunes I've been playing for five years and might hear something different, but it seems like that 3/4 has kind of got a straight jacket on us there!

"I try to pick a song that sounds good and that might be familiar and then try to have parts in the song where we can play a solo. But it seems like we are into this thing where we want to solo on a modal perspective more or less, and therefore we end up playing a lot of vamps within a tune. I don't know how long we're going to be in that, but that's the way it's been. So the song is usually picked primarily as a vehicle to blow on."[2]

About his own composing, Coltrane said:

"I've been going to the piano and working things out, but now I think I'm going to move away from that. When I was working on those sequences which I ran across on the piano, I was trying to give all the instruments the sequences to play and I was playing them too. I was advised to try to keep the rhythm section as free and uncluttered as possible and if I wanted to play the sequences or run a whole string of chords, do it myself but leave them free. So I thought about the way we're going to have to do it. I won't go to the piano any more. I think I'm going to try to write for the horn from now on, just play around the horn and see what I can hear. All the time I was with Miles I didn't have anything to think about but myself so I stayed at the piano and chords, chords, chords! I ended up playing them on my horn.

"I tell you one thing, I have done so much work from within, now what I've got to do is go out and look around me some and then I'll be able to say I've got to do some work on this or on that."

John was taking in information at an incredible rate. Reggie Workman, exhausted after playing in a group more intense than he had ever been exposed to before, would be up nights practicing. One night he knocked on John's door. He was surprised to find him also up practicing, fingering his horn in silence. On other night visits to his room, John would either be practicing or sitting on the floor among nineteen or twenty books, all of which were on the floor and opened. These books were on topics such as African-American or African culture, Eastern culture, improvement of one's personal character, spiritual concepts, science, math — any number of topics. During the day the books were stuffed into a satchel in which he carried them around. He was absorbing knowledge as if there were something he had to do soon. Friends noticed that he was still warm as before – with as much time as he would give them. He took less time in conversation – always giving the impression that he was involved with the music. In his playing, just as that of Charlie Parker, there was an urgency that seemed to push him always further on before – druma – teti – yo – bas.

On a broader level his mind was synthesizing the throb of the times, the diverse musical streams, and the history and tradition of his people. He married these entities to an uncompromising investigation of his inner being to fashion excitement and vivid emotional contours. However, his group was not yet settled.

Reggie Workman began to feel the strain of a group so spiritually and physically demanding. He had never been in a group where few explicit directions were given and where each man was heavily depended upon to make his own contribution. He felt that he wasn't progressing fast enough and told John: "On this particular tune I don't seem to have a good concept of what's going down. If you feel that there's something specific that you want on it, then let me know, otherwise, I'm going to do what I'm going to do."

Emphatically, John answered, "Look man, I can't tell anybody how to play their instrument. I can just about play the saxophone. I'm busy working on that. I can't tell anybody how to play their instrument, so don't ask me. This [the music] is the subject matter. This is what we're doing."

Another concept began to take shape around this time. On his many visits through Chicago, John would visit a bassist named Donald Garrett, with whom he would exchange ideas. Garrett recalled: "I had this tape where I was playing with another bass player. We were doing some things rhythmically, and Coltrane became excited about the sound. We got the same kind of sound you get from the East Indian water drum. One bass remains in the lower register and is the stabilizing, pulsating thing, while the other bass is free to improvise, like the right hand would be in the drum. So Coltrane liked the idea."[3]

Soon another bassist, Arthur Davis, was added to the group. John liked his deep resonant tone and technical mastery of the instrument. Davis and Workman played together to create a sound similar to what Garrett described.

Rhythm also began to be explored more but not by trying different meters such as 12/8, 5/4, for example. It was on one of his trips to Los Angeles that he came across the idea of using African rhythms instead of a strict 4/4 meter. His approach to rhythm was a natural one. One of his personal records had on it two African men imitating the sounds of conga drums with their voices. From this record he obtained the rhythm for a composition entitled *Dahomey Dance*. His concept of an African hunt also went into the creation of this composition.

Drums beat hypnotically. Hayah! Hayah! They formed a circle around a desperate animal hopelessly trying to find a weakness in the tightening noose. The ring closed tighter. The drums beat louder. The ring closed tighter. The drums beat louder. The animal cringes as they near. He is so bewildered by the tightening noose of sound that he is unable to avoid the piercing spear.

It is likely that John's interest in rhythm, and his desire to learn more of his cultural heritage, made him receptive to two African drummers, Michael Olatunji and Chief Bey, who were playing around New York at this time. Olatunji had an Afro-jazz band at New York's Birdland. Once after listening to him, John greeted him with "Brother! Fantastic! One day we'll have to do an album together." He went on to express his desire to know more of Olatunji's music. Around this time he approached Chief Bey with the idea of playing together.

Much of the knowledge he had obtained was being assimilated into the music. His search for rhythm took him to Africa. His search for the drone led him to the East. The changes in his playing are clearly heard in a record which he made with Miles Davis on March 20 or 21, 1961. Though no longer a member of the group, he just dropped in one day to play on the recording session. He played on two tunes, *Someday My Prince Will Come* and *Teo. Teo* especially shows how his playing, compared to his previous records with Miles, had changed to sound more like a musician from the Middle East.

The drone, rhythmic impulses, and a multitude of colors came together in a composition entitled *Africa*, on the album "Africa Brass." This album was done with Impulse Record Company, with which John signed after being with Atlantic. Prior to the final recording, Folks wrote some music and convinced John to use it for "Africa Brass." A demonstration record was made, which John liked. Three days before the record date, Folks and his aide, Romulus, began the difficult job of copying the music for a large band. On the day of the recording session, they were still trying to organize the music. Folks had been having financial difficulties, and had suffered a series of nervous breakdowns with a long-standing case of insomnia. In the studio one of the musicians gave him a bottle of gin, half of which he drank. Behind this he took some Seconal tablets and fell flat on his face. His assistant couldn't finish without him, and the music was never recorded. John paid him for the date. But he was hurt and was leery of Folks for many years later.

On May 23, 1961, John assembled a band to record one of the selections for the "Africa Brass" album, *Greensleeves*. This rendition of *Greensleeves* was much different from the traditional. The concepts of steady pulsation and multiple rhythms and John's blaring, smooth sound put a rejuvenating vigor into the beautiful melody – as he says, "It's one of the most beautiful folk melodies I've heard. It's written in 6/8, and we do it just about as written. There's a section for improvisation with a vamp to blow on."[4]

Greensleeves is a good example of what John did to many songs, including *My Favorite Things*. The song would be played very close to the melody. But he would take one section and extend the amount of time alloted to it. On this section he or another member of the group would spin an Eden of improvisation. Even when playing close to the melody, the wailing sound of the saxophone and the steady pulse of the band created an hypnotic trance. "For me, *Greensleeves* is most enjoyable to play. Most of the time we get a nice pulse and groove. It was a challenge to add the band to it. I wanted to keep the feeling of the quartet. That's why we took the same voicings and the same rhythm McCoy comps in."[5]

Two days later material for another album, "Ole," was recorded on his last known date for Atlantic, before recording exclusively with Impulse. The big band was not used on this date. Instead he used a small group composed of himself on tenor, and soprano saxophones – Eric Dolphy, alto sax and flute; Freddie Hubbard, trumpet; McCoy Tyner on piano; Reggie Workman and Art Davis on bass; and Elvin Jones on drums.

His desire to use music with a Spanish theme was realized in *Ole* the title composition, which was based on a Spanish folksong and played with an Arabic feeling. *Dahomey Dance* was recorded, as well as a touching composition by McCoy Tyner for his wife, *Aisha*, which John played tenderly.

On June 7th the big band was reassembled to finish the "Africa Brass" album. *Blues Minor*, a composition close to *Bag's Groove*, by vibraphonist Milt Jackson, was recorded. In this rendition some sections of the original were left out, producing a more compact feeling within which an explosiveness was created.

The combination of instruments on "Africa Brass" was unusual:

Booker Little, trumpet; Britt Woodman, trombone; Carl Bowman, euphonium; Julius Watkins, Donald Corrado, Bob Northern, Robert Swisshel, french horns; Bill Barber, tuba; Eric Dolphy, also sax, bass clarinet, flute; John Coltrane, tenor sax; Laurdine (Pat) Patrick, reeds; McCoy Tyner, piano; Reggie Workman and Art Davis, basses; and Elvin Jones on drums. Eric Dolphy, who did the orchestrating, explained the use of these instruments, "John thought of this sound. He wanted brass. He wanted baritone horns. He wanted that mellow sound and power."[6]

In the creation of *Africa*, he had listened to many African records from which he drew inspiration for rhythmic ideas. One record had a deep bass sound that was like a chant. This sound was intimately involved with the drone he had heard in his dream. "I had a sound I wanted to hear and what resulted was about it. The main line carries all the way through the tune. One bass plays almost all the way through. The other has rhythmic lines around it. Reggie and Art have worked together and they know how to give and take."[7]

One bass maintains a constant pulse, while the other improvises with agility and richness. This improvisation and pulse continue, joining soon with a mellow and powerful group of horns that splash out drooping leaves of color. The saxophone floats within, creating figures that move forward, backward, or in both directions somehow at once. Some listeners hear screams of elephants, lions, gazelles and other animals. John was satisfied with the record, though *this* was not completely the drone that he was seeking. "It's the first time I've done any tune with that kind of rhythmic background. I've done things in 3/4 and 4/4. On the whole I'm quite pleased with *Africa*."[8]

By the summer of 1961, *My Favorite Things* had been released and eventually became a "gold record." This achievement placed John in the rare category, in Western culture, of those who in their lifetime attain both artistic and public success. In July the group played at the Village Vanguard, and an article appeared in *Newsweek* covering the event:

> John Coltrane put down his tenor saxophone and acknowledged the applause of the assorted beatniks, pseudobeatniks, and uptown jazz lovers, who came to his opening last week at New York's Village Gate. Then the husky, 34-year-old musician picked up a smaller, golden horn, thrust its mouthpiece between his lips, and began flooding the cheerless cellar with the lilting, heart-stopping sounds which they had all come to hear.

At first, playing the theme from Rodgers and Hammerstein's fragile waltz, *My Favorite Things*, Coltrane produced the sinuous wail of a snake charmer — eerie, tremulous, faintly melodic. Then the tone shifted, the timbre became more strident, the rhythm more insistent. His eyebrows knit in an agony of concentration, his fingers moving in a studied frenzy, Coltrane hammered away relentlessly, sweeping the audience along with him. Slowly the tension mounted until in a final convulsion of sound, Coltrane found his release and slipped back to the graceful cadences of the opening theme. The audience, which had been stunned into momentary silence, suddenly exploded in successive waves of applause.

It was a typical demonstration of why many eminent jazzmen consider Coltrane — who last week won three awards in *Down Beat*'s International Jazz Critics' Poll — one of the finest musicians alive.

Much of Coltrane's shimmering freshness is due to his finesse with the soprano saxophone, an instrument all but ignored by most other modern jazzmen. Not since the late Sidney Bechet was in his musical prime has anyone employed the clarinet-shaped soprano sax with such skill and imagination.

"It's hard to say whether I prefer the soprano or tenor," says Coltrane. "I find myself playing the soprano more and more, though. You can play lighter things with it, things that have a more subtle pulse. After the heaviness of the tenor, it's a relief to shift to the soprano."

Coltrane, who has been criticized for being "too far out," is a horn innovator who insists that there are still "quite a few avenues open for jazz and they're all going to be explored. I know that I'm going to try everything."[9]

Art Davis had this to say about the performances: "John Coltrane would play for hours a set. One tune would be like an hour or two hours, and he would not repeat himself, and it would not be boring. I would be there, and people would just be shouting, like you go to church, a holy roller church or something like that. This would get into their brains, would penetrate. John had that spirit — he was after the spiritual thing, and he had that. You could hear people screaming and this was something, despite the critics who tried to put him down. Black people made him because they stuck together and they saw — look what's going down — let us get some of this — and you know all the hard times that John had at the beginning, even when he was with Miles, and when he left starting out, everybody tried to discourage him, but I'd be there and the brothers and sisters would be there and they supported him. You see what happens, he made it despite people pushing down — as you know so many people are pushed up, made into images, but John had this power of communication, that power so rare it was like genius — I'd call him a prophet because he did this."[10]

Many began to hear John as a prophet. Others considered him a God, and some felt that he could not possibly be from this planet. There were those who were consumed by the music, buying and playing only Coltrane records. There was one brother named Spliby who was a drummer. He could play anything on a piece of paper with brushes, but on an actual set of drums he would sometimes get leery, because he could never afford a set of his own. Spliby could also play John's intricate solos on the kazoo, and amazed John by doing it for him. Also, more and more saxophonists, as well as those on other instruments, were being influenced. Another review of the Village Gate performance appeared in *Variety* magazine.

> The John Coltrane Quintet is about as solid and swinging a group as there is on the modern circuit today. It is smooth, well-controlled and inventive, with each of the members a fine jazzman in his own right. The combo demonstrates an ability to blow, arrange, from far out originals to crisp interpretations of pop tunes. Among its standouts is a charged rendition of *Favorite Things*, which features Coltrane on soprano sax. This tune exemplifies the group's ability to build from a theme through varied and often complex variations, without losing sight of the basic melodic structure of the tune, building to climax after climax in an exciting and driving sound.
>
> Coltrane's sax work is the driving core of the group. McCoy Tyner is a solid piano interpreter whose playing is smooth and inventive. Alvin Jones [sic] dishes up some crisp and elaborate figures, especially in *Favorite Things*, on drums, and Reggie Workman and Art Davis are bassists of fine caliber.[11]

The summer of 1961, Eric Dolphy joined the group on an on-and-off basis. If John could be said to have had a "best friend," it was Eric. "Eric and I have been talking music for quite a few years, since about 1954. We've been close for quite a while. We watched music. We always talked about it, discussed what was being done through the years, because we love music. What we're doing now was started a few years ago."[12]

John felt that as far as a musician who knew his instrument was concerned, Eric Dolphy was foremost. Speaking of how Eric joined the group, he recalled, "Eric was in New York, where the group was working, and he felt like playing, wanted to come down and sit in. So I told him to come on down and play, and he did — and turned us all around. I'd felt at ease with a quartet until then, but he came in, and it was like having another member of the family. He'd found another way to express the same thing we had found one way to do.

"After he sat in, we decided to see what it would grow into. We began to play some of the things we had only talked about before. Since he's been in the band, he's had a broadening effect on us. There are a lot of things we try now that we never tried before. This helped me, because I've started to write – it's necessary that we have things written so that we can play together. We're playing things that are freer than before.

"I would like for him to feel at home in the group and find a place to develop what he wants to do as an individualist and as a soloist – just as I hope everybody in the band will. And while we are doing this, I would also like the listener to be able to receive some of these good things . . . "[13]

Some time after Eric began playing with the quartet, John was considering the addition of a sixth instrument. McCoy asked Booker Little, a trumpeter who had played extensively with Eric Dolphy, to join the group. But Booker answered that he didn't like to work hard. Neither did McCoy, nor did most others know, that Booker was gravely ill and would be dead by the end of the year. Though John sought additional voices for the group. the other musicians of the band felt strongly that remaining a quartet would be most viable.

Eric Dolphy was from Los Angeles. He had developed into a musician of great skill on the flute, bass clarinet, and alto saxophone. He was unique in using the bass clarinet as a solo instrument. Physically he was tall, thin, and had a whispery, pleasant voice. In his music he strove to produce a warm, human-like quality which at times sounded like shouts, phrases or even sentences. There was a young, 16-year-old piano player named Bobby Neloms from Detroit who had a special communication line with Eric. Bobby would sit in the audience and make numerous faces, from which Eric would draw ideas for his next musical statement. Prior to joining John, Eric played with bassist Charlie Mingus. They made a record on which a conversation is carried out on their instruments, and it is not difficult to imagine what they are saying. Eric also had different ideas about playing chords. He felt that there was no need to play in the key suggested by a chord, or even one which is considered by Western theory to be related. For him the key which *sounded* correct was the right one. When playing, he achieved an effect which startled – causing your attention to shoot straight up. Then there would be contortions, turns and leaps of connected notes.

Once when the group was playing a New York nightclub, Eric had not arrived by show time. The club owner made some heated remarks. John ignored the owner, as if he didn't even exist, and continued setting up his instrument. Eric arrived shortly, came calmly on stage, and the frustrated club owner walked away.

Many who knew Eric knew him as a friend. He would have difficulty finding work, and was usually low on money. Still, when he did get a gig, the next thing he'd do was to buy groceries for other musicians. One night a close friend of his, bassist Richard Davis, had a flat tire which he couldn't fix because his jack was broken. He called Eric late at night to ask what to do about the jack. Eric jumped out of bed and drove the long distance to help him.

Eric and Richard went to John's house and spent a casual day talking about music, taking care of one's mind and body, and various physical exercises. John was munching on sunflower seeds much of the time. Eric had a composition for which he couldn't find the right tempo. John went over it with him, and they played some of Eric's other compositions. John also mentioned his desire to form a big band, in which everyone played freely — without reference to chords.

Frequently Eric and John were invited to give solo concerts before various organizations. They accepted the invitations on the basis of how sincere they felt the organization to be.

Eric made many visits to John's house. When John was away, he would leave Eric to take care of Naima, Toni, and also Mary who was living in New York. In practicing together, they would go through a piece only enough to gain a familiarity with it, rather than rehearse it over and over again. In nature, vines twist, knot and dive. Instead of making rigid intersections, grass unfailingly cracks man's "perfectly" aligned cement walks. Red sometimes comes with a twirling ribbon of brown, a person may fall up, a straight line may really curve, and a gasp may be ecstasy or death. John and Eric felt that there should be some raggedness about what they played, thereby moving closer to the imperfect perfection of nature.

Both were serious about their instruments, practicing long hours and looking into every facet of their horns. John could take a saxophone apart and put it back together. Once Eric tracked down a flute teacher who had knowledge of a minute aspect of the instrument. John's mouthpieces were not giving him the sound he wanted, so he began a long, long search for one that would. He even went so far as to go to Florida to stay with a man named Link, who made mouthpieces. Naima went with him.

Link made a mouthpiece to John's exact specifications. But it didn't work. Another was made out of old German tank metal. The older the metal, the better the sound was supposed to be. But this didn't work either. After a week of similar failures, John and Naima returned to New York. Mouthpieces in a store cost from twenty to thirty dollars each, and John would buy boxes of them, without getting what he wanted. This search for a mouthpiece continued through the years.

While in San Francisco, John wanted to shop for more mouthpieces. A man named Scotti was supposed to take him to the local music stores, but was unable to go. A friend who had been searching for a replacement called John, saying that there was a Cat who played much like him and loved him. The friend arranged for Farrell Saunders, then also called "Little Rock" because he was from Little Rock, Arkansas, to take John to the stores. John wanted to start early, at eight in the morning.

They met, and before going to the stores, John bought a bushel of bananas. By the end of the day, he had eaten them all. Neither man was very talkative, so they walked in a peaceful silence to each store, speaking only occasionally. At one store, John had looked at all the mouthpieces which were piled up on the counter without being satisfied. He joked, "If you put them all together, it might sound like something." – and bought them all.

When they did talk, John would say something like, "I hear a sound. It's like putting a seashell to your ear, or like New York at four-thirty or five in the morning."

Later in the day, Farrell showed him the twenty-five or thirty mouthpieces he had and was not satisfied with. John liked one of them, though it still wasn't exactly what he wanted. Farrell gave it to him. In their conversation they talked about meat, why Farrell didn't eat meat, and spiritual matters. Both men thought a large part of the day about the Creator. After hearing Farrell play, John excitedly told Neet, when he returned home, how Farrell's sound gave him a feeling that made him sit up straight – as he made a straightening motion with his back.

On either the same or another trip to San Francisco, guitarist Wes Montgomery sat in with the group, which now included Eric Dolphy. John hired Wes for an engagement, and asked him to join on a permanent basis. Wes declined the offer, possibly because he wanted to work with his brothers, Buddy and Monk Montgomery. Also, Wes may have been going in another musical direction. Occasionally he would say, "Now you guys are gettin' too far out for me there."

One club owner in California became worried over the length of the performances. He felt that it had cost him a lot of money to get the group there, lines of people were waiting outside, but each performance would last two hours or more. He wanted a more rapid turnover of audiences. He knew Wes well, and asked him to convince John and Eric to shorten their solos. Wes proposed to them that, since John was the leader, he should solo as long as he wished, but that he and Eric could keep their solos to a minimum. A stare shot from Eric's eyes which abruptly ended this suggestion.

For John, 1961 brought widespread acceptance by the critics and the public. Most records on which he was leader or sideman received 4½ to 5 stars by their infantile grading system. He had never before placed first in any category of the International Critics' Poll. This year he was first in four areas: new star, the regular saxophonist category, miscellaneous instruments (for the soprano saxophone), and new combo. However, in the regular combo listing, the group was only 11th. John was now at the epitome of success with the "Jazz Establishment." This caused him to worry.

One evening at the Half Note, a Greenwich Village club, George Russell, with whom John recorded in 1958, spoke briefly to him. John expressed his concern over the success of *My Favorite Things*. He felt pressed between two alternatives: (1) continue playing in the same manner, making albums like "Our Favorite Things," "Your Favorite Things," "Son of My Favorite Things," "My Favorite Things Parts II and III," etc., etc., or, (2) to follow his essence, continue to play honestly and grow, but risk the loss of the audience it had taken so long to build and possibly draw new attacks from critics. He decided to follow his essence, as he said, "The real risk is not changing."

Events arranged themselves, leading to another personnel change in the group. Ornette Coleman began a personal protest against the low salaries paid musicians in clubs. The focus of attention was The Five Spot. The usual salary for a sideman was ninety to a hundred dollars per week. When Ornette first took his group there with bassist Jimmy Garrison, his sidemen got one hundred and fifty dollars per week. Crowds were waiting in lines to hear them play. Before agreeing to play there again, Ornette demanded more money so he could pay his men more. He thought that the group deserved more money because of the high level of their art and the simple fact that they drew large crowds. Negotiations reached an impasse, and Ornette decided not to play in any clubs until they came up with a decent salary. This move caused a financial strain on his sidemen. Jimmy Garrison, because his weekly salary had jumped from one hundred dollars a week to one hundred and fifty, had just moved his wife and three children into a larger apartment. It was against this background that John called him to play on a live recording at the Village Vanguard, as a substitute for Art Davis, who was unable to make the date.

Five tunes were recorded at the Vanguard on November 2, 3 and 5, 1961. These were *Spiritual, Softly As In A Morning Sunrise, India, Chasin' the Trane* and *Impressions*. In his personal library John had a book by James Weldon Johnson entitled *200 Negro Spirituals*. It is possible that the spiritual on which *Spiritual* is based came from this book. His comments on the composition were, "I liked the way it worked out. I feel we brought out the mood inherent in the tune. It's a piece we'd been working with for some time because I wanted to make sure before we recorded it that we would be able to get the original emotional essence of the spiritual."[14]

Softly As In A Morning Sunrise, the only one of the five that John hadn't written, was included " ... because I like to get a sensible variety in an album. It seems to me to round out the two originals, and I especially liked the swinging by Jones in this particular take."[15]

Chasin' The Trane was a completely improvised piece. John honked, screamed, played the blues, and in general tore the place up, moving the audience to applaud wildly. "Usually I like to get familiar with a new piece before I record it, but you don't have to worry about the blues unless the line is very complicated. In this case, however, the melody not only wasn't written, but it wasn't even conceived before we played it. We set the tempo, and in we went."[16]

Two months later he spoke of his overall goals, and on *India*. "I've got to write more music for the group. I've really got to work and study more approaches to writing. I've already been looking into these approaches to music – as in *India* – in which particular sounds and scales are intended to produce specific emotional meanings. I've got to keep probing. There's so much to do."[17]

By this time John and McCoy had studied and discussed many different scales, including Indian ragas in which the notes ascending are different from those descending. John was also making up his own scales from a few notes, or by mixing Indian ragas and Western scales. One of his own scales was used in writing *Impressions*, as well as the chords of the Miles Davis composition, *So What*. On *Impressions* the group is tight, playing as one flexible soul. The horn and drums are right on top of each other, one pushing while the other tugs, rising while the other recedes. Waves of intensity surge higher and stronger as the music is built to a thrashing level. It sounds like a blues stretched to its straining limits.

Jimmy Garrison was recorded on *Impressions* and *India*. John told him that if he ever thought about leaving Ornette, to call him. Right away Jimmy answered that he was considering leaving because Ornette wasn't working, and he needed money for his family. John told him that he would call him after the group returned from Europe.

Before leaving, the *Down Beat* critics had been wining and dining John as a result of his success. They heaped praise and compliments upon him, and John began to feel more at ease with critics. But the pendulum of opinion, now so highly in his favor, was rapidly swinging in the direction of abyss.

The group left for London shortly after the Vanguard engagement, accompanied by Dizzy Gillespie's band. On November 9th, a review appeared in *Down Beat* by Don DeMichael, which covered a summer performance of the group, with Wes Montgomery, at the Monterey Jazz Festival. DeMichael wrote that Wes had given the best solos, John's were good, but that Eric Dolphy sounded as if he were "trying to imitate birds."

The pendulum swung to its lowest, with this article by John Tynan, in *Down Beat*, November 23rd:

> Go ahead call me reactionary. I happen to object to the musical nonsense currently being peddled in the name of jazz by John Coltrane and his acolyte, Eric Dolphy.
>
> At Hollywood's Renaissance Club recently, I listened to a horrifying demonstration of what appears to be a growing anti-jazz trend exemplified by these foremost proponents of what is termed avant-garde music.
>
> Melodically and harmonically their improvisation struck my ear as gobbledegok . . .,
>
> The sincerity of Coltrane and Dolphy is not the question here . . . to these ears the sum of the sounds remains musical nonsense.[18]

In London, the audience reaction was unfavorable. Writer Bob Dawbarn of *The Melody Maker* wrote a review just as opposed as Tynan's, but considerably less caustic. Part of the response in London may have been due to the time lag between release of records in the United States and their later exposure in England. From records available to them, the English had no preparation for what they heard.

> BAFFLED, bothered and bewildered! That just about sums up my reactions to the John Coltrane Quintet.
> In a rash mood of prophecy I wrote in last week's Melody Maker that with Coltrane and Eric Dolphy playing together something was bound to happen.
> It did. But what was it?
> The Coltrane group opens the programme of Norman Granz's latest "Jazz at the Phil" offering, with the Dizzy Gillespie Quintet occupying the second half.
> I caught the second house at Kilburn on Saturday and, frankly, the Coltrane Quintet was so far out it made Gillespie sound as formal and easy to follow as Acker Bilk.
> An afternoon preparing myself with Coltrane records – all of which I like and admire – proved to be no preparation at all.
> Between them, Coltrane (on tenor and soprano) and Dolphy (alto, flute and bass clarinet) produced the most extraordinary sounds I have ever heard.
> And the rhythm section!
> Pianist McCoy Tyner, bassist Reggie Workman and drummer Elvin Jones were all apparently playing in different tempos and frequently in different time signatures.
> Coltrane's soprano was used during a 25-minute *My Favourite Things* and sounded so Eastern I kept looking into the wings for Wilson, Keppel and Betty.
> Dolphy's flute tone would have given Julius Baker a heart attack.
> Despite the most intense concentration, I had no more idea at the end of the group's hour-long programme what it was all about, than I had at the beginning.
> There just seems to be no logical basis to any of it.
> My general feeling is that it belonged more to the realms of higher mathematics, than music.
> Perhaps if this were on a record which could be played over and over, one might begin to see what lay behind the apparent chaos.
> As music for a jazz concert it is just too much.
> Fortunately there was still an hour of Dizzy Gillespie to come.
> Familiarity bred from Dizzy's many British visits has only confirmed his place as a true Jazz Great.[19]

In the next week's issue Dawbarn wrote of his visit to John's hotel room.

> JOHN COLTRANE is undoubtedly the most controversial jazz musician to make a concert tour of Britain.
> On my way to see him at his London hotel last Friday I reflected

that, if his music was any guide, he was probably an aggressively dedicated character crusading for a new approach to jazz.

I was quite wrong. This quiet American turned out to be a man of great personal charm and remarkable honesty.

Far from showing the expected contempt for those who failed to understand his musical attitudes, his chief desire seemed to be to communicate with his audiences.

Here are some of the questions I put to Coltrane, and his frank, if sometimes complex, answers.

I found your Quintet's music completely bewildering. Can you explain what it is you are trying to do. Surely, you and Eric Dolphy are not following the normal chord sequences?

"I can't speak for Eric — I don't know exactly what his theory is. I am playing on the regular changes, though sometimes I extend them.

"I do follow the progressions. The sequences I build have a definite relationship to the chords. Can you give me a particular example of something that puzzled you?"

Take your two soprano solos on *My Favourite Things*. The first I found reasonably easy to understand. The second I couldn't follow at all.

"That tune has a melody in the major key and a short vamp in the minor. In the first solo, I played straight through. You could follow the melody in it.

"The second was more ad lib. It was in the same form except that the vamp parts were stretched out."

It seemed to me that the three members of the rhythm sections were playing completely different often in different time signatures.

"They are free to play anything they feel. Tyner plays some things on piano. I don't know what they are, but they are based on the chords.

"The bass works from nothing but the basic E natural and plays it in as many different rhythmic ways as possible. The drummer is playing basically in 3/4 time."

Your playing seemed so different from anything we have heard on your records here.

"So many people have told me that, it must be true. I've got to listen to those records again. I guess I've changed in the last year. I'm in the process of changing things around and finding areas that haven't been exploited."

Does the soprano present special problems?

"It certainly does. You need to play it with such a tight embouchure that I've been frightened of losing my tenor embouchure.

"I have my suspicions that that is beginning to happen. I'm not getting the tenor tone I'd like at the moment.

"The soprano seems to take over and I may have to choose between them."

Do you plan to keep this Quintet together?

"I'm not sure, but it will probably revert to a Quartet. Eric just came in and played with us one night. He wasn't doing anything else so we invited him along.

"Most of our things were conceived for a Quartet, and the group sounds more like a quartet plus one than a quintet."

Have you enjoyed the British tour?

"We're very inexperienced at playing concerts. We're used to playing at great length in clubs and find it hard to cut things to fit a concert. I don't get a chance to stretch out. With Dolphy added it makes things even harder.

"Some people sound as good on concerts as in clubs. Dizzy is one – he really knows how to put it over. I haven't the ability yet. I'm just becoming aware of the problems involved.

"Since we went out of London I've been trying to play things the audiences are more familiar with. It seems we might get it right too late – at the end of the tour."

I see a guitar on your bed. I didn't know you played it.

"I just bought it for company. I got lonesome and had read everything I had. I can't play it, but every instrument has its own personality. Maybe I'll stumble across something I wouldn't get on piano."

Any other comment on the tour?

"I would really like to come back, particularly if I could work in a club – I really want to communicate with the audiences."[20]

The band went on to other cities, among them Copenhagen, Helsinki, Berlin, and Munich, where Naima, who had just flown over, met John. After London the reaction had been much more favorable, either because more familiar material was played or because of the different nature of the audiences. The tour ended in Paris where John began work on a new composition, *Crescent*. This composition was derived from the figure of the moon's crescent.

John would use other figures from which to compose, such as a church steeple. These drawings may have been what he had in mind in seeking other approaches to writing. He was combining the visual with the auditory sense, and drawing upon the open road to his youth, when he sketched futuristic cars and other figures with Franklin Brower. Before returning home, Nita and John wanted to visit Africa. However, they were told that to go to Africa would be easy, but the trip back would take two weeks. Having commitments in New York, John decided not to go.

On returning, his bassist, Reggie Workman, was confronted with personal problems. The Selective Service wanted to draft him. He told them bluntly that he didn't believe in the policy of the country and that he wasn't going to put his life on the line. He was not going to fight for something that might take his life away any minute, when there was a fight right here in this country with which he should be involved. These statements combined with the fact that his older brother and sisters were members of the National Youth for Democracy, then considered a "radical" organization by the government, caused him to be harassed. Without hesitation, he told them how positive he thought the organization was. After which the Selective Service went berserk.

The Service would frequently call him to their office for interviews. Agents would come to his hotel room while the band was playing in distant cities. They questioned friends, and even came to the clubs where the band was performing. They told him to report for induction. At the same time, Reggie's father was dying of cancer in Philadelphia. Having lost much of his peace of mind, and having to go home to take care of his father, Reggie decided to leave the band.

He told John, who had not mentioned quitting to him. John answered that leaving the band would be alright because he had been working on a change – Jimmy Garrison.

Jimmy was well prepared to enter a band of such intensity. From various influences, and his own work, he had synthesized a distinctive way of playing. His notes were warm, elastic-like, slowly stretching, and collapsing rubber bands, but were always on the beat. Amidst the resonance he produced would spurt forceful outpourings of notes. At these times his face would frown, showing the energy he was putting in. When it came to walking a bass, he did more than walk it. He ran it. Also, over the years he had developed a means of playing chords on the bass, enabling him to create sounds like a soothing flamenco guitar.

Being in Ornette's band put him in the role of a major soloist rather than in the traditional bassist's role of accompanist. Ornette placed him at the front of the bandstand with the horns, instead of to the side. He demanded as much from him as from a horn. Rehearsals with Ornette were long, hard, and numerous. He would expect as much energy in the rehearsal as in actual performance. This demanding situation prepared Jimmy for the Coltrane band, which he joined just two days before the end of 1961. Jimmy's introduction to the informal nature of the group came early when he asked what tune they were going to play. John only answered, "You'll hear it" and they went on and played it.

John appreciated his contribution, having this to say of Jimmy, after he had been in the group for some time: "Jimmy has been a great influence within the group. Certain things have occurred in the ways in which our music has gone that definitely reflect his approach to bass playing. The way, for example, he solos without rhythmic accompaniment. That influenced us. And the mood that his solos set. Knowing what he is capable of helped a lot of music to take shape. He was always in mind. It's difficult for me to put into words what makes it so outstanding. Of course, there's more than that. There's an intuitive sense at work too – he just knows what to hit and when to hit it."[21]

McCoy could tell when John was in a good mood, and when he was sad. Elvin could sometimes tell by listening to him play. But it was difficult to tell by his playing, since most of it had so much beauty. When happy John would relax in the audience, sipping juices or health food drinks, smoking a cigar and enjoying the playing of his rhythm section. They would build the music up to such an intensity that one couldn't see how it could possibly go any higher. After the music reached a certain level, John would step in to take the energy out of the belief sphere of Neptune. Afterwards, he would buy McCoy, Jimmy and Elvin whatever they were drinking from orange juice to liquor.

But when sad or disturbed, there was no stopping him. It seemed as though he wanted to play the keys off the horn. One night in Detroit, no one knew what was wrong with John. He came in and just played, played, played for two hours. Whatever the reason that sparked John's outpouring of music, a new era for the group was begun. They now knew that they had the strength to create freshly for hours, and began doing it regularly at performances.

When with Ornette, Jimmy had to play long and hard, but not as long, and not as hard, as with this group. Each man's solo would sometimes be an hour or more long. Jimmy usually soloed last after everyone had left the bandstand. As a matter of pride, he would put out as much as the others. Each night on coming home, he would lie exhausted in bed, with his finger hanging over the edge. It would be swollen at the end, painful, with throbbing blood, blistered, and raw red from intensive use. Eventually he had to wear tape on his fingers to be able to play. This band, now a quartet, with Eric having left, was the unit that would carry out the music John had heard. They were close on stage, as well as off. Jimmy recalls of John, "There was a love that he emitted that is rare to find, a thing you recognized immediately on meeting him . . . This force had become a part of the band. We were like four brothers in the deepest sense of the word."[22]

The group was in Philadelphia playing at the four o'clock matinee at the Showplace. John was playing in pants he had just bought, with the label still on the side, and his cuffs bent over. They played *Afro-Blue* until 5:30 and the audience responded with a ten-minute standing ovation. John hardly acknowledged the applause, going off stage as soon as they finished, to a backroom to practice – during the half-hour intermission. At six o'clock the group went on again.

At one point during the performance, John and Elvin sailed upward, playing without bass or piano. Frequently, the two of them would become involved in a thunderous duet, playin so closely that they became one terrible force. The second performance lasted until 7:45 – past the usual 7:00 ending time.

Jimmy Heath, who had a concurrent engagement at the nearby Sahara club, invited John to his mother's house for dinner. He knew that since he played so much overtime, John would have difficulty getting all the way to his own mother's house and back. The two old friends spoke briefly about Ravi Shankar and Indian music. John felt that the music of the Indians was more highly spiritual than that of musicians of this country who played pop and show tunes, which resulted in selling these tunes for those who wrote them.

When they arrived at Jim's house, the meal wasn't quite ready. They all sat at the table for about a minute, after which John asked Jimmy if it would be alright to go upstairs and work on something he was trying to do. He practiced until the meal was on the table, ate, and returned to the club for the nine o'clock show.

John was completely enveloped by *the music*, seeking to advance it as far as he could. The group had become so tight that they would begin each performance at a high level of intensity and be striving to take it even a few steps higher. The emotionalism had reached insane levels. Once in Los Angeles, a trumpet player sat in when the music was leaping and burning. He struggled to keep up until a sound crashed KuBoom!! He had fainted, and before anyone knew it, two men were carrying him off the stage. John played once so hard that his nose bled. Some musicians would leave the club, not believing what they had just heard.

Many young musicians, inspired by the music, would ask to sit in with the band. John would invariably welcome them. Jimmy Garrison became tired of this. He reasoned that each member of the band had at least fifteen years of experience, and that someone with only three or four years of experience shouldn't be playing with them. Jimmy broke out one night with, "Man, wait a minute, man! I can't be playing with people [with so little experience]. What are you doing, man?"

John answered frankly, "Man, look, I need other people." There was nothing Jim could say after this. He had much respect for John, and if John needed other people, then there must be something to it. Sometimes after a young musician who could barely play had finished, John would follow by playing ideas he had drawn from him. He was wide-opened musically and for him the *music* was more important than personal ego.

At one performance at the Showboat, a young musician who would later become an important member of the group asked to sit in. Rashied Ali had been wanting to sit in for a long time. But because of the power of the music, he was afraid to ask. This night, in order to reinforce his confidence, he drank a lot of wine.

In the club he waited patiently until the storm that the quartet created had subsided, and asked John if he could sit in. John saw the condition he was in and told him, gently, "Well, look, man, Elvin is playing with the band right now, and actually we don't want anybody to sit in right now."

Elvin was standing beside them as Rashied started hollering, "Man, I can play. I can play as well as Elvin. You need me, man. I know what you're doing. I can complement what you're doing. This cat [Elvin] can't."

John unexcitedly changed the subject and gave him some advice. "I think maybe you should leave Philly, man. Because in Philly, there's only a certain amount of growing you can do in Philly. Go to New York, man, and check out playing with the cats in New York for a while."

It was time to play again, and the members of the quartet stepped onto the bandstand. Rashied, meanwhile, was walking angrily back and forth around the club, catching Elvin's eye whenever he could and saying, "Motherfucker, you can't play. Get the fuck off the drums! ... " Rashied was asked to leave by the management and needed a little assistance to "help" him out. They told him to go home and get some rest, treating him with care since he was well known in the club.

In Rochester, New York, the band received an enthusiastic response. One man, however, irately told John that he didn't come to hear him play no soprano saxophone. He paid his money, and wanted to hear him play tenor. As the man flailed about, John said nothing – just stood and looked straight at him. This ended the confrontation.

Also in the audience was Larry Young, who would later become John's good friend. They sat at the table together. Larry noticed how polite John was. When cutting his fingernails, one popped up and hit Larry. John very apologetically said "Oh, excuse me," and turned away rather than have it happen again. They exchanged lifesavers and talked about music. John asked why he played organ instead of piano, letting Larry know that he preferred the piano sound. Only a few months later, however, John had broadened even further musically, telling him, "You can play a shoestring if you're sincere about it."

Success on the road did not mean success with the critics who had mounted an attack against the new steps *the music* had taken. These steps were rich improvisation from one or just a few chords, the use of new scales and ragas, and the more abandoned manner in which the group played. In France there were signs of acceptance. But in the United States rancorous opposition increased. *Down Beat* magazine was at the front of this opposition. An example is a review of "Africa Brass" by Martin Williams, from *Down Beat*, January 18, 1962:

> Certainly no one could question Coltrane's particular skill as a tenor saxophonist. Nor that his ear for harmony, his knowledge of it, and his use of it can fascinate . . .
>
> What I do question is whether here this exposition of skills adds up to anything more than a dazzling and passionate array of scales and arpeggios . . .
>
> In these pieces, Coltrane has done on record what he has done so often in person lately, make everything into a handful of chords, frequently only two or three, and run them in every conceivable way, offering what is in effect, an extended cadenza to a piece that never gets played, a prolonged montuna interlude surrounded by no rhumba or son [sic], or a very long vamp 'til ready.
>
> *Africa* is African by the suggestions of its rhythms. It has some bars figures that, for me, get a bit too monotonous to add variety and which are also in general too much in the background to add much of their own.[23]

Critics were now flinging telling darts against the change in the music. John was upset and could not understand why he was attacked so viciously.

There was also public reaction. Letters to *Down Beat*, in response to Tynan's attack, were about equally divided pro and con on the music. *Ole* was reviewed in the February issue, and received a lukewarm review. In mid-March, however, John received a letter from

ABC-Paramount Records informing him that "Africa Brass" had received an award from the Academie Charles Cros in France.

March 15, 1962

Dear John:

Today I received a letter from our French affiliate, Vega Records, that your Impulse album, AFRICA BRASS, has just received an award from the Academie Charles Cros.

I would like, at this time, to add my congratulations to those of Vega on this wonderful achievement.

Sincerely,

ABC-PARAMOUNT RECORDS, INC.

(sgd.)

Samuel H. Clark
President

SHC:mld

P.S. When the award is received by us, which may be some time in the future, we will have it suitably framed and presented to you.[24]

Also in March he received a favorable review of his "Live at the Village Vanguard" album in a California paper.

"John Coltrane at the Village Vanguard / John Coltrane Quintet" (Impulse A-10). John Coltrane, tenor and soprano; Eric Dolphy, bass clarinet; McCoy Tyner, piano; Reggie Workman, bass; Elvin Jones, drums.

John Coltrane continues to be one of the most creative jazz musicians alive. Today you can hear elements of his playing not only in other tenor players but in pianists and other hornmen as well.

This is primarily because his entire conception and approach is wholly individual and completely valid to the point of being accepted by all other jazz musicians (as opposed to Ornette Coleman, who is wholly individual but not totally accepted).

Spiritual opens with Trane starting the theme out of tempo over somber chords by the rest of the group. The piece then moves into an easy but very down 3/4.

Trane's initial solo is not based so much on the thematic material as on the emotional content of the piece.

Following his brief solo are Dolphy, sounding much better than usual; Tyner, sounding as marvelous as ever, then Trane is back for an extended solo on soprano sax. Throughout is the incomparable drumming of Elvin Jones. His playing is great at any tempo, but at this particular 3/4 time his playing transcends any purely verbal description.

I have never heard a drummer play so much and do so many things and yet have it all fit. The extreme excitement this group is capable of generating is due in great part to his drumming.

The piece concludes with Trane playing the opening motive on soprano over the same somber chords.

In Trane's typical manner, the closing chord resolves back into tempo and fades out after another fifteen bars.

Softly As In Morning Sunrise opens with Tyner and the rhythm section (Jones uses brushes). After an extended solo Trane enters on soprano and imparts that peculiar emotional intensity he is so capable of.[25]

The second side is taken up with a spontaneous blues called *Chasin' the Trane*. At a very fast tempo be blows 16 minutes of constantly inventive, hard swinging blues.

During the course of the piece he displays a remarkable range of tonal color.[25]

But the overwhelming tide of establishment critics in this country was unfavorable. In the April 21st *Down Beat*, a momentous article appeared entitled "John Coltrane and Eric Dolphy Answer the Jazz Critics." Critic Don DeMicheal, who in writing of the Monterey Jazz Festival, had stated that Eric Dolphy sounded as though he were "trying to imitate birds," was the interviewer.

John Coltrane has been the center of critical controversy ever since he unfurled his sheets of sound in his days with Miles Davis. At first disparaged for his sometimes involved, multinoted solos, Coltrane paid little heed and continued exploring music. In time, his harmonic approach — for the sheets were really rapid chord running, in the main — was accepted, even praised, by most jazz critics.

By the time critics had caught up with Coltrane, the tenor saxophonist had gone on to another way of playing. Coltrane II, if you will, was much concerned with linear theme development that seemed sculptured or torn from great blocks of granite. Little critical carping was heard of this second, architectural, Coltrane.

But Coltrane, an inquisitive-minded, probing musician, seemingly has left architecture for less concrete, more abstract means of expression. This third and present Coltrane has encountered an ever-growing block of criticism, much of it marked by a holy-war fervor.

Criticism of Coltrane III is almost always tied in with Coltrane's cohort Eric Dolphy, a member of that group of musicians who play what has been dubbed the "new thing."

Dolphy's playing has been praised and damned since his national-jazz-scene arrival about two years ago. Last summer Dolphy joined Coltrane's group for a tour. It was on this tour that Coltrane and Dolphy came under the withering fire of *Down Beat* associate editor

John Tynan, the first critic to take a strong – and public – stand against what Coltrane and Dolphy were playing.

In the Nov. 23, 1961, *Down Beat* Tynan wrote, "At Hollywood's Renaissance club recently, I listened to a horrifying demonstration of what appears to be a growing anti-jazz trend exemplified by these foremost proponents [Coltrane and Dolphy] of what is termed avant garde music.

I heard a good rhythm section . . . go to waste behind the nihilistic exercises of the two horns . . . Coltrane and Dolphy seem intent on deliberately destroying [swing] . . . They seem bent on pursuing an anarchistic course in their music that can but be termed anti-jazz."

The anti-jazz term was picked up by Leonard Feather and used as a basis for critical essays of Coltrane, Dolphy, Ornette Coleman, and the "new thing" in general in *Down Beat* and *Show*.

The reaction from readers to both Tynan's and Feather's remarks was immediate, heated, and about evenly divided.

Recently, Coltrane and Dolphy agreed to sit down and discuss their music and the criticism leveled at it.

One of the recurring charges is that their performances are stretched out over too long a time, that Coltrane and Dolphy play on and on, past inspiration and into monotony.

Coltrane answered, "They're long because all the soloists try to explore all the avenues that the tune offers. They try to use all their resources in their solos. Everybody has quite a bit to work on. Like when I'm playing, there are certain things I try to get done and so does Eric and McCoy Tyner [Coltrane's pianist]. By the time we finish, the song is spread out over a pretty long time.

"It's not planned that way; it just happens. The performances get longer and longer. It's sort of growing that way."

But, goes the criticism, there must be editing, just as a writer must edit his work so that it keeps to the point and does not ramble and become boring.

Coltrane agreed that editing must be done – but for essentially a different reason from what might be expected.

"There are times," he said, "when we play places opposite another group, and in order to play a certain number of sets a night, you can't play an hour and a half at one time. You've got to play 45 or 55 minutes and rotate sets with the other band. And for those reasons, for a necessity such as that, I think it's quite in order that you edit and shorten things.

"But when your set is unlimited, timewise, and everything is really together musically – if there's continuity – it really doesn't make any difference how long you play.

"On the other hand, if there're dead spots, then it's really not good to play anything too long."

One of the tunes that Coltrane's group plays at length is *My Favorite Things*, a song, as played by the group, that can exert an intriguingly hypnotic effect, though sometimes it seems too long.

Upon listening closely to him play *Things* on the night before the interview, it seemed that he actually played two solos. He finished one, went back to the theme a bit, and then went into another improvisation.

"That's the way the song is constructed," Coltrane said. "It's divided into parts. We play both parts. There's a minor and a major part. We improvise in the minor, and we improvise in the major modes."

Is there a certain length to the two modes?

"It's entirely up to the artist — his choice," he answered. "We were playing it at one time with minor, then major, then minor modes, but it was *really* getting too long — it was about the only tune we had time to play in an average-length set."

But in playing extended solos, isn't there ever present the risk of running out of ideas? What happens when you've played all your ideas?

"It's easy to stop then," Coltrane said, grinning. "If I feel like I'm just playing notes . . . maybe I don't feel the rhythm or I'm not in the best shape that I should be in when this happens. When I become aware of it in the middle of a solo, I'll try to build things to the point where this inspiration is happening again, where things are spontaneous and not contrived. If it reaches that point again, I feel it can continue — it's alive again. But if it doesn't happen, I'll just quit, bow out."

Dolphy, who had been sitting pixie-like as Coltrane spoke, was in complete agreement about stopping when inspiration had flown.

Last fall at the Monterey Jazz Festival, the Coltrane-Dolphy group was featured opening night. In his playing that night Dolphy at times sounded as if he were imitating birds. On the night before the interview some of Dolphy's flute solos brought Monterey to mind. Did he do this on purpose?

Dolphy smiled and said it was purposeful and that he had always liked birds.

Is bird imitation valid in jazz?

"I don't know if it's valid in jazz," he said, "but I enjoy it. It somehow comes in as part of the development of what I'm doing. Sometimes I can't do it.

"At home [in California] I used to play, and the birds always used to whistle with me. I would stop what I was working on and play with the birds."

He described how bird calls had been recorded and then slowed down in playback; the bird calls had a timbre similar to that of a flute. Conversely, he said, a symphony flutist recorded these bird calls, and when the recording was played at a fast speed, it sounded like birds.

Having made his point about the connection of bird whistles and flute playing, Dolphy explained his use of quarter tones when playing flute.

"That's the way birds do," he said. "Birds have notes in between our notes — you try to imitate something they do and, like, maybe it's

John Coltrane's birthplace in upper floor of this two-story building, Hamlet, N.C. Picture was taken in 1972.

Reverend Blair's church, appearing almost exactly as it did in 1926, Hamlet, N.C. Picture was taken in 1972.

Parsonage next to church, where Rev. and Mrs. Blair lived, Hamlet, N.C. Picture was taken in 1972.

The family house where the Blairs, Coltranes and Lyerlys lived, High Point, N.C. Picture taken in 1972.

Underhill Street, High Point, N.C., as it appeared in 1972.

William Penn High School, unidentified man in foreground who graciously agreed to add his presence to the photo, High Point, N.C. Picture taken in 1972.

John's first girlfriend, Doreatha Nelson; high school photo courtesy of James Kinser, from old local newspaper.

John Coltrane in Navy band, 1945, seated in first row, second from left, with shades on.

John Coltrane seated second from right in Joe Webb's band. Webb is standing. Big Maybelle, then 17 or 18 years old, is seated at the far left.

John Coltrane seated with cigarette, engrossed in Charlie Parker's soloing. The cigarette eventually burned John's hand and dropped from his hand, as he was so enrapt by Bird. Jimmy Heath, the bandleader, has his back to the camera. Philadelphia, 1948, courtesy of Jimmy Heath.

Taken in 1955 in Philadelphia.

In 1955, Philadelphia, at Naima's apartment.

In 1955 with step-daughter, Saida. All photos on this page by courtesy of Naima Coltrane.

Photo taken at Randall's Island Jazz Festival, New York City. © Kwame Braithwaite

John Coltrane, Cannonball Adderley & Miles Davis, Randalls Island N.Y.C.: 1959 ©
Kwame Braithwaite

John Coltrane, Miles Davis, Randall Island 1959. © Kwame Braithwaite

1959 Taken in his New York City Apartment. © Kwame Braithwaite

1959 Taken in his New York City Apartment. © Kwame Braithwaite

Coltrane on soprano saxophone around 1961, courtesy of Naima Coltrane.

Photo of Coltrane taken around 1961, courtesy of Naima Coltrane.

Place and occasion unknown, taken around 1961, courtesy of Naima Coltrane.

Sulieman Saud on piano, Elvin Jones on drums, place unknown, courtesy of Sulie-man Saud.

From left to right, John Coltrane, Jimmy Garrison, Rashied Ali, Elvin Jones, Sulieman Saud. Courtesy of Sulieman Saud.

Jimmy Garrison in Japan, 1966. Photo by courtesy of Rashied Ali.

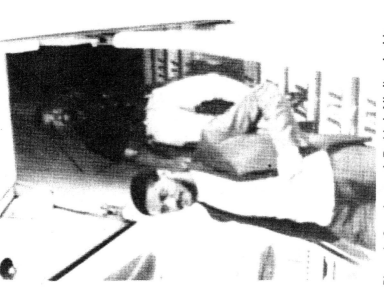

Pharoah Saunders and Rashied Ali disembarking from plane in Japan, 1966. Photo by courtesy of Rashied Ali.

Alice and John on train in Japan, 1966. Photo by courtesy of Rashied Ali.

John Coltrane in Japanese airport, with hand over area of abdominal pain. Photo by courtesy of Rashied Ali.

Harold Lovette, John's lawyer, riding train in Japan. Pharoah Saunders seated behind him, April, 1966. Photo by courtesy of Rashied Ali.

John Coltrane practicing soprano saxophone backstage in Japan. Also in picture are Alice Coltrane and Rashied Ali. Photo by courtesy of Rashied Ali.

John Coltrane resting against a column and holding his hand over the pain in his abdomen. Also from left to right are Jimmy Garrison with back to camera, Harold Lovette, Pharoah Saunders, and Alice Coltrane. Photo by courtesy of Rashied Ali.

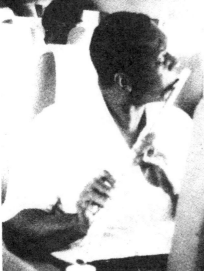

John Coltrane practicing flute while on plane over Japan. Photo by courtesy of Rashied Ali.

Shrine at site of WW II atomic bomb explosion, where John prayed. Photo by courtesy of Rashied Ali.

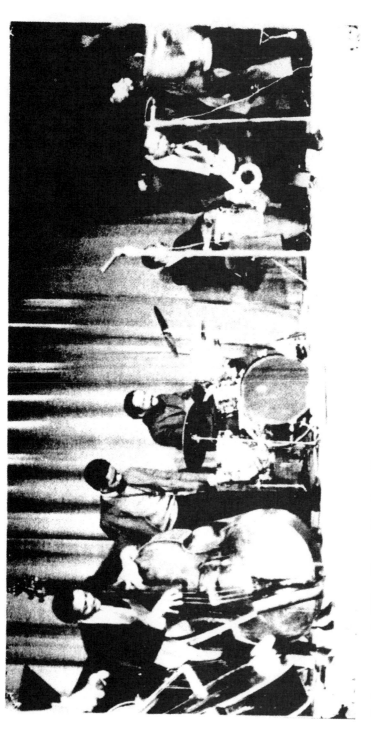

Performance at the Village Theater, New York City. Right to left, Algee DeWitt, John Coltrane, the late John Salgado (second cousin of Rashied Ali), Omar Ali (brother of Rashied Ali), Rashied Ali, Pharoah Saunders, Jimmy Garrison, Sonny Johnson (not seen on photo, but playing the bass to the extreme left). Winter, 1966. Photo by courtesy of Rashied Ali.

Rhythm written out for drums
By John Coltrane
In his hand writing., during recording session.

Rhythms written out for drums by John Coltrane in his handwriting during recording session in early 1967. Photo by courtesy of Rashied Ali.

Photo from around 1966, by courtesy of Rashied Ali.

Flyer for the performance at the Olatunji Center of African Culture. Photo by courtesy of Naima Coltrane.

Performance at Olatunji's Center of African Culture in New York City. Right to left, John Coltrane, Alice Coltrane (mostly obscured), Rashied Ali, Algee DeWitt playing the Bata drum, Jimmy Garrison, and Pharoah Saunders. April 23, 1967. Photo by courtesy of Rashied Ali.

between F and F-sharp, and you'll have to go up or come down on the pitch. It's really something! And so, when you get playing, this comes. You try to do some things on it. Indian music has something of the same quality – different scales and quarter tones. I don't know how you label it, but it's pretty."

The question in many critics' minds, though they don't often verbalize it, is: What are John Coltrane and Eric Dolphy trying to do. Or: What *are* they doing?

Following the question, a 30-second silence was unbroken except by Dolphy's, "That's a good question." Dolphy was first to try to voice his aims in music:

"What I'm trying to do I find enjoyable. Inspiring – what it makes me do. It helps me play, this feel. It's like you have no idea what you're going to do next. You have an idea, but there's always that spontaneous thing that happens. This feeling, to me, leads the whole group. When John plays, it might lead into something you had no idea could be done. Or McCoy does something. Or the way Elvin [Jones, drummer with the group] or Jimmy [Garrison, the bassist] play; they solo, they do something. Or when the rhythm section is sitting on something a different way. And that is what it does for me."

*   *   *

Coltrane paused, deep in thought. No one said anything. Finally he went on:

"It's more than beauty that I feel in music – that I think musicians feel in music. What we know we feel we'd like to convey to the listener. We hope that this can be shared by all. I think, basically, that's about what it is we're trying to do. We never talked about just what we were trying to do. If you ask me that question, I might say this today and tomorrow say something entirely different, because there are many things to do in music.

"But, over-all, I think the main thing a musician would like to do is to give a picture to the listener of the many wonderful things he knows of and senses in the universe. That's what music is to me – it's just another way of saying this is a big, beautiful universe we live in, that's been given to us, and here's an example of just how magnificent and encompassing it is. That's what I would like to do. I think that's one of the greatest things you can do in life, and we all try to do it in some way. The musician's way is through his music."

This philosophy about music, life, and the universe, Coltrane said, is "so important to music, and music is so important. Some realize it young and early in their careers. I didn't realize it as early as I should have, as early as I wish I had. Sometimes you have to take a thing when it comes and be glad."

When did he first begin to feel this way?

"I guess I was on my way in '57, when I started to get myself together musically, although at the time I was working academically and technically. It's just recently that I've tried to become even more aware of this other side – the life side of music. I feel I'm just beginning again. Which goes back to the group and what we're trying to do. I'm fortunate to be in the company I'm in now, because anything I'd like to do, I have a place to try. They respond so well that it's very easy to try new things."

Dolphy broke in with, "Music is a reflection of everything. And it's universal. Like, you can hear somebody from across the world, another country. You don't even know them, but they're in your back yard, you know?"

"It's a reflection of the universe," Coltrane said. "Like having life in miniature. You just take a situation in life or an emotion you know and put it into music. You take a scene you've seen, for instance, and put it to music."

Had he ever succeeded in re-creating a situation or scene?

"I was getting into it," he said, "but I haven't made it yet. But I'm beginning to see how to do it. I know a lot of musicians who have done it. It's just happening to me now. Actually, while a guy is soloing, there are many things that happen. Probably he himself doesn't know how many moods or themes he's created. But I think it really ends up with the listener. You know, you hear different people say, 'Man, I felt this while he was playing.' or 'I thought about this.' There's no telling what people are thinking. They take in what they have experienced. It's a sharing process – playing – for people."

"You can feel vibrations from the people," Dolphy added.

"The people can give you something too," Coltrane said. "If you play in a place where they really like you, like your group, they can make you play like you've never felt like playing before."

Anyone who has heard the Coltrane group in person in such a situation knows the almost hypnotic effect the group can have on the audience and the audience's almost surging involvement in the music. But sometimes, it is said, the striving for excitement *per se* within the group leads to nonmusical effects. It was effects such as these that have led to the "anti-jazz" term.

Such a term is bound to arouse reaction in musicians like Coltrane and Dolphy.

Without a smile – or rancor – Coltrane said he would like the critics who have used the term in connection with him to tell him exactly what they mean. Then, he said, he could answer them.

One of the charges is that what Coltrane and Dolphy play doesn't swing.

"I don't know what to say about that," Dolphy said.

"Maybe it doesn't swing," Coltrane offered.

"I can't say that they're wrong," Dolphy said. "But I'm still playing."

Well, don't *you* feel that it swings? he was asked.

"Of course I do," Dolphy answered. "In fact, it swings so much I don't know what to do – it moves me so much. I'm with John; I'd like to know how they explain 'anti-jazz'. Maybe they can tell us something."

"There are various types of swing," Coltrane said. "There's straight 4/4, with heavy bass drum accents. Then there's the kind of thing that goes on in Count Basie's band. In fact, every group of individuals assembled has a different feeling – a different swing. It's the same with this band. It's a different feeling than in any other band. It's hard to answer a man who says it doesn't swing."

Later, when the first flush of defense had subsided, Coltrane allowed:

"Quite possibly a lot of things about the band need to be done. But everything has to be done in its own time. There are some things that you just grow into. Back to speaking about editing – things like that. I've felt a need for this, and I've felt a need for ensemble work – throughout the songs, a little cement between this block, a pillar here, some more cement there, etc. But as yet I don't know just how I would like to do it. So rather than make a move just because I know it needs to be done, a move that I've not arrived at through work, from what I naturally feel, I won't do it.

"There may be a lot of things missing from the music that are coming, if we stay together that long. When they come, they'll be things that will be built out of just what the group is. They will be unique to the group and *of* the group."

Coltrane said he felt that what he had said still did not answer his critics adequately, that in order to do so he would have to meet them and discuss what has been said so that he could see just what they mean.

Dolphy interjected that the critic should consult the musician when there is something the critic does not fully understand. "It's kind of alarming to the musician'" he said, "when someone has written something bad about what the musician plays but never asks the musician anything about it. At least, the musician feels bad. But he doesn't feel so bad that he quits playing. The critic influences a lot of people. If something new has happened, something nobody knows what the musician is doing, he should ask the musician about it. Because somebody may like it; they might want to know something about it. Sometimes it really hurts, because a musician not only loves his work but depends on it for a living. If somebody writes something bad about musicians, people stay away. Not because the guys don't sound good but because somebody said something that has influence over a lot of people. They say, 'I read this, and I don't think he's so hot because so-and-so said so.' "

Dolphy had brought up a point that bothers most jazz critics: readers sometime forget that criticism is what *one* man thinks. A critic is telling how he feels about, how he reacts to, what he hears in, a performance or a piece of music.

"The best thing a critic can do," Coltrane said, "is to thoroughly understand what he is writing about and then jump in. That's all he can do. I have even seen favorable criticism which revealed a lack of profound analysis, causing it to be little more than superficial.

"Understsnding is what is needed. That is *all* you can do. Get all the understanding for what you're speaking of that you can get. That way you have done your best. It's the same with a musician who is trying to understand music as well as he can. Undoubtedly, none of us are going to be 100 percent — in either criticism or music. No percent near that, but we've all got to try.

"Understanding is the whole thing. In talking to a critic try to understand him, and he can try to understand the part of the game you are in. With this understanding, there's no telling what could be accomplished. Everybody would benefit."

Though he said he failed to answer his critics, John Coltrane perhaps had succeeded more than he thought.

None of the critics accepted John's offer to meet with them.

The article did set up a reaction within one listener, George Russell, a non-musician, otherwise known as "Big George."

He was angry over the way DeMicheal approached and questioned John and Eric. One night, at around 4 a.m., the anger seethed over. George sat at his desk, set up two bottles of wine, put on some sounds, "Live At The Village Vanguard," "Coltrane Jazz," *My Favorite Things, Giant Steps* and poured out this letter to Don DeMicheal,

Dear Mr. DeMicheal:

I am writing in reference to your critical article about the music of John Coltrane and Eric Dolphy. Your article seems to have been written as an outsider. You and your fellow critics should observe more of Trane's music before you write such an article. Any time someone can say that the above two musicians don't swing, they must be outsiders. When these two cats play a blues, the sound has all kinds of movement; it swings, bounces, drives, strolls, according to the mood or beat of the rhythm section. Listen to Trane on "Blues Minor," "Traning In," "Summertime." Dig Dolphy on "Blues in the Abstract Truth."

The solos are long because Trane and other musicians that play extended solos bring out some of the many ideas of the tune. For example, when you write a letter to a friend you haven't seen in some time and you have a great many things to tell him. While writing this letter you can just briefly explain what you have to say, or you can go into detail about each instance. This is one reason I think solos are as extended as they are. The musician improvises on the melody, then the bridge, then the melody again. When Trane stops playing a tune there is not too much more that can be said about it. The Trane you heard two weeks ago is not the same Trane you are hearing this week.

In the statement about Eric Dolphy sounding like birds, I believe bird music has some genuine soul and beauty myself. I think what Eric was trying to do was to express some of the things he has observed in his environment. He may have grown up in an area where birds are constantly present. Therefore, his influence from birds may be evident in his playing. You can't expect a guy who has been speaking one language and living in one society to speak another language and adjust to another society. Also, Eric might have been trying to represent a certain mood where the sound of birds is a necessity such as in Africa on the Africa/Brass Album on Impulse Label.

When a critic asks what a musician is trying to do when he is playing, it shows a lack of understanding or narrow-mindedness. Either way they both equal the same thing: being in the dark.

What I think musicians are trying to do is to paint a picture of their inner feelings. They express how a tune should be written or how a story should be told. For example, the title of the tune can be *Giant Steps, Africa, Oleo,* or what have you. The musician will explain to the listener what he sees and hears.

Actually, to understand what musicians are trying to do you have to get into the music with them. By finding the groove it will help you to understand what the musician is trying to say. If you are an outsider, this may be a little difficult to do.

The way musicians play their instruments is a reflection of their personality. Their personalities reveal some of their influences and thoughts that come to their minds. It's like having a down to earth talk with someone where there are no punches pulled. I have felt many times that I was inside the music, as if I were the one who was taking the *Giant Steps* or the person in *Africa.* This was a story being told by another human being like myself that was coming true. This was reality. Whether they are playing jazz, bird music or nursery rhymes, this is how the musician communicates to the listener. This is their way of expressing themselves. No musician is forcing the public, critics included, to come and hear them at the jazz spots or to buy their records.

The trouble with most jazz critics is that they are outsiders. The elements that outsiders are lacking are feeling and understanding. The basic blues are the roots of jazz. This is the foundation, and it must be felt in order to explore other ideas. The environment enters into the picture again. Some people can hear a beat and immediately they find a groove. Then they hear a melody where they get a few ideas. At this point they sense a direction and they can almost anticipate what the musician's ideas are building up to. It's pretty easy if you have that basic blues background. From this you can improvise and stray as far away from the original theme as you care to without losing the basic idea.

When you grow up in this basic background, these things come natural. Some of the squares who are playing and digging jazz cannot feel this basic idea. Their basic idea may have originated when they were seniors, playing in the high school band. Others who have this precious basic thing have inherited it. Their backgrounds go all the way back to the time when their ancestors were slaves, singing folksongs in the fields. From these folksongs came the blues, then from the blues came jazz. It's a long story and some people can't expect "to come in the middle of it" and understand it.

I am not a personal friend of John Coltrane, but I feel that through his music I know him and can understand him. I don't know a concert "A" from a high "C" or "G" major, but I can feel this man's ideas. Trane's music and jazz to me, in general, is the inner feelings of this environment. His ideas on horn both tenor and soprano, combined with the rhythm section have painted some very beautiful pictures for me.

My suggestion to you Mr. DeMicheal is to really listen to Trane, not just sip highballs or chat with your date all night. Trane's music is not meant to be background music. I would also suggest that you listen to some of Trane's records, the earliest "Coltrane" to "Live at the Vanguard." Try listening to some of the earlier things with Miles. Maybe as one who understands the sound and the development of this genius I can bring you along slowly so that you and your fellow critics can reach a point where you learn to appreciate some of the more beautiful things in music. As an outsider you may be limited but at least you will have an understanding of jazz.

Truly jazz

George Russell

P.S. Not to be confused with the pianist of the same name.[27]

Big George lived in Baisely Park, an area near John's house. A friend had told him that John had a harp. On a walk one day he saw a house from which music was dancing and which had a harp in the picture window. He realized that this was John's house but didn't venture to knock on the door. Instead he sent John a copy of the letter with a note saying that he would meet him where the band was performing, at the Blue Coronet in Brooklyn.

The night that George introduced himself John looked up at him.

"Oh, you're George Russell?"

"Yeahhh."

"I'm pleased to meet you. Man, I really appreciate what you wrote. I think you hit the nail on the head. I'm glad *somebody* can dig it."

George answered in his deep round voice,

"Man, like that's how I felt. Man, like I was so drugged I couldn't sleep."

John invited him,

"You come by, man, and check out this juicer and have some carrot juice."

'Carrot juice?' George thought. Then said,

"How does that taste, man?"

"Man, it tastes good!!"

On his first day at the house, he and John were in the kitchen drinking carrot juice and eating chicken when John's thoughts fell abruptly into words.
"Excuse me, I'll be right back."
He went straight upstairs and started blowing his horn, brooomm, bowrocay boorrouuum. Bewildered at being left so suddenly, Big George accepted it. As time moved on, he came to understand that a musical feeling would come over John which he would have to immediately express and begin to develop. This was why his horn was usually near him wherever he went.
The stinging wave of critical ignorance had not subsided. In the April 26th issue of *Down Beat*, a review entitled "A 'Double View' of Live at the Village Vanguard" by Ira Gitler and Pete Welding appeared.

> *Chasin' the Trane*, a blues that consumes all of the second side, is more like waitin' for a train – a 100-car freight train – to pass.
> Coltrane may be searching for new avenues of expression, but if it is going to take this form of yawps, squawks, and countless repetitive runs, then it should be confined to the woodshed. Whether or not it is "far out" is not the question. Whatever it is, it is monotonous, a treadmill to the Kingdom of Boredom. There are places when his horn actually sounds as if it is in need of repair. In fact, this solo could be described as one big air-leak . . .
>
> (I.G.)

*   *   *

The fault is less in Coltrane than in the task he has set himself. Perhaps the fullest appreciation of the monumental difficulties involved in the approach may be seen in the Coltrane-improviser that he so often is unable to bring it off, to control and direct it with the strength and surness of purpose it needs.

In a real sense, the first two pieces, the successful ones, are much less ambitious in scope than is the lengthy *Chasin'*, and in this lies much of the reason for their success.

They are more interesting melodically, for one thing, and, for another, they are much more closely allied with conventional jazz improvising than is the unorthodox *Chasin'*, where the interest is primarily rhythmic and emotional. This piece, with its gaunt, waspish angularities, its ire-ridden intensity, raw, spontaneous passion, and, in the final analysis, its sputtering inconclusiveness, seems more properly a piece of musical exorcism than anything else, a frenzied sort of soul-baring. It is a torrential and anguished outpouring, delivered with unmistakeable power, conviction, and near-demoniac ferocity – and as such is a remarkable human document. But the very intensity of the feelings that prompt it militate against its effectiveness as a musical experience. It's the old problem of the artist's total involvement as a man supplanting his artistry, which is based, after all, to some greater or lesser degree, in detachment.

As for the other participants, their supporting work (for that's what it is) is excellent throughout, especially that of Jones, whose primary role cannot be too strongly stressed. The rhythm section furnishes Coltrane exactly the solid bedrock he needs for his constructions. Strangely enough, after Coltrane's solo on *Spiritual*, Dolphy's brief vocal-dominated bass-clarinet segment sounds surprisingly tame, albeit appropriate.

The degree of Coltrane's striving on *Chasin'* in no wise mitigates the failure in attainment. If anything, the very loftiness of the goal tends to magnify it out of all proportion. It is, however, one of the noblest failures on record.[28]

Though John was concerned with the critics' babble, his predominant involvement was with the music. He ate no solid foods and his entire diet consisted of juices. Other musicians, he felt, could benefit from this diet. This was a very creative period during which music flowed.

On April 11th or 12th, 1962, he brought the quartet into the recording studio. They did a delightful song which John wrote for an older musician he admired, *Big Nick*. On June 29th, another composition, dedicated to African drummer Michael Olatunji, and entitled *Tunji*, was recorded. *Tunji* is an example of the use of few chords and new scales. On the same day, a rearrangement of the popular song, *Out of This World*, was recorded. This reinterpretation put new, healthier blood into the original body of the song.

It begins with a briskly plucked bass note and broad dancing rhythm. John surges into a stirring oration. A feeling is generated like the wave of a leader's hand, that can spear a shudder through the crowd and instantaneously snap them into rage or rhapsody. Briefly, rises the tune of *Wade In The Water* from within the enchanting fervor.

Between the recording of *Big Nick* and *Out of This World*, John wrote a letter to Don DeMicheal, in which he emphatically stated his beliefs on Black music. DeMicheal had sent him a book by Aaron Copeland on music.

June 2, 1962

Dear Don,

Many thanks for sending Aaron Copland's fine book, 'Music and Imagination.' I found it historically revealing and on the whole, quite informative. However, I do not feel that all of his tenets are *entirely* essential or applicable to the 'jazz' musician. This book seems to be written more for the American classical or semi-classical composer who has the problem, as Copland sees it, of not finding himself an integral part of the musical community, or having difficulty in finding a positive philosophy or justification for his art. The 'jazz' musician (You can have this term along with several others that have been foisted upon us.) does not have this problem at all. We have absolutely no reason to worry about lack of positive and affirmative philosophy. It's built in us. The phrasing, the sound of the music attest this fact. We are naturally endowed with it. You can believe all of us would have perished long ago if this were not so. As to community, the whole face of the globe is our community. You see, it is really easy for us to create. We are born with this feeling that just comes out no matter what conditions exist. Otherwise, how could our founding fathers have produced this music in the first place when they surely found themselves (as many of us do today) existing in hostile communities where there was everything to fear and damn few to trust. Any music which could grow and propagate itself as our music has, must have a hell of an affirmative belief inherent in it. Any person who claims to doubt this, or claims to believe that the exponents of our music of freedom are not guided by this same entity, is either prejudiced, musically sterile, just plain stupid or scheming. Believe me, Don, we all know that this word which so many seem to fear today, 'Freedom' has a hell of a lot to do with this music. Anyway, I did find in Copland's book many fine points. For example: 'I cannot imagine an art work without implied convictions.' – Neither can I. I am sure that you and many others have enjoyed and garnered much of value from this well written book.

"If I may, I would like to express a sincere hope that in the near future, a vigorous investigation of the materials presented in this book and others related will help cause an opening up of the ears that are still closed to the progressive music created by the independent thinking artist of today. When this is accomplished, I am certain that the owners of such ears will easily recognize the very vital and highly enjoyable qualities that exist in this music. I also feel that through such honest endeavor, the contributions of future creators will be more easily recognized, appreciated and enjoyed; particularly by the listener who may otherwise miss the point (intellectually, emotionally, sociologically, etc.) because of inhibitions, a lack of understanding, limited means of association or other reasons.

"You know, Don, I was reading a book on the life of Van Gogh today, and I had to pause and think of that wonderful and persistent force – the creative urge. The creative urge was in this man who found himself so much at odds with the world he lived in, and in spite of all the adversity, frustrations, rejections and so forth – beautiful and living art came forth abundantly . . . if only he could be here today. Truth is indestructible. It seems history shows (and it's the same way today) that the innovator is more often than not met with some degree of condemnation; usually according to the degree of his departure from the prevailing modes of expression or what have you. Change is always so hard to accept. We also see that these innovators always seek to revitalize, extend and reconstruct the status quo in their given fields, wherever it is needed. Quite often they are the rejects, outcasts, sub-citizens, etc. of the very societies to which they bring so much sustenance. Often they are people who endure great personal tragedy in their lives. Whatever the case, whether accepted or rejected, rich or poor, they are forever guided by that great and eternal constant — the creative urge. Let us cherish it and give all praise to God. Thank you and best wishes to all.

Sincerely,

P.S. Congratulations to the writer of Article, "Thunder in the Wings." I think it was Bill Mathieu. He is consistently proving himself one of the best in musical theory. Thanks also to Martin Williams for his very fine discourse in the same issue.[29]

In August, the International Critics' Poll appeared in *Down Beat*. John was still rated first in the soprano saxophone category, but was placed second on tenor saxophone behind Sonny Rollins. The reaction to the music, especially the Gitler article, began to affect Bob Thiele, the representative of Impulse Records, who was present whenever John recorded. Thiele recalls:

"I think he was less affected by the reviews than I was. After you've been in the record business for years and years, you're always concerned about the commercial aspects, although you try to record as many artistic things as possible. You're always concerned with how well the record will sell.

"I read reviews in *Down Beat* which really, I guess, were upsetting things, mainly because I knew that Coltrane was so sincere. I think the fact that Coltrane was sincere and was such an honest and genuine musician affected me and I knew that I was concerned as to why the so-called critics were not as affected as I was. In other words, I am not a critic and I am deeply affected, but the critics of *Down Beat* were almost like demons in their attacks about what they called the new music and wrote that Coltrane was just rambling and blowing . . . they seemed very unfair and almost irresponsible, almost as if they hadn't given any thought to what he was doing."[30]

For the remainder of the year, and the beginning of the following year, many of the records made were slower and more adherent to the ballad form. The reason for this change is revealed in both Thiele's and John's recollections. Bob Thiele continues:

"Here I was working for a record company and concerned about how well our records would sell and we have a critic who comes along and says John Coltrane's records are windy, flat and need editing, etc. . . . I figured we had better go in and see if we can get John to do some melodic things, do some standard tunes. . . . John accepted them and was enthusiastic about them."[31]

At a later date, John spoke of these records. "I think Impulse was interested in having a balanced sort of thing, a diversified sort of catalog, and I find nothing wrong with this myself. You see, I like — in fact, most of the songs that I even write now, the ones I consider songs, are — ballads. So there's something there that I mean I really love these things.

"And these ballads that came out were definitely ones which I felt at this time. I chose them; it seemed to be something that was laying around in my mind — from my youth, or somewhere — and I just had to do them . . . "[32]

He told Naima as long ago as 1959, "I can't play ballads," and went on in 1962 to record some of the most beautiful renditions of ballads ever done. Thiele suggested that the group record with Duke Ellington. John was elated to play with a great contributor to the music, one whom he had admired for so long. This work with Duke affected his approach to the recording studio. Previously, he strove for perfection to the smallest detail in his recordings. Once he had the quartet return to the studio to re-record one note. Thiele spoke of the effect of Duke.

"He would do a tune, maybe 12, 15 or 20 times before he was satisfied and even though we did a tune 20 times he might go back to, or agree to go back to the second or third take or something like that. The first tune we did with Ellington was *In A Sentimental Mood*. We did that in one take, and I'll never forget my reaction. I figured, when the tune ended, now I've got a real problem. Ellington, I know from past experience, is going to say *that's it*, great, and Coltrane would say, I feel we should go over this a few more times. Immediately I ran out of the studio and though I didn't know how I would handle it, I had to get the two guys together. I said, Duke (he was the oldest of the three of us there), what do you think, knowing he would say it was great, which it was. He said, "That's fine," and I said, John, do you think we should do it again, giving him the opportunity to say something. Duke immediately interrupted, and said, "Well, what for, you can't say it again that way, this is it." John said, "Yes, Duke you're right," and from then on the album went very smoothly. Also, from then on John's recordings were really based on one and two takes. I must say that after that meeting with Ellington, Coltrane never spent that much time on a take, on a tune. He would like to get it in one or two takes, and if it didn't happen, we would scrape it. That would be the end of it, and he would go on to something else. I think it was a very, very important point in Coltrane's recording period, the meeting with Ellington, and I think they both liked the record. Johnny Hodges told me quite emphatically that, as long as he had been playing *In A Sentimental Mood*, the best reading of the tune was Coltrane's."[33]

Music for another album entitled "Ballads" was recorded by the quartet alone on November 13th, 1962. With the exception of *It's Easy to Remember*, none of the tunes had been played by the quartet before. They arrived at the recording studio with sheet music of each tune, discussed them, wrote changes on the sheets, and rehearsed loosely for one-half hour. Afterwards, each tune except one was done in one take.

All Or Nothing At All, on which John had written "Arabic feeling," was more complex rhythmically, and got off to a couple of false starts. After these starts, they played it without difficulty. The album has a floating feeling. There is a high, motionless motion, and John shows his ability to play romance.

But this was a difficult period for him. In an interview with writer and history professor Frank Kofsky, he referred to his view on the critics, and briefly about difficulties at home that were beginning to appear.

Kofsky: Why do you think there's been all this hostility to the new music, especially in your case?

Coltrane: Oh, man, I never could figure it out! I couldn't even venture to answer it now. Because as I told them then, I just felt that they didn't understand.

Kofsky: Do you think they were making as conscientious and thorough an attempt to understand as they could have?

Coltrane: At the time, I didn't feel they were, because I did offer them, in an article in *Down Beat*, that if any of you men were interested in trying to understand, let's get together and let's talk about it, you know? I thought if they were really genuinely interested or felt there was something here, that instead of just condemning what you don't know about, if you want to discuss it, let's talk about it. But no one ever came forth, so I don't think they wanted to know what I had to say about it.

Kofsky: I think it frightened them. Bill Dixon and I talked about this at great length; and he said "Well, these guys, it's taken them years to pick out *I Got Rhythm* on the piano." And now the new music comes along and undermines their entire career, which is built around understanding things based on those patterns.

Coltrane: Yes, I dug it like that too. I said, "Well, this could be a real drag to a cat if he figures this is something that he won't be able to cope with and he won't be able to write about." If he can't write about it, he can't make a living at this; and then I realized that, so I quieted down. I wouldn't allow myself to become too hostile in return. Although there was a time I kind of froze up on those people at *Down Beat*. I felt there was something there that wasn't – I felt that they were letting their weakness direct their actions, which I didn't feel they should have. The test was for me. They could do what they wanted to do. The thing for me to do was to remain firm in what I was doing. That was a funny period in my life, because I went through quite a few changes, you know, like home life – everything, man – I just went through so many . . . everything I was doing.[34]

These were difficult times during which his confidence was challenged, and he would have to summon all his resources to emerge spiritually intact. Nineteen sixty-two brought a decline in his popularity among establishment ranks. The choice he had made to advance the music was exacting some heavy dues. There were also the personal problems between him and Naima. On another level struggle was burning around the country. Blacks were finding themselves becoming less and less tolerant of oppression. Whites wanting to perpetuate their system began to retaliate with violence: bombing churches, masonic lodges, homes, killing leaders' families, terrorizing communities, and committing bestial atrocities. Only a fraction of these actions reached news media.

In Albany, a protracted battle between the city administration and a non-violent Black community led by Rev. Martin Luther King was lost, after striking successes in other cities. There was no doubt now that an adamant city government could withstand a massive non-violent campaign, regardless of pressure by the Federal government. The battle lines were becoming clearer and clearer, as Black people searched and found strength within themselves.

XII

The Prophet Reigns

> I have a basic desire
> to go
> to
> the basic elements of music
> and come out
> with value
> to go right
> into the heart
> strip myself of the old
> and be truly creative.[1]
>
> *John Coltrane*

Elvin, the terrible panther; James, the mighty-taloned eagle; and Saud, the lion with the fleetness of a gazelle, would beat the unclean air until it begged for mercy. John, the all-embracing sun, stood quietly, bobbing his head in affirmation. Trying to escape Elvin's madman' pounding, the bass drum would slide away. John would tip it back, with his foot, to its original position.

> Dance, Saud!! Dance your fingers over
> the piano keys!!!
> Elvin, don't bust them drums!!!!
> Tear at the bass, James. Tear it up!!
> Strum the deep hum of the soul.

Those in the audience who knew him would wave shyly, "Hey, John," "Hi, John." His only response would be a short nod or brief wave of his hand. It was time for the music now.

> Roaring upward, thrashing, bashing;
>> God damn!!

John's eyes focused only on his thoughts and on his horn. He held it sideways, fingering it in his own silence.

> twisting, surging, rolling, leaping
>> Can it go higher!!
> Where can it go?
> Air Flames red
> like dark red lipstick on a Black woman's lips
> like water of the fertile Nile
> like the fruit of the planet Mars

Heart pushing outward, horn gliding high, Rev. John William Coltrane could set the people on fire, make them shout, make them weep, make them thunder the floor with stomping feet.

> Snap!!

Searing, screaming necklaces of sapphire notes writhed beyond the outer reaches of belief. Sound beckons afar, magnetically drawing you to its midst, like a muezzin calling the people to prayer.

> Come Come praaaay with me
>> Come praaay with me
> Let meee take you down to the valley of God
>
> That's where ittt's so beautiful
> That's where itttt's so beautiful
>
> So cooome praaay with me
> Come on and praaay with me
> Let me take you to the Valley of God.

Wonderful, rising, wavering, wail leaps into your body. The soul gurgles with the warmth of goodness. As the sun set foot upon each jewel of the necklace, they smiled back their own color: coral blue, lava red, joyful yellow, infinite purple.

Leaning back slightly, eyes closed, eyebrows up and down, his face strained with each jumping note.

> Haah!
> Haya!!
> Haya!!!

The energy pierces upward and his body sways side to side.

> Patterns form
> Air bristles red and blue with cleanliness
> Inverted volcanos emit liquid suns
> Preach, Trane! Preach!!

His body bends forward erupting long curves of plush notes. Notes flow so fast they trip over themselves to become just sound. Skewed laughing sounds drop out, tightening his body, twisting him sideways. The rhythm in his playing strikes like pistons of air.

> Get Ge' Ge' Get it, 'Trane!
> Whoooooooooooooooooo!

The horn shoots up, swaying from side to side. Then the horn swings down, almost scraping the floor. How did he keep the horn in his mouth? His skilled fingers seemed hardly to move, though so much was created. Bearing down, sweating, walking across the floor, possessed by his own power, he trembled, flinging spirits into the audience.

> "Col - trane! Col - trane!!!"

Some forgot to breathe; some danced, some were afraid, and some whirled into the miracle insanity of momentary paradise.

> Ride the lavender triangle through
> a pillow of Black oblivious to the
> spring yellow circles whizzing erratically
> by, over the Harlem bridge
> > Into
> > the
> > Helical
> > Universe
> Falling losing track of our steed, to
> spiral into a multitude of variations
> who protested and put us in front of bars
> > Saturn
> > Save
> > Us
> From this straight line who intends
> to embrace us, tremble us, little ones — entwine
> us to be judged before the galactic court of
> > The
> > Last
> > Note

Thankful applause erupted. John would disappear, acknowledging the crowd with only a small nod. After playing, he would be inspired and want to practice in a secluded area of the club. When he didn't leave the audience area, he would sit at a table, drawing lines and abstract patterns that he related to music. Or he might read a math book from which relationships to the music were found. Sometimes he would be dissatisfied with his playing. His approach to *the music* was in many ways like that of a scientist. He would formulate technical problems for himself and try to solve them in playing.

Certain basic elements might be used such as a scale, a set of chords, a seemingly random set of notes. These elements would be developed in ways that most musicians would say was impossible or at least very difficult. When he solved the problem he would be ecstatic. But when he did not, his mood was one of dejection and self-criticism, even though listeners would glowingly say how much they received from the music. Regardless of his inner feelings, listeners' comments were always received graciously. Along with his powers of analysis he combined a desire to give good things to people.

> "Sometimes I let technical things surround me so often and so much, that I kind of lose sight . . . basically, all I want to do would be to play music that would make people happy."[2]

He went deeply into himself to reveal more of the ebony, red and fiery, yellow-winged beauty that swirled energetically within him – and resides in different colors within us. The music opened people up to their own capacities for creation. An important part of this "self" that he sought to reveal to people comes from the African legacy. There is a recording of a Kenyan chief directing a chorus of 1,000 men and women with instruments. Most prominent among the instruments is an African horn that sounds identical to the high human tone John exacted from the saxophone. The sound of the horn creates excitement. The women in the choir yell rolling screams around its sound that advance and recede, like warm, pressing waves.[3]

More musical creations reached the recording studio this year. John had spoken to Naima, with a sense of wonder, of the freshness of the air after a rain which he referred to as "rain-washed skies." From this wonder came the composition *After the Rain* in which the water-cleansed air moves, and yet does not move. With his horn, John cradles the notes that sound like the phrase, after-the-rain. The group recorded this composition on April 29th, 1963, with Roy Haynes substituting for Elvin Jones.

Around this time John met a female musician who was to become his second wife. His and Naima's problems had created a distance between them. The musician's name was Alice McLeod. She was from Detroit and from a musical family. Her mother played piano and sang in a church choir. Her brother was a bassist. After working in Detroit with a trio, she spent a year, 1962-63, on the road with vibraphonist Terry Gibbs, who said that she " . . . was always seeking, trying for something else." The "first indication was (playing) Jewish songs (which were based on) minor melodies." These "seemed to fit what (she) was trying to do." Alice played vibraphone as well as piano. Gibbs introduced her to John. "From the first evening (she) listened intently to his music."

In September, this same year, the quartet, unaccompanied by any other group, made its European tour. The reception was much more favorable than it had been on the first tour. European ears had become accustomed to the music.

"Musical nonsense!" snorted John Tynan, West Coast editor of *Down Beat*. "A horrifying demonstration of what appears to be a growing anti-jazz trend." Tynan, one of the most good-natured of critics, was not merely trying to stir up a controversy when, in 1961, he wrote this assessment of John Coltrane; he was, in fact, echoing views that had long been uttered privately by countless respected jazzmen.

Yet for every musician or critic who fears that the Coltrane approach is destroying swing, the vital essence of jazz, there is another who sees in him the wave of the future; and for every moment of what some of us have called anti-jazz there is another moment of Coltrane music, past or present, that reveals the man's prior relationship to swinging, tonal jazz as well as his probing challenging nature. It is as misleading to generalize about all his music under the anti-jazz heading as it is to brand Ella Fitzgerald a pop singer. Some writers, present company included, have been remiss in not pointing this out.

The avant garde pianist Cecil Taylor, who recorded with Coltrane a few years ago, says significantly: "Coltrane has a feeling for the hysteria of the times."

*   *   *

Answering his critics, Trane says: "I wish they would explain what they mean by anti-jazz. People have so many different definitions of jazz, how can anti-jazz be defined? And as for swinging, there are so many different ways to swing, too; a heavy four, or the Basie type feeling, or the kind that our group gets. How can you answer someone who says you don't swing?" Trane's success, it seems to me, is based partly though inadvertently on a sort of musical hypnosis.

Often he develops a mood in which audiences find consistent, building intensity, with influences from many cultures: West Indian, Oriental, African, Arabic. Often a single montoona-like performance in a club, built on one or two chords, may go on for a half hour, an hour or even 90 minutes.

Coltrane once admitted: "If I'm going to take an hour to say something I can say in ten minutes well, I'd better say it in ten minutes." A few of his records, mainly ballads and studio recordings, prove he can achieve a mood and make his point in four or five minutes, yet his latest LP devotes almost all its space to two 14-minute tracks.

A quiet, intense, articulate man whose manner reflects none of the seeming anger and frustration of his music, Coltrane continues to experiment as player and composer.

"I want to find new avenues, look into different approaches to music. You have to keep on examining everything that's going on around you, in music and in life."

Those who hear in his music only ugliness and nihilism should consider what he once told Don DeMicheal: "It's more than beauty that I feel in music . . . The main thing a musician would like to do is give a picture to the listener of the many wonderful things he knows of and senses in the universe. That's what music is to me."[4]

Physically, this was an especially grueling tour. A typical day found them up at six in the morning. At seven, there would be a "continental" breakfast — toast and juice. At eight o'clock, they would board a plane to the next country, and arrive during late afternoon. There would be only a few hours for dinner, sightseeing, rest or practice. Early evening the concert would begin in a huge auditorium. In Europe, Black music was much more respected than in its native United States. Performances were held in each city's best concert hall, instead of in cramped dens called nightclubs, where the smell of alcohol made one sick.

During performances, sweat poured down each member of the group's face as he was caught in cascades of emotion. Sometimes two concerts were given in one night. They would get to bed late with the next day promising only more of the same routine. In spite of this strenuous schedule, the quartet put all of its enormous energy into each performance. By the end of the tour they were exhausted.

On the plane back to the United States, John was sitting next to the aisle, Elvin was at the window and James was between them. McCoy was sitting a few seats ahead. John appreciated the effort the others had put into the tour. He leaned over and said deeply, "Thanks, fellas," and kissed Elvin and Jimmy on the lips. Tears came to Jimmy's eyes, and Elvin also was touched.

During the time of their tour, the turmoil of the early sixties had culminated in several abominable murders. On April 3rd, Birmingham police used dogs and firehoses to beat back Black demonstrators, many of whom were of high school age or younger. A few months later about 2,500 Blacks attacked police with bricks and bottles, wrecked cars and burned buildings. President Kennedy stationed a force of 3,000 outside the city. In June, the Black leader Medgar Evers was killed in an ambush while in the garage of his home. Soon afterwards, on a Sunday, the Christian sacred day, a church was bombed, killing four little girls and injuring other children while attending Sunday school. Hours later, police killed a little boy, and two white youths killed another. Reverend Martin Luther King spoke in memory of the little girls.

While riding a plane on the way to a performance in the United States, John read this speech. From its rhythm, he wrote the composition, *Alabama*. This composition sounds like a mournful chant, filled with sorrow; bottomless, endless despair of having lost a loved child. But amidst the hopelessness, there is a surging defiance that swears vengeance on the murderers of children.

> May their lives be taken on their happiest of days
> May they bleed a million tortures before knives of fire.
> May they sink endlessly into the quicksands of torment
> May their wives and children be enslaved to crushing masters.

On October 8th, a live performance was taped at Birdland in New York City. *The Promise, I Want to Talk About You*, and *Afro-Blue* were recorded. On November 18th, *Your Lady* and *Alabama* were recorded in a studio. *Your Lady* gets its name from Naima. This was the term she used when speaking to John in reference to Alice. These selections were released on an album entitled "Coltrane Live At Birdland." The music is at a highly energetic level. It strains the air like tight skin over a talking drum, whose sound breaks into a multitude of dancing rainbows, feverish moons and deep-voiced lions.

Nineteen sixty-three was a year of rage. The end of this rage was not soon to come. Into the Black consciousness anger was evolving, as well as a broad love for mankind. John was an integral part of this consciousness and infused his force of love and strength. This was not love in the sense of submission. For even the slow compositions were assertive and definitive, like the unequivocal music of Malcolm X's speech.

While Europe opened its concert halls to Black musicians, those in the United States were firmly closed. Pianist Randy Weston and others had fought the barriers of New York's Philharmonic Hall. By 1963 there had been several performances of Black music in the auditorium that had once been firmly shut. These efforts by Weston probably led to the appearance of John's group and others at Philharmonic Hall.

It was just before the end of 1963

The quartet with Eric Dolphy was to perform in Philharmonic Hall. Also on the program were saxophonist Albert Ayler, pianist Cecil Taylor, and drummer Art Blakey with his band. John was given first choice in his group's place on the program. He wanted to go on first in order to be able to play as long as he wished. However, it was customary for the most popular group to appear last. Many in the audience were surprised to see the quartet come on first. The group performed. The audience was responsive. But John was sad. While playing a harp backstage, John called his friend, Folks, over. "Folks, I got something I want to talk to you about." Folks looked into his face and knew that something was wrong. He had a hint in his mind of what it might be, but kept it to himself. After the next performance, John called, "Come here, man." They walked to a secluded area where he explained, "Neet and I have separated. Nobody else knows. But you know that's the first woman in my life − Neet. I still have respect for her and we still have an understanding, and she never will want for anything as long as she lives. I have it fixed that way."

Folks thought, wishing desperately that John had come to him before. Maybe he could have mended their problems. But realizing that it was too late, he said with resignation, "You can't do no more than that, man."

The page of 1963 was turned to the following year. On April 27th, and June 1st, of 1964, the quartet recorded an album entitled "Crescent." The title composition was the result of John's drawing the figure of the moon's crescent in Paris. Deviating from his practice of recording quickly, the group made seven or eight tapes of "Crescent," trying to capture a feeling of listening in on a performance that had already begun. The result is a majestic composition with great measured sweeps of sound. It has the swaying sadness of a spiritual, and the grandness of an anthem. *Lonnie's Lament*, on the same album, is a composition which is beautiful in its despair. It sounds like a slave's song asking God for bread, and freedom for his child.

The Drum Thing rumbles gently with Elvin's deep drumming. The feeling is a mysterious rain forest in which a horn chants its solemn meditation. *Bessie's Blues* is a dedication to Bessie Smith, and *Wise One* is a prayer for Naima, which he wrote because of his respect for her wisdom and intelligence.

In New York's Greenwich Village, a confluence of musical and political ideas was smouldering. A few of the musicians involved were Albert Ayler, Don Ayler, Sonny Murray, Rashied Ali, Archie Shepp, Marion Brown, George Braithe, and Dennis Charles. These and others found each other in New York. Most were engaged in a desperate battle for survival in the "Big Apple."

The glitter of publicity, record dates, and playing in clubs all turned to puff. Instead, there were few record dates. If a musician cut a record, he rarely made enough money from it to pay rent. Club dates were few and publicity was limited even after an artist had a successful record.

These musicians represented a broad spectrum of ideas: some felt that one should just play, without reference to chords, melody, or any system except that of their feelings. Others adhered to more traditional systems. A fertile field of ideas and energies filled the air. These would eventually come to the surface and become lumped by the label makers as the "New Wave" or the "New Thing."

Many of the musicians directed themselves to the cleansing of the human spirit through music, as saxophonist Albert Ayler so aptly expressed: " . . . we are the music we play. And our commitment is to peace, to understanding of life. And we keep trying to purify our music, to purify ourselves — and those who hear us — to higher levels of peace and understanding. You have to purify and crystallize your sound in order to hypnotize. I'm convinced, you see, that through music, life can be given more meaning. And every kind of music has an influence — either direct or indirect — on the world around it so that after a while the sounds of different types of music go around and bring about psychological changes. And we're trying to bring about peace."[5]

Ayler also expressed the alignment of the young musicians with the developments within the Black consciousness. " . . . I think it's a very good thing that Black people in this country are becoming conscious of the strengths of being Black. They are beginning to see who they are. They are requiring so much respect for themselves. And that's a beautiful development for me because I'm playing their suffering, whether they know it or not. I've lived that suffering. Beyond that, it all goes back to God. Nobody's superior, and nobody's inferior."[6]

John knew most of the younger musicians by first name. For them he was an example of clean living, diligence in work, kindness, and a spiritual way of life. Because of the respect they had for him, those who smoked marijuana would not do so in his presence. Inspiration came from his words of reassurance and his spirit, as it showed itself in his playing. He would often take time and advise them, lend money freely, and receive phone calls to discuss personal problems. One difficulty all shared was getting record dates.

John would help by using his influence with Impulse. Bob Thiele spoke of this, "John Coltrane really had very little to say. It was quiet action. If he heard a young musician he would call me and all of a sudden the player would be recording. He was really helping an awful lot of people. I think that if we signed everyone that John Coltrane recommended, we'd have four hundred musicians on the label. He was very much concerned about the young musician."[7]

Archie Shepp continued his relationship with John. New York had been very frustrating for Shepp. Having reached a high degree of mastery of his instrument and possessing a good knowledge of theory, Shepp felt that he should at least be making a decent living from music. Such was not the case. He was on welfare, and spent his dimes trying to call Bob Thiele for a record date. One night, after accompanying a group at a dance concert, he felt very frustrated and went to the Half Note where John was playing. John let him sit in, and later expressed his enjoyment of Shepp's contribution. In a straightforward manner Shepp spoke to him, explaining that he had made a record with Savoy Records, but that they didn't seem to want to push it. Without saying much else John asked, "What do you want me to do, Shepp?" Shepp answered, "I want you to talk to the cat, man." The next day Shepp was able to reach Thiele on the telephone. Soon he had a record date with Impulse which was entitled "Four for Trane." On this album, Shepp played four of John's compositions.

One night George Braithe was jamming in the Village, playing his two horns at once. Someone tapped him on the shoulder saying, "Gee, what tune was that? That was really fantastic." George turned around, looked up, and to his disbelief, it was Coltrane! John left for a couple of minutes and returned with his own horn. "I decided to come back. I want you to play my horn."

Fearing that he might break it, George refused, "No, I can't touch that." John answered, "Try it. What kind of mouthpiece do you use?" George had never thought of using any particular mouthpiece and could only say, "This is the mouthpiece I got out of the shop." He felt good, playing John's magical horn. Afterwards they talked. George told him how he felt the critics were absolutely wrong and how much he admired his playing. John accepted this graciously. He advised George to select the "pretty tones" and practice them, because there were so many different ideas about music at the time in the air.

The musical storm of the time reflected the torrential political atmosphere. Malcolm X Shabazz had made a dramatic break with the Muslims in May, 1964, after the assassination of President Kennedy. He was making speeches in New York, trying to consolidate his own organization, the Organization of Afro-American Unity. John attended one of these speeches and expressed, briefly, his opinion in an interview.

Kofsky: " . . . I wanted to know how many times you have seen him, what you thought of him and so forth."

Coltrane: "That was the only time."

Kofsky: "Were you impressed with him?"

Coltrane: "Definitely. That was the only time. I thought I had to see the man, you know. I was living downtown. I was in the hotel. I saw the posters, and I realized he was going over there, so I said well, I'm going over there and see this cat, because I had never seen him. I was quite impressed."

Kofsky: "Some musicians have said that there's a relationship between some of Malcolm's ideas and the music, especially the new music. Do you think there's anything in that?"

Coltrane: "Well, I think that music, being an expression of the human heart, or of the human being itself, does express the whole thing — the whole of human experience at the particular time it is being expressed."[8]

Within life's mosaic, John's plateau of success, the fertile thought of the period, and horrible death occurred in the same basket of time. Later in 1964, anguish ran through the music community on hearing of the death of Eric Dolphy on June 29th, in Germany. He had left this country because of difficulty in getting work. An article then appeared in *Down Beat*, giving Eric more space in the magazine than he had while alive. The article ended with John's sentiments: "Whatever I say would be an understatement. I can only say my life was made much better by knowing him. He was one of the greatest people I've ever known, as a man, a friend and a musician."[9]

In the July 11th issue of London's *Melody Maker*, an article appeared, covering John's engagement at the Half Note in New York. This article provides many insights into his thinking:

> At 4:15 one morning, after an incredible five-hour session at New York's famous Half Note jazz centre, John Coltrane sat down. Perspiration was pouring from his brow.
>
> Understandably, because the final tune took an hour to play, and this was nothing unusual. Earlier, *Greensleeves* had lasted an hour and a quarter.
>
> The waiter delivered "the usual" to Coltrane, who was ending his stint at the club. It was a big cup of hot water. The poll-winning tenorist drank it feverishly, then relaxed with a cigarette as the crowds trickled out in search of taxis.
>
> His music depicts him as a man of fervour and intensity, but in person he shows few, if any, moments of drama. He is quiet and retiring, and speaks softly, in direct contrast to his instrumental tone.
>
> Two years ago he came to Britain and admitted that he was not sure which direction his playing was taking. Is he any more certain today?
>
> "Yes, I am," he told me.
>
> "If anything, I think it is going back a little. For the past few years we have been playing a more modern form of jazz rather than progressive. The next thing for me is for more rhythmic aspirations.
>
> "I may do some work with some more drums — on record, anyway. Not necessarily featuring any one drummer more, but featuring more than one drummer. If this works out in the early stages, I may extend it to stage work.
>
> "I am beginning to get more interested in the drum itself. I feel that since we have used fewer chordal progressions, we need more rhythm, and I want to experiment."
>
> Coltrane's music has often been said to have some Eastern influences at work, and during the session that night with his regular quartet — McCoy Tyner (pno), Jimmy Garrison (bass) and Elvin Jones (drs) — it was again evident. Did he agree?
>
> "Yes, I find that my moods in music sometimes have that flavour, and I am often influenced by what sort of sounds I am listening to privately.

"At the moment, I am listening to records featuring an African drummer and a Chinese flute player – two different works entirely – different works entirely – but to me it sounds like they made the records together!

"Right now I am very concerned with African rhythms. But I do listen to all kinds of music all the time."

Which album by the Coltrane Quartet had given him most satisfaction?

"None. I like parts of all of them, but not one of them entirely."

Was John ever dissatisfied with his playing to the point of thinking that he had been wasting his time?

"Oh, yes, sometimes. I can feel when things have not gone properly. Not that anything I do is regulated. If I feel something coming on during a performance, I just let it go and it just goes on. Then it's not a case of 'did it work out,' but 'it took its course!'

"Sometimes I start a tune with a set pattern, sometimes not. It depends on how I feel at the time."

Coltrane made no announcements that night at the Half Note, and I asked him for his comment on the perennial "presentation" controversy.

"I don't announce things because – well, over here they've got used to it. They know most of the things we are doing, anyway. I think it would be superfluous."

What was his answer to critics who attacked him for "practising in public"?

"They are right," he answered. "But they should remember that I have been playing for almost 25 years. I have always practised in public.

"But then, that's the wrong word. If you are playing jazz, you have to play what comes out at any moment – something you have never said before. So the word should not be practise, but improvise."[10]

Folks had been seeing very little of John, who was busy with club engagements. Folks was still undergoing recurrent periods of illness. One day, most likely in 1964, he saw John with a Bible, and told him that he had read it when he was 16. He asked John what the Bible did for him. John answered that it " . . . brought him closer to God."

As a small child he had desired to be close to God. Through music he was able to cross the river galaxies to reach the overjoyed hands of the Creator. For John capturing the feeling of a moment was more important than following the rules of music. This direction was deeply entwined with the colors of his own soul where the possibilities for creation were infinite, as he said, "There is never any end. There are always new sounds to imagine, new feelings to get at, and always there is the need to keep purifying these feelings and sounds, so we can really see more and more clearly what we are. But to do that, at each stage, we have to keep on cleaning the mirror."[9]

Many new sounds and feelings were discovered in 1963-64. John explored the saxophone, and found depth and color on the instrument that sprang from his inner being. These years closely predated the advent of a new group of musicians, many of whom had come to New York in the early 1960's. This was a rich period of discovery on the saxophone, piano, trumpet and every other instrument. The capacities for sound and uses to which instruments could be put were being expanded. A new musical revolution as complete as that of the 1940's was in progress.

Many white writers of the period were frightened of a music they did not understand. They immediately linked the unchained emotion of the music to the bitterness that prevailed among our people. The writers took their parallels no further.

There was bitterness. There was violence. There was anger over the years of suffering. The centuries of atrocities continued − in the murder of Medgar Evers and the robbing of little Black children of their lives in Birmingham. This anger was appropriate, a sign of being alive, thinking, and at our best.

The music spoke of kindness, beauty, the Creator and humanistic values. This was us at our most creative, for when an oppressed people are quiet, they are not creative. They are the walking dead.

The voyage upward, on which John had been since 1957, continued at a cosmic rate. His music revealed the fire of his grandfather, Rev. Blair, though exteriorally he was still quiet, humble, though intense. For John life was like clay which he could mold into a musical composition. The cleansed air after a rain, the figure of the moon's crescent, and the tragedy of Birmingham were fashioned into masterpieces. He made extensive use of the pentatonic scale, a scale composed of five notes. This scale gave him great flexibility and a deep emotional impact. His roots into the common denominator of Black music is shown by the fact that this scale is widely used in Africa as well as in the "rhythm and blues" of African-Americans.

But the kaleidoscope of life compressed ecstasy with grief. Eric Dolphy was taken, by time, in 1964. John and Naima were no longer together. Alice and he became closer and were soon to marry. Yet the resultant was toward God. His soul continued to overflow with wonders. Studies of music, spiritual matter, and other subjects continued to be assimilated. The urgency was still present. Why was he moving so fast? Why so fast?

John was undergoing another spiritual awakening which was as meaningful as his experience in 1957. He was coming ever closer to the Creator through music, as well as through readings in the Bible, pre-Koranic texts and other sacred works. He and Elvin Jones would discuss these readings. John once told Elvin of a series of notes which when played, could eliminate all friction in the universe. The consequences of this, John explained, would be to cause all matter to fall away from itself, since there was no friction to hold it together.

Just as John had evolved, the quartet had developed with him. Since 1962 they had played portions of music which in late 1964 culminated in an extended spiritual masterpiece, *A Love Supreme*. This composition was a bridge which linked John's earlier plateaus to his attainment of wider heights after late 1964. During this time, as he told Naima, he was even more resolute in his feelings about God, and that after *A Love Supreme*, ninety percent of his playing was actually prayer. Around this time, he called Nita from Los Angeles saying, "God is! I know it now!!" He said that he had seen God. John was ecstatic. But his mother was afraid for him. She felt that one who saw God was soon to die.

The quartet went to the studio to record *A Love Supreme*, on December 9th and 10th, 1964. On the 10th they were joined by Archie Shepp on saxophone and the bassist, Art Davis. The version done on the 9th was released. To the listener of his work, John wrote a message which appeared within the album cover.

Dear Listener:
ALL PRAISE BE TO GOD TO WHOM ALL PRAISE IS DUE.

Let us pursue Him in the righteous path. Yes, it is true: "seek and ye shall find." Only through Him can we know the most wondrous bestowal.

During the year 1957, I experienced, by the grace of God, a spiritual awakening which was to lead me to a richer, fuller, more productive life. At that time, in gratitude, I humbly asked to be given the means and privilege to make others happy through music . . .

As time and events moved on, a period of irresolution did prevail . . . I do perceive and have been duly reinformed of His OMNIPOTENCE, and of our need for, and dependence on Him. At this time I would like to tell you that NO MATTER WHAT . . . IT IS WITH GOD. HE IS GRACIOUS AND MERCIFUL. HIS WAY IS THROUGH LOVE, IN WHICH WE ALL ARE. IT IS TRULY A LOVE SUPREME.

This album is a humble offering to Him. An attempt to say "THANK

YOU GOD" through our work, even as we do in our hearts and with our tongues. May He help and strengthen all men in every good endeavor. . . .

Our appreciation and thanks to all people of good will and good works the world over, for in the bank of life is not good that investment which surely pays the highest and most cherished dividends?

May we never forget that in the sunshine of our lives, through the storm and after the rain — it is all with God — in all ways and forever.

ALL PRAISE TO GOD.

With love to all, I thank you.,

(sgd)[10]

In the last section of the composition, he plays the words of a poem entitled "A Love Supreme," which he wrote. It was also placed inside the album cover.

XIV

Ascension

The Lord is my shepherd;
I shall not want.
He maketh me to lie down
In green pastures:
He leadeth me beside the still waters.
He restoreth my soul:
He leadeth me in the path of righteousness
For his name's sake,
Yea though I walk through the
Valley of the shadow of death,
I will fear no evil:
For thou art with me;
Thy rod and thy staff
They comfort me.
Thou preparest a table before me
In the presence of mine enemies,
Thou annointest my head with oil.

My cup runneth over.
Surely goodness and mercy
Shall follow me all the
Days of my life
And I will dwell in the house
Of the Lord Forever.

A Love Supreme

A cavernous gong begins the composition. Then powerful horn signals the way to paradise. Piano pronounces the steps, and John emits a far-reaching cry. It is Okonkwo, the mighty warrior, doing his dance to Chukwu. Okonkwo screams, flinging the frenzy higher, with hands clenched in the desperate search for Chukwu. Suddenly in a moment within a moment, which is eternity, the horn is quieted while John sings in his deep voice, a voice that seems to vibrate his entire chest: A Love Supreme, A Love Supreme, A Love Supreme, A LOVE SUPREME, A LOVE SUPREME. While the drum shakes a maddening rhythm, piano lays a crystalline mirror, reflecting only beauty. Singing stops and the bass hums the song: A Love Supreme, A Love Supreme. Quietly, the chant whispers hotter until it catches afire as Okonkwo kneels before beginning his dance of *Resolution*.

Oooooh Talk about the Love of God, I love Allah, I really, really, really, really, really do love Allah. Thrashing piano chords disintegrate into tiny drops of water. The dancer Okonkwo is possessed. Legs go as high as arms, each down step cuts into the earth. He becomes an egwugwu, speaking in the uncanny manner of the movements of his body. Wild streams of spirits run through the land in the ocean of the ancestors. Little beings dance and disappear as the mystic enters the next stage of *Pursuance.*

Pursuit begins on a blues line as Okonkwo chases desperately after the elusive Karma. Searching, wrestling, the warrior's muscles strain against the demon that blocks the path. Again the blues: Okonkwo has won, riding triumphantly on a carpet of lions' backs. Saturn's ring carries him to the serenity of the bass.

Time's gap between *Pursuit* and *Psalm* is almost indistinguishable. John is now at one with the Omniscient. Harps of tree branches and grass play soothing melodies. The wind refreshes with its kiss. Then the caves howl as a crushing power manifests itself.

It destroys all of that which destroys: envy, greed, hatred, fear.

Boundaries are no more – no beginning, no end, no breath, no death, no small, no large, no warm, no cold, no lines, no body, no daggers of distress. There is only the one substance. Tears become pears for mothers to feed their children. Spears become light to carry travelers through the night. Tremulous torrents of violet burst upon ebony light – the universe trembles with Elation – Elegance – Exaltation.

After recording *A Love Supreme*, the quartet went on another European tour later in December, 1964. In Paris, the music was well received by a capacity audience. However, after the performance, Jimmy and John were sitting on stage when one Frenchman addressed himself to John,

"Monsieur Coltrane, I 'ave never 'eard anyzing so jive. You are a jive motherfucker . . . " blah, blah, blah.

Jimmy shot up, "Man do you know who in the fuck you're talking to? This is John Coltrane. Where's the respect, baby?"

John, still seated and not having said a word, nudged Jimmy, "Sit down, Jimmy. Sit down and let the man say what he has to say."

The Frenchman rambled on and on, after which John politely said, "Thank you."

This article, by Leonard Feather, appeared in the December 19th, 1964, *Melody Maker* during the time of the quartet's tour:

> The path of the avant-gardist in jazz is a precarious one, strewn with critical contumely and with aesthetic decisions that lead to economic hazards.
>
> John Coltrane is one of the handful of new wave performers who can claim artistic and commercial success. His quartet, formed soon after he left Miles Davis in 1960, is widely accepted in night clubs, on recordings and overseas tours.
>
> Though a real understanding of his music demands technical knowledge and intense attention, Coltrane's most devoted followers are young listeners, many of whom may be musically illiterate. Recently, at Shelly's Manne Hole in Hollywood, he discussed his audiences.
>
> "I never even thought about whether or not they understand what I'm doing," he said. "The emotional reaction is all that matters.
>
> "As long as there's some feeling of communication, it isn't necessary that it be understood. After all, I used to love music myself long before I could identify a G Minor Seventh chord.
>
> "Audiences haven't changed much. They say Dizzy and Bird had to face a lot of hostility, but they had their good audiences, too. Eventually, the listeners move right with the musicians.
>
> "Jazz is so much a music of individuality that every new artist with any originality effects a change in the overall scene. Lester Young

represented as great a change in his time as some of the things that are happening now. So did Bird."

The ethos of Coltrane's music is a hypnotic quality, achieved through variations on a simple modal of harmonic basis. He has moved into areas that were once the exclusive preserve of Indian music.

I asked him how he hoped to extend the audience for this process of acculturation: "You've had no television exposure at all. How long do you think it will be before the layman is ready for what you're doing?"

"I don't know – do you think they ever will be? Anyhow you can't really do what you want to do in television. You're restricted."

His meaning soon became clear. In the next set it took Coltrane an hour and 15 minutes to play two tunes. Both were framed by a 20-second theme; everything in between was improvised.

The first tune ran 50 minutes, with Coltrane playing tenor sax mercurially and uninterruptedly, with unbelievably complex ideas and execution, for the first half-hour.

The second tune, which included a 13-minute drum solo by the phenomenal Elvin Jones, featured Coltrane on soprano saxophone, an instrument he rescued from limbo almost single-handedly.

Since that chance discovery, saxophonists from Paris to Tokyo have taken to doubling on soprano, in the Coltrane style. But the cult is modestly shrugged off by its leader:

"I don't think people are necessarily copying me. In any art, there may be certain things in the air at certain times.

"Another musician may come along with a concept independently and a number of people reach the same end by making a similar discovery at the same time."

Despite this disclaimer, Coltrane is shaping a musical revolution.[1]

By the end of 1964, John's popularity was indisputably established, and his audience was still growing. In the International Critics' Poll, he was voted number one on tenor saxophone and second in the miscellaneous instrument category for the soprano sax. First was Roland Kirk, who played manzello and stritch. These results were practically duplicated in the Readers' Poll. The album, "Live at Birdland," received unanimously favorable reviews, although Bill Mathieu in *Down Beat* claimed that John was avoiding a challenge by using the principle of improvising on one or two chords instead of many:

" . . . today my critical ear whispers into my receptive ear that seesaw convention is a cop-out. I wish Coltrane would use it less often. The alternative? More creative attention to harmonic thought."[2]

This contention, shared by Mathieu as well as Martin Williams who reviewed "Africa Brass," was opposed by another critic, John A. Sinclair, writing on "Live At Birdland" in *Jazz and Pop*:

> "It has been (and will undoubtedly continue to be) remarked that certain of Trane's tunes, e.g., *Afro-Blue* are 'boring' in their harmonic make-up, making use of at most a few and often only one or two chords; when Trane was utilizing extremely dense harmonic frameworks for his improvisations a few years ago, however, there was an equally great number of protests against this practice. John Coltrane has most certainly proved his virtuosity with regard to chords and harmonic complexity in the past; the critics of his current experiments are denying themselves a musical experience that no one should miss."[3]

Larry Young, whom John had met in Rochester, in 1962, shared the feeling of Sinclair and was inspired by John's music in his own explorations on the organ. In 1965, Young became Khalid Yasin, and converted to Islam. He and John had been seeing each other regularly in the nightclubs. Once John had on a facial oil which Khalid recognized, "Ah, Secret of Venus." It was the brand of oil John was wearing. John was surprised by his recognition of the scent. In their conversation, he told Khalid how thankful he was to Ornette and Sun Ra, who were contributors to some of the musical advances he made. He also told Khalid that he sent Ornette a telegram saying something like "Bless You," and that he had finally reached the laws of music that Ornette discussed with him in 1960. With the telegram, he sent $30.00.

John asked about Khalid's new religion and wanted to know if there were any separatism in it. Khalid answered that sects did exist but that Islam basically was concerned with unity, not sects and differences between people. John told him how yoga breathing exercises, or sitting still for a long time with his finger in his ear produced sounds within his body which he could express in music. To Khalid, John radiated an inner peace which beckoned to others and brought out the best in them. His personality had not changed.

Though now in the public spotlight, his speech was the same: slow, deep, and clear. His laugh was still high and unrestrained, like sitting around a Mississippi fireside. His walk was smooth, cool, with a little hop that characterizes the natural walk of many Black men. He still had problems with his weight, going through cycles of strict dieting; then enjoying large meals and regaining the weight.

He and Alice, by 1965, had married and eventually there were four children in the household: one girl, Mickey, Alice's daughter prior to their marriage; and three boys, John Jr., Ravi, and Oran. These children brought him much happiness. He loved many things — music, art, people who loved each other, people who gave of themselves, people who were honest. He enjoyed metaphysical conversation and would buy books from a metaphysical bookstore in California. These books would cover many topics such as Yoga, the Torah, one's improvement as a person, and Islam.

He preferred being at home to running the streets, and would usually come directly home after a performance. He stayed in Manhattan only when something special was occurring such as a performance by Sonny Rollins. He liked to rise early in the morning and to go to bed around 10 or 11 at night. One of his favorite pastimes was gardening, or fixing things around his new house.

It was a modern 12-room house built on three acres of land, far from the noisy city, in Dix Hills, Huntington, Long Island. For many years he had wanted to leave New York City. He would be bothered by a constant "vibration" he said he felt in the ground.

Behind the house was a healthy forest, and at the entrance was a high wrought iron gate. Inside was filled with rich purples, reds and yellows. One room had each wall painted a different color. Rugs were scattered about among low tables, fireplaces, African and other types of art, and a wide variety of instruments. There were: a grand piano where he sketched his music; tenor saxophone; an alto sax; an Indian sitar; conga drums; flute; bagpipes; and a small African horn. He also possessed a bass clarinet, and other instruments of Eric Dolphy's which Eric's mother had sent to him. After her son's death, she would have frightening nightmares of him practicing, as he had in life, in their garage where his instruments were left after he died. She felt that John was the best person to have Eric's instruments and sent them to him in an effort to stop her horrifying dreams.

Music, as before, occupied most of John's time. For whatever reason he went into New York City, he always carried his horn with him. Even when he and Alice went shopping he would bring a flute along, practicing as she selected the food.

His search for a mouthpiece continued as he tried different ways of obtaining the sound he wanted. Sometimes he would file his reeds down. Once he went so far as to have dental work done. Over the years his tone had become even richer: plush and beautiful with a widely undulating vibrato. There was no doubt even by his most stubborn critics that he was a technical master. In spite of this general consensus, he continued long hours of practice and composing.

Most musicians welcomed his unequivocal declaration of the connection between the Creator and the music. Other musicians said that he had gone mad and were jealous because he was so popular, and was getting an abundant share of night club jobs.

His income had risen to a gross of between $175,000 and $200,000 a year. Harold Lovette was his lawyer and close friend. All of John's holdings were part of a personal corporation. The houses he owned in Philadelphia and New York were under Coltrane Realty. His music was published under Jowcol. His finances were intact, but he often expressed the wish that he had thought more of the financial aspects of the music earlier in his career. Even with the large number of records he sold, he only received at most 10 percent of the retail price.

Most of the "Jazz" magazines were replete with praise of each record release. The exception was *Down Beat*, whose critics continued to condemn, or give at most tongue-in-cheek praise. Criticism, however, bothered him much less, if at all, by this point. He bluntly proclaimed, once while riding in a car with Big George, "If a motherfucker can't dig it, man, I can't wait. I got to play it now." His concern was the advancement of *the music* and he knew that if it was valid, people would eventually come to enjoy it.

The music, after *A Love Supreme*, reached another level of creativity. The intensity of the quartet had reached an awesome height, and John's movements on stage were even wilder than before. His, and the quartet's, playing was freer. Together they formed one total, overwhelming, living force. On May 26, 1965, *Dear Lord* was recorded. It is a tender song of love and wonder for the Creator. There is a delicate feeling like a small happy child who is just learning to walk and perpetually tumbling, but never falling. On June 10th, the group recorded *Transition*. A strong straining blues-like theme begins the composition. Rages of force overwhelm. They may make you howl and dance in a manner which is bizarre, only because it is so natural and we are so far from nature. A suite consisting of five parts was recorded on June 16th. The sections were: *Prayer and Meditation; Evening; Affirmation; Prayer and Meditations; 4 a.m.* This suite also begins with a blues theme, but continues on to the multitude of feelings of one who meditates with the Creator into the early morning hours.

Also on June 16th, a composition entitled *Living Space* was recorded. Personnel and instrumentation were different from the usual format. These were: John, tenor saxophone; McCoy Tyner, piano; Jimmy Garrison, bass; Elvin Jones, drums; John's son, Oran, on bells and strings; and Alice Coltrane on harp and tamboura.

This slow piece, with its expansive feeling of vibrant, infinite space is a contrast to the highly charged pieces that he was mainly involved with at the time. This gives evidence of his wide breadth of musical exploration. The music has a sweeping grace, and a feeling of slow moving endlessness. His words depict the spiritual journey he was involved with at this time.

> "To perceive again and this time it must be said, for all to read to know no matter what, it is all with God. He is gracious and merciful. His way is in love, through which we all are. Whenever and whoever you are, always strive to follow and walk in the right path and ask for aid and assistance . . . herein lies the ultimate and eternal happiness which is ours through His grace."[4]

Incresha is a lavender form where all sincere emotions find their way in the universe. This form is highly energetic and bustling furiously on its far-reaching travels. Flames of love and peace flick outward and return. Incresha is immortal, and will not die when the universe melts away. Within its realm John created music that would be better called forms rather than compositions. They are emotions unhampered. On June 28th two forms were recorded, *Vigil* and *Welcome*, of which he spoke:

> *Vigil* " . . . implies watchfulness. Anyone trying to obtain perfection is faced with various obstacles in life which tend to sidetrack him. Here, therefore, I mean watchfulness against elements that might be destructive from within and without. I don't try to set standards of perfection for anyone else. I do feel everyone does try to reach his better self, his full potential, and what that consists of depends on each individual. Whatever the goal is, moving toward it does require vigilance."[5]

> *Welcome* " . . . is that feeling you have when you finally do reach awareness, an understanding which you have earned through struggle. It is a feeling of peace. A welcome feeling of peace."[6]

Another dream came, concerning the idea he had nurtured since

1961, of recording with a band in which everyone played without reference to chords. John asked Jimmy Garrison, "James, would you like to play in a big band?" James answered that he would, and John told him that he had dreamt of a band of "fifteen or twenty cats" with everyone playing "free." This dream was followed by the creation of a form entitled *Ascension*.

John called the men for the session: Freddie Hubbard, trumpet; Dewey Johnson, trumpet; Marion Brown and John Tchicai, alto saxophones; Archie Shepp and Pharoah (formerly Farrell) Saunders, tenor saxophones; Art Davis, bass; and the members of the regular quartet. Most of these musicians were a part of what was labelled the "Avant Garde" or the "New Thing" to which considerable opposition had been voiced by critics and some audiences.

Marion Brown's comments give an idea of what the date and resulting music were like, describing the session as, " . . . wildly exciting. We did two takes, and they both had that kind of thing in them that makes people scream. The people who were in the studios were screaming. I don't know how the engineers kept the scream out of the record . . . Spontaneity was the thing. Trane had obviously thought a lot about what he wanted to do, but he wrote most of it out in the studio. Then he told everybody what he wanted. He played this line, and he said that everybody would play that in the ensemble. Then he said he wanted crescendi and decrescendi after every solo. We ran through some things together, until we were together and then we got into it."[7]

Archie Shepp also commented on the music: "It achieves a certain kind of unity; it starts at a high level of intensity with the horns playing high and the other pieces playing low. This gets a quality of like male and female voices. It builds in intensity through all the solo passages, brass and reeds, until it gets to the final section where the rhythm section takes over and brings it back to the level it started at. . . . The idea is similar to what the action painters do in that it creates various surfaces of color which push into each other, creates tensions and counter tensions, and various fields of energy."[7]

Marion Brown spoke of the technical aspects: "In the ensemble sections you get a different idea of what harmony is, or can be. Certain chords were used, but they were stretched out and orchestrated."[7]

Shepp adds, "The ensemble passages were based on chords. But these chords were optional. What Trane did was to relate or juxtapose tonally centered ideas and atonal elements, along with melodic and non-melodic elements. In those descending chords, there is a definite tonal center, like B-flat minor. But there are different roads to that center . . . In the solo plus quartet parts there are no specified chords. These sections were to be dialogues between the soloists and the rhythm section. The whole work, beginning with Trane's solo was keyed, especially in McCoy's playing, to a minor blues . . . The emphasis was on textures rather than the making of an organizational entity. There was unity, but it was a unity of sounds and textures rather than like an ABA approach."[7]

The manner in which John wrote and directed *Ascension* demonstrated the flexibility-within-unity he created. The ensemble passages were written, as usual, with notes and time values. But in the parts where collective improvisation was intended, four sets of four notes each were used. These notes were only pitch designations without time values. Their interpretation was left to each musician. When playing the piece, John would indicate which of the four sets he wanted the band to improvise on by raising one finger when he wanted set one, two fingers for set two, and so on.

Before the band began playing, he told each musician when he wanted him to solo. He insured a constant change of textures by making sure no two similar instruments followed each other. The alto saxophone followed the trumpet rather than following another alto saxophone.

The resulting music is awesome. It envelops your body and imparts the desire to act. The hugeness and complexity of emotions obtained from such a superficially simple structure was termed by one writer as "the most powerful human sound ever created."

During the summer the quartet went to Europe again, this time to Antibes, France. Two concerts were given. These articles from the *Melody Maker* describe what occurred:

> For sheer breathtaking musicianship, passionate sincerity and immense vitality, the John Coltrane Quartet completely dominated the sixth International Jazz Festival at Antibes.
>
> Their concert on Monday night, to a jam-packed audience, was the supreme moment so far in the Festival. Yet the applause at the end was lukewarm and even included a few boos.
>
> Even organist Jimmy McGriff, making his European debut and playing unsophisticated, hard-swinging and intellectually undemanding music, raised only moderate enthusiasm.
>
> It really makes you wonder just what festival audiences want. I have a sneaking suspicion that if Coltrane had played "Girl from Ipanema"

and McGriff had played "Goldfinger," the audience wouldn't have let them leave the stage.

But happily, there was no such sell-out to easy commercialism.

Coltrane was simply fantastic. His Quartet played just one piece — "A Love Supreme" — and it lasted 47 minutes. It was played with the conviction that this was the definitive jazz work.

This is a quartet of musical giants, all of whom exploit the whole compass of their instruments to the limits. The leader, who played only tenor throughout, blew with immense authority. His controlled use of harmonics is no gimmick.

He fashions these notes into sublime and intensely moving music. He builds his solos, developing his ideas to the full extent of the tenor's capabilities and straining to go beyond them, threatening almost to blow the horn straight.

McCoy Tyner, a fresh, incisive pianist, has developed tremendously and is one of the most inventive and invigorating piano talents on the scene.

Jimmy Garrison, who was left alone on the stage at one point for a magnificent, virtuoso bass solo, has a superb attack and a rich, singing tone. He plays bass sometimes like a harp, sometimes getting a tremendous flamenco effect by passing the bow on the strings, and sometimes even using the spine of the bow.

And Elvin Jones, of course, just defies description. In this context he is simply irreplaceable.

This is probably the greatest jazz quartet playing today.

Earlier, Jimmy McGriff, playing very much in the Jimmy Smith idiom, with an occasional touch of cinema organ but swinging his way through three 12-bar blues and an appealing version of "Round Midnight," sympathetically accompanied by Thornel Schwartz (gtr) and Richard Easley (drs).[8]

Melody Maker, July 31st, 1965

Of all the jazz musicians currently exploring new directions, John Coltrane has always seemed to me to be the only one with a map and compass.

To begin with, Coltrane was way-in before he became way-out. His evolution from rhythm and blues has been constant and logical.

He is a musician of many virtues. He has a passionate sincerity, a simple dignity and a command of the tenor saxophone which, in my view, is without equal in the jazz world.

No other musician to my mind has broken away with such consummate success from the "theme-solos-fours-theme" format over 12 or 32 bars which has, for many, become the ball and chain of jazz.

If you want a contemporary equivalent of Charlie Parker, then you need look no further than Coltrane. As his bass player, Jimmy Garrison, says: "Now that Ornette don't come out, John is the only one who's keeping things alive."

When I met Coltrane in his hotel room during the Antibes Jazz Festival, I was immediately impressed by the apparent contrast between the man and his music. He is a big, slow-moving man with an extremely gentle disposition and an economy of conversation. You have the impression that he expresses himself so completely and comprehensively in his music that when it comes to interviews there is little left to say. In the music of Coltrane you can find anger, bitterness, anguish, sadness. In the man you are conscious only of a great inner peace and serenity.

It was a fascinating meeting. Because for the first hour and a half Coltrane expressed himself through his tenor and soprano. He stood at the table, blowing into a portable tape recorder and then playing it back. Unhurriedly he changed reeds, adjusted mouthpieces, tore off characteristically intricate and extended runs. He was practising for the concert that evening.

When he finally laid down the tenor I asked him how long his reeds lasted. "A good reed lasts me three weeks – but it doesn't seem too easy to get a good one these days." Then he picked up the soprano and practised for another half an hour.

My appointment had been for 4 o'clock. By the time we got to talk it was 6:30 p.m. . . . and even then I somehow felt that Coltrane would much rather have played than talked. But as he touched into a slightly bizarre dinner of two raw egg yolks, clear soup, milk, iced water and fresh peaches (he's trying to keep his weight down) he answered my questions amiably and thoughtfully.

"How often do you practise like that?"

"Not as often as I should. I have been thinking about writing so much recently that I haven't done too much practising. I think four hours' practice a day would be good for me. That little bit of practising just then – well, I didn't play a thing I didn't know. But after four hours I would get through all that and then maybe I'd break into something new."

"What were you listening for on the playback?"

"Just to see how the notes were coming out – whether they were coming through clear and in tune."

"Do you have intonation problems with the soprano?"

"Funnily enough, I have more problems with the tenor than with soprano. I was lucky with my soprano. I've had it five years – it was the first one I bought. It was a good one, but it's beginning to go off a little now."

"How do you think your playing now compares with your work with Miles Davis five years ago?"

"I don't think it has changed basically – though I suppose I've grown a little, musically. But then in some respects I think I might have been a little more inventive in those days."

"What would you say were the faults in your playing – do you feel there is anything missing?"

"That's hard to answer. I don't know if you can ever be a complete musician. I'm not. But I don't think I'll know what's missing from my playing until I find it – if you understand me. Perhaps my main fault at the moment is that I have a natural feeling for the minor. I'd like to do more things in the major. I want to work to bring that up – and there are many other modes I've got to learn."

I asked him if, in his search for new directions, he ever found himself in a musical dead end.

He laughed. "I doubt if there are any dead ends." Then, on reflection, he added: "There may be, though, I suppose I've had some things which didn't work out. But usually if you get on a new thing you just keep on playing it until you get it together. I'm very lucky – I work with very fine musicians. They are very inventive. I don't have to tell anybody what to do. When we have a new thing, I just define the different sections and leave the rest to them.

"We have great confidence in one another. That's essential – that's how it hangs together. They're with me in always wanting the band to move into a new area. We generally don't believe in standing still."

A philosophy which, while thoroughly commendable, also raises an audience problem. At the first Coltrane concert at Antibes, the audience was a little puzzled and disappointed to hear just one piece, "A Love Supreme," played for 47 minutes.

"What about giving audiences a chance to catch up?" I asked Coltrane.

"This always frightens me," he said candidly. "Whenever I make a change, I'm a little worried that it may puzzle people. And sometimes I deliberately delay things for this reason. But after a while I find that there is nothing else I can do but go ahead." (In fact – and this underlines Coltrane's anxiety to carry his audiences along with him – he changed the programme for the second concert and featured some more established pieces like "Impressions" and "My Favourite Things" – but without sacrificing any of his individuality or inventiveness.)

Coltrane says he hasn't yet composed anything he is completely satisfied with. "I plan to do more extended works – I have sketches of them in my head. I want to get to a point where I can feel the vibrations of a particular place at a particular moment and compose a song right there, on the spot – then throw it away. I try to avoid repeating things as much as I can."

It has been said that Coltrane has recently discovered God. I asked him about this.

"Rediscovered would be a better word. Religion has always been with me since I was a kid. I was raised in a religious atmosphere and it has stuck with me throughout my life. Sometimes I feel it more strongly than others."

"Do you listen very often to your own records?"

He smiled. "No. Perhaps two or three times a year I'll take them out and evaluate them – but I'm more concerned with how I'm playing right now."

More often Coltrane listens to African and Indian music. "There's a harp record I play quite a lot, too. I got very interested in harp for a while. But now I think when I get tired of blowing, I'll take up guitar or piano."

"How far have you extended the range of the tenor?"

"Well, you can't get below B-flat. But there's at least another octave above the normal top limit which can be fingered."

"And talking of extending limits, which musicians do you think are making important contributions in seeking new jazz expressions?"

"I think the Jazz Composers' Guild are doing good things — I admire Albert Ayler, Archie Shepp, Dewey Johnson, Pharoah Saunders and John Tchicai."

Has Coltrane definitely abandoned the more orthodox jazz frameworks?

"Not necessarily. I've been thinking of doing another album of ballads — just playing them straight. Though generally I do feel that normal forms have pretty well been used up. I'm also thinking of doing an album with a couple of horns and Latin percussion."[9]

Melody Maker, August 14th, 1965

The recording output for 1965 continued at a prolific rate. Each recording differed from the previous one, thereby providing excellent documentation of John's meteoric rise toward . . .

Sun Ship, Dearly Beloved, Amen, Attaining, and *Ascent* were recorded on August 25th. At least three concepts are evident on this album. One was the utilization of rhythmic patterns as a basis of improvisation instead of chords. These rhythmic patterns were those which conga or bongo players commonly used, and were played on his horn with a percussive effect imparted to each note. *Sun Ship* and *Amen* both are very much based on such patterns.

Attaining and *Ascent* have a solemn, powerful, chant-like quality that he had employed before in *Alabama*. Also, on this record was the demonstration [not the first] of his mastery of overtones. This mastery took him beyond the capacity conceived for the saxophone by Western musicians.

His exploration and synthesis of different music of the world continued in what he saw as a never-ending endeavour. His analytical mind, and search for unity and harmony among all things, led him naturally to the Hindu concept of Om which he defines: "Om means the first vibration — that sound, that spirit which sets everything else into being. It is the Word from which all men and everything else comes, including all possible sounds that man can make vocally. It is the first syllable, the primal word, the word of Power."[10]

In Washington, D.C., on October 1, 1965, *Om* was recorded. Pharoah Saunders had joined the group and played tenor saxophone. John had this to say of Pharoah: "Pharoah is a man of large spiritual reservoir. He's always trying to reach out to truth. He's trying to allow his spiritual self be his guide. He's dealing among other things, in energy, in integrity, in essences. I so much like the strength of his playing. Furthermore, he is one of the innovators, and it's been my pleasure and privilege that he's been willing to help me, that he is part of the group."[11] "What I like about him is the strength of his playing, the conviction with which he plays. He has will and spirit and those are the qualities I like most in a man."[12]

Donald Garrett on bass, and Joe Brazil on flute, were also contributors to *Om*. The music began with an incantation, part of which was,

> I the oblation and I the Flame into which it is offered
> I am the fire of the world and this world's mother and grandfather . . .
> I am Om Om Om Om Om! Om![13]

It is a 30-minute piece in which time no longer exists. Notes as understood in European music no longer set limitations. There is only flowing sound like the confluence of seven mighty rivers, which gushes into a field of gentle lambs. John spoke again of his concern for the listener: "I wish I could walk up to my music as if for the first time, as if I had never heard it before. Being so inescapably a part of it, I'll never know what the listener gets, what the listener feels, and that's too bad."[14]

Critic Nat Hentoff, who years before had condemned John severely, wrote the liner notes for *Om* and admitted to a change of his attitudes on a deep level. In doing this he dealt with narrow-minded concepts that critics had tried to apply to individualistic and creative Black musicians.

> "In my own case a lot of my walls are still up, but some have cracked. Certainly those have cracked that maintained there is only one standard of beauty, of sound, one standard of 'form,' one standard of 'cohesiveness.' . . . As one listener, I can attest that I get from it a sense of the limitlessness of what man can express . . . each new album by Coltrane [is] almost as if I were learning his music for the first time. For there was no way to predict what would happen, and although there were past experiences to act as a bridge to the start of each new

adventure, once that adventure began, I was on my own."[15]

Later in October, the quintet was in Los Angeles, performing and recording. John met a conga drummer, Juno Lewis. Juno not only played drums, but also made them, and played unusual instruments like a conch shell, and the water drum. He and John collaborated on an album entitled *Kulu Se' Mama* which reflected Juno's Louisiana Afro-Creole background. Juno composed a poem which was sung in his own dialect, while the quartet with bassist Donald Garrett and drummer Frank Butler accompanied him with music that brought images of potent voodoo and gri-gri. Expressed in the poem was pride in being of African ancestry and the desire of Juno to build an African-American music center.

> The ritual, JUNO SE MAMA, begins in a
> Mighty cloud burst
> And the rippling of the water drum
> begins beating against the
> air cups of the world.
> Moon children . . . ready to be born.
> Signs of sky, earth, water.
> One is born called JUNO.
> His father's house is the bird.
> You can hear him teaching his son
> how to fly.
> Fly, till you reach the sky. Float,
> Float
> Fly,
> till you make a boat
> Be strong my son and show your arm.[16]

John was fulfilling his desire to explore rhythm more, which he had expressed five years before in the *Down Beat* interview with Don DeMicheal. He often used two drummers instead of the traditional single set of drums. It had become common practice for him to call another drummer in whatever city he was in. Returning from California, he called Rashied Ali to work with Elvin at the Village Gate.

Previously, he had asked Rashied to join Elvin on *Ascension*. Rashied at the time answered, "Will I be the only drummer on the date?" John stated that he planned to use Elvin too. Rashied refused, "Naw, man, I don't want to do it unless I'm playing by myself." Without any show of displeasure John accepted his decision. Still, the gambling net of time would have Rashied later become an important contributor to the music. Rashied was born in Philadelphia, on July 1, 1933.

In the late '50's, Rashied knew that there was something else to be played on the drums. Listening carefully to Max Roach, Elvin Jones and Philly Joe Jones, he could feel that these men, though labeled as being distinct from the "avant garde," were expressing something beyond what was considered traditional drumming. Rashied thought much about various time signatures and other experiments with time. Before meeting John he would make frequent trips to New York where the effect of Ornette Coleman and Cecil Taylor reached him. John was also a major influence during this period. Rashied felt that the strength and character of John's playing demanded a different approach to the drum. However, other musicians in Philadelphia would shun him, and sometimes not let him play whenever he put into practice what he learned in the city and his own feelings. After his encounter with John, in 1961, Rashied took his advice and moved to New York. There he played with other men who were interested in advancing the music, such as Archie Shepp, Sun Ra, Albert Ayler, Paul Bley, Cecil Taylor, Bill Dixon and Sonny Rollins. He would often see John in clubs but would say nothing.

In New York he gained confidence in his ability and had no need now to prepare himself before talking to someone he admired, or meeting any other challenge. One night at the Half Note Rashied spoke to John for the first time since 1961. He asked to sit in. Elvin was nearby and John told him, "I don't know. I'll see." Rashied was cool — no rage, no apprehension. He sat back down in the audience. Later John let him play on one tune. Even after sitting in the audience so many times Rashied did not experience the full power of John's sound until he was finally on the bandstand with him. When John played the first note Rashied was stunned and unable to play. John glanced at him and Rashied regained his senses. After playing John complimented him. Rashied was satisfied, feeling that he had gained enough ability to be in control of the mammoth music. That night Rashied resolved never again to play in any manner that was not an honest expression of his feelings.

Two days later, he went again to the Half Note. Elvin missed the entire first performance, and John let Rashied play its entire length. Wherever John was playing, Rashied would come. Soon he found that he was playing more and more frequently as Elvin kept missing more and more performances. Often if Rashied played an entire set, John would give him $20 to $50, which he would do with many of the young musicians who sat in with him. However, after seeing that he was playing frequently with John, Rashied became swell-headed, "Shit, I'm good enough to play with Trane! He digs the way I play." This attitude led to his refusal to accept working with another drummer on the *Ascension* recording session.

Afterwards, he felt left out when he realized that most of the musicians on the record were from his group of friends. Consequently, when John returned from California and was to perform at the Village Gate, Rashied didn't wait for him to call. He called John. Without any display of hostility, John informed him: "Yeah, well you know, I'm using two drummers." Rashied answered, "Yeah, well, that's cool. I don't really care how many drummers you're using."

Opening night was set for November 9th, but on that day a complete BLACKOUT struck the entire East Coast, giving blind men an infrequent advantage. Opening night was cancelled. New York City subways stopped. People were stranded in elevators, and the old and infirm were unable to walk home. Surprisingly, there was very little looting. Instead of thinking to commit crime or take revenge in the darkness, people banded together and the birth rate made a significant jump nine months later. Drivers gave rides to older people who had to walk home. Songs, love, compassion and concern welled within the collective human soul, gripped by the flood of night.

After this event, Big George and John talked over the phone. Their conversation began on the topic of flying saucers and went on to noting how the crime rate was so low that night. They agreed that the BLACKOUT was more than an electrical mishap. It was a test for people, to see if they would allow their better selves to emerge.

The day after the BLACKOUT, power was restored and the Village Gate performance went on. Elvin didn't arrive until the last performance of the evening, so Rashied played alone most of the night. Archie Shepp and alto saxophonist Carlos Ward sat in. Black writer A. B. Spellman, writing in *Down Beat*, December 30th, 1965, gave his version of what occurred:

> The band John Coltrane showed at the Gate Nov. 10 might be called "J.C. & After." Coltrane, who put the kinetic field back into the tenor saxophone after it had been lost when the Illinois Jacquets disappeared from Respectability (a small, affluent suburb of New York), assembled an aggregation of reed men who were learning their fingering when he was cutting *Blue Trane*; their harmony when he was cutting *Milestones*;

their selves when he was cutting *Coltrane's Music.*

Trane, with his *Ascension* record date and with the augmented quartet he uses in the clubs, is not only creating a band with more power than Con Ed but is also introducing some of the best of the New Jazz musicians to the World of the Living Wage and, thereby, performing a double service. Shepp and Saunders, by virtue of the discomforting weight of their music, get precious few gigs, and Coltrane, by presenting their music in its proper musicological context, is performing a great service to their generation. Both these men have highly distinctive styles. They really sound nothing like Coltrane, but it is clear that they have benefited from Coltrane's line, harmonics, and dissection of a song's melody.

On this night, the two sets consisted of long interpretations of one tune each: *Afro Blue* and *Out of This World.* The difference between the two sets was that Jones didn't show for the first. And the first was, to my ear, far better.

Coltrane played theme on soprano, and Shepp, in very good voice, took it from there. Shepp's style is reiterative − a kind of supercharged theme and variations. He stated a motif, broke it down to its elements, and returned to it every few bars. After carrying one idea through innumerable permutations he would start another. Shepp is a bluesy player who roars his masculinity. He plays at both ends of the horn, and he may spot his intensities at any part of the register. He makes heavy inflections on the notes he wants to emphasize. His opening solo, about 10 minutes long, was a strong one, as it had to be, for this is deep water.

This was the first time I'd heard Panamanian altoist Ward. He seemed to be neither a screamer nor a singer, but a talker. He seemed to be engaged in some kind of a dialog with himself, playing a rapid series of terse, self-contained, but related phrases. I liked Ward; his ear is different. I couldn't sort out his influences in this cauldron, however, and I look forward to hearing him in a smaller group.

Saunders followed Ward, and his is the damnedest tenor player in the English language. He went on for minute after minute in a register that I didn't know the tenor had (actually, I did − I've heard Saunders before). Those special effects that most tenor men use only in moments of high orgiastic excitement are the basic premises of his presentation. His use of overtones, including a cultivated squeak that parallels his line, is constantly startling. He plays way above the upper register; long slurred lines and squeaky monosyllabic staccatos, and then closes with some kind of Bushman's nursery rhyme. Pharoah is ready, and you'll all be hearing from him soon. Or should.

Trane soloed on soprano which, as usual, seemed a few months behind his tenor. Here, in this reed chorus, it had the effect of stretching out the sonic boom.

The orchestral composition of the group had been expanding all along. No one was ever idle − a man would finish his solo and pick up a rattle, tambourine, or some other rhythm instrument and start shaking away. The reeds also were free to provide filler or comment for the soloist, and the effect was of an active, highly charged environment. With the constantly shifting rhythms of Rashied on drums this was free large-group improvisation at its best. Rashied's playing is an everflowing pattern that defies time signature. He once said he was after a drone effect that flowed with the horns. At the Gate, he showed how well he achieves this effect.

Garrison's bass was strong and witty, and Tyner's chords are necessarily more dissonant than before.

The difference in the second set was, to me, the unnecessary addition of Jones. It was interesting to hear this band with Rashied, who, unlike Jones, disperses the rhythm centers. It has always been an aweful, pleasurable experience to have Elvin tear up my nervous system for me. I have also heard two drummers used with laudable results, e.g., the intimate communication of Billy Higgins and Ed Blackwell in Ornette Coleman's monumental Free Jazz LP and some work Rashied did with another drummer in a Sun Ra concert.

I think I see what Coltrane wants — an ever evolving ground swell of energy that will make the musical environment so dangerous that he and the others will have to improvise new weapons constantly to beat back all the Brontosaurs. However, if Jones is to be one of the two drummers, then Lincoln Center at least is needed to contain and separate all that sound. One simply couldn't hear anything but drums on *Out of This World*. I had no idea what the soloists were saying, and I doubt that the players could hear each other. Garrison (who played a truly virtuoso solo to open the second set) was completely swallowed up. At one point, I saw Coltrane break out a bagpipe (another demon in the forest) and blow into it, but damned if I heard a note of what he played.

Note: Coltrane played bass clarinet in some ensemble sections. I was told that the instrument had belonged to Eric Dolphy and had been given to Coltrane by Dolphy's mother.

— A.B.Spellman.[17]

During the next few weeks, Rashied found that he was somehow playing with the band with increasing regularity, even making out-of-town jobs. He became a permanent member, though John never said that he was permanently hired. It just happened that he was.

Rashied brought a new concept into the band. He tried to make the drums completely unrestrictive for the soloist. He visualized his sound as a constant, hovering cloud from which a soloist could expand in any direction. John spoke of his contribution. "The way he plays allows the soloist maximum freedom. I can really choose just about any direction at just about any time in the confidence that it will be compatible with what he's doing. You see, he's laying down multi-directional rhythms all the time. To me, he's definitely one of the great drummers."[1][8]

However, a new problem within the group began to form. There was a pronounced antipathy and competition between the two drummers. Each was trying to outdo the other by making the sound of the drums unreasonably large and out of balance with the others in the group. John's experiment with two drummers was being thwarted by the human factor. This problem was submerged in the recording on November 23rd of the form entitled *Meditations.*

Meditations consists of five parts. *The Father, And The Son, And The Holy Ghost; Compassion; Love; Consequences;* and *Serenity.* The first part begins with a never-before-heard sound that seems to defy all physical laws of nature, rising and falling, involuting and expanding at the same time. The form moves through several immense and touching moods as in *Love* where John shows his ability to vary a simple theme in many ways.

Around the time *Meditations* was recorded, John spoke more of his thoughts. He was asked by Nat Hentoff if *Meditations* was an extension of *A Love Supreme*: "Once you become aware of this force for unity in life, you can't ever forget it. It becomes part of everything you do. In that respect, this is an extension of *A Love Supreme* since my conception of that force keeps changing shape. My goal in meditating on this through music, however, remains the same. And that is to uplift people, as much as I can. To inspire them to realize more and more of their capacities for living meaningful lives. Because there is certainly meaning to life."[1][9]

He also commented on the rhythm that resided within him: "I feel the need for more time, more rhythm, all around me. And with more than one drummer, the rhythm can be more multi-directional. Someday I may add a conga drummer or even a company of drummers."[2][0]

On *Meditations* Elvin and Rashied complemented one another like two rumbling forces, each thunderous in its own right but when surged together becoming innumerable vortices of healing helical helices, within the center of time.

By late 1965, John's popularity had risen to unprecedented heights. The music was played throughout the world. Folks and Archie Shepp were in Algeria when they heard *A Love Supreme* on the radio. They heard John's music in many of the countries they traveled to, commenting that John was following them wherever they went. This year, John dominated the polls. In the *Down Beat* Readers' Poll, he was voted number one saxophonist, Jazzman of the Year, and was elected to the Hall of Fame. *A Love Supreme* was voted record of the year.

All the furor that had arisen contrasted with the man's involvement with *the music*. He wasn't aware of the fact that *A Love Supreme* had sold a landmark number until he saw a gold record on the wall of the record company. The music he played in the clubs was always months ahead of the records by the time they were released. Just as in 1961, after *My Favorite Things* made its impact, he risked losing a sizable audience by continuing the natural evolution of the music. However, now he was less concerned. His eyes saw forward. He had committed his music to the Creator.

In Philadelphia, at the Showboat, the audience reacted strongly against the change in the music. It was late 1965. Many walked out grumbling that they could go home and hear Trane play the way they wanted to hear him on their old records. An additional problem arose because John Coltrane had become an established figure.

Some musicians would impose on his good nature, asking too frequently to sit in. Once a musician sat in for the last set of the night. He wouldn't come off the stage but continued to play until an hour had passed and it was time for the club to close. John had to speak to him, "I don't want you to feel bad about it, but don't come up here and play with me no more, 'cause you ain't got no consideration for anyone else but yourself."

Another common tactic was for a listener to introduce himself to John, sit at his table and ask what he was drinking. Then the listener would order two drinks saying, "This drink is on Trane." John and tenor saxophonist Wayne Shorter spoke of the poor audience reception and those who were trying to take advantage of him. He realized that he would have to be stricter with people, saying: "Man, I can't afford no more handouts with my life. I can't afford no meal tickets." Still he maintained a soft spot for those he thought could contribute to the music.

It had been a tragic year. On February 21st, 1965, Malcolm X was brutally assassinated while on the rising slope of his power and influence. The philosophies of Reverend King and Malcolm had been seen as vehemently opposed entities. But recently they had shaken hands in a warm gesture of the cessation of hostilities and the birth of a true unity. Black people from all classes of society began to embrace Malcolm's philosophies. He was the only man who had the respect and trust of the African leaders. He went to Africa. In Egypt, he was poisoned, and as the doctors pumped his stomach, Nasser stood over him, crying like a baby. He survived the poisoning, but he knew that his life was in danger, telling confidantes that the Muslims were not the ones who were trying to kill him. It was a larger entity — large enough to work on an international scale. Before his death, his house was bombed while he and his family were asleep. No one was hurt, but the police refused to give him or his family protection, and laughingly said that he was trying to get attention by bombing his own house. A week later, our Black Prince was dead.

By 1966, the anger of Black voices and fists had not abated. A process had begun of expelling whites from Black organizations. Black groups were changing from depending on white contributions and support to the long struggle toward self-sufficiency. Differences in tactics between groups who preached pacifism and an attitude of doing "whatever necessary" were widening. Stokely Carmichael, in Mississippi, enunciated a new password — *Black Power*.

Riots exploded in many cities during the summer: Cleveland, Los Angeles, Jersey City, Atlanta, Chicago. Bobby Kennedy began to emerge as a strong presidential candidate. Rev. King continued massive protests in several cities. Both men were rising in power on their way to — *drumatieyobast*. Against this background, the group consisting of John, McCoy, Elvin, Jimmy, Rashied and Pharoah played.

Audiences continued to react against the music. An article in *Variety* magazine, covering a Chicago appearance reflects the disapproval but respect that John had established:

> Although he has never been easy to understand musically John Coltrane's current stand at Boniface Mike Pierpoli's Plugged Nickel even gets the Coltrane bufls [sic] puzzled. Besides the normal aggregation of two saxophones, piano, bass, and drums, Coltrane has added a second drummer to the group. When both percussionists are going at it — which is most of the time — it's almost impossible to hear anything except the drums.
>
> The sets during the current engagement have been longer (several have reportedly gone over three hours, with the result being one show per night) than the usual hour-and-a-half stints the jazz musician seems to find palatable. Many patrons have found the shows to be almost endurance contests, pitting the musicians against the auditors. More times than not Coltrane is the winner.
>
> Pierpoli probably reflected most of the audience's feelings when he opinioned that he had no idea what Coltrane is searching for, but that for everyone's sake he hoped he found it soon.
>
> Coltrane has been in the front lines of the whole group of jazz musicians who have freed themselves from the restriction of timing and

chord structure. They apparently are attempting to make sense out of
what outwardly seems to be musical chaos.[21]

Since 1964, McCoy Tyner had been considering the starting of his
own group. He had formed definite ideas on the direction he wanted to
take, just as John had done before leaving Miles. McCoy's decision to
leave was precipitated by the volume of the two drummers who were
still trying to outdo each other. He felt that the listeners could not hear
him, and that the volume was diminishing what he could give to the
audience as well as its response to him. Always sensitive to the quality
of the pianos on which he had to play, McCoy was very annoyed when
he was unable to tell that the D-sharp was out of tune, because of the
battling drummers. Norman Simmons, the pianist with singer Carmen
McRae's group, which was alternating on stage with John's group, had
to inform McCoy of the bad key on the piano. He called John, telling
him of his decision to leave, saying that he felt he wanted to do
something else. John replied by saying that he was very proud that
McCoy felt strong enough to go on his own, and had made the decision
to leave.

Alice replaced him. The transition was not entirely smooth and easy
for her: "He was very patient with me; because I hadn't played or even
practiced in almost two years and I was blowin' in some wrong chords.
But he showed me how to build the sort of impact he wanted. He
always made you feel you could do it yourself if you really tried."[22]
" . . . he'd teach me not to stay in one spot and play one chord pattern.
'Branch out . . . you have a whole left register – use it. Play your
instrument entirely.' "[23] "Because he was a master, he saw that I was
playing with only a few octaves. He told me to play the whole piano,
utilize the range so I wouldn't be locked in. It freed me."[24]

He taught her some of his personal views on music. One point he
stressed above all others: "Don't ever play down to anyone. Play just
what you feel yourself."[25] He would draw an analogy between his horn
and mankind, saying that one group might represent the higher register,
another the mid-range, and still another the deeper notes, but that it
took all the groups together to make the whole.

When she asked how he would classify his music, he answered: "I'm
looking for a universal sound."[26] In an interview Alice explained her
understanding of John's answer: " . . . I think what he was trying to do
in music was the same thing he was trying to do in his life. That was to
universalize his music, his life, even his religion. It was all based on a

universal concept, all-sectarian or non-sectarian. In other words, he respected all faiths, all religious beliefs. In music it was the same way because he had such a combination of concepts and ideas, some interwoven with each other."[26]

In addition to playing the piano and vibes, Alice also learned the harp after meeting John: "John wanted a harp in the family . . . "[26] "He was using the harp for some of his studies, and that's how the harp got into the family in the first place. He used it for his own music. You know, just like he did with other instruments — the bass clarinet, drums, things like that."[26] "He had a book he referred to in regards to tuning and things. He used to tune it his own way, though. Sometimes he'd just leave it because he said he liked to hear the air, if it was blowing through the house, just passing over the strings. The harp then gave its own sounds. John liked that. He'd say that's a beautiful thing."[26]

She described the way in which he created, bringing together all things to fashion a new whole. His enjoyment of drawing futuristic cars as a child with Franklin Brower, now appeared in his creative work: "He was doing something from a map he drew — sort of like a globe, taking scales from it, taking modal things from it. And he was continually changing and continually doing things like that, and another day it would be something else, working with harmonics, working with chromatics, microtones, working with overtones, adding octaves to his instrument."[26]

The broad scope of his music especially belied the term "jazz." Alice also spoke of this word with respect to his music: "A higher principle is involved here — some of his latest works aren't musical compositions. I mean they aren't based entirely on music. A lot of it has to do with mathematics, some on rhythmic structure and the power of repetition, some on elementals. He always felt that sound was the first manifestation in creation before music."[26]

John had this to say of Alice's contribution to the group: "She continually senses the right colors, the right textures of the sounds of chords, and in addition she's fleet. She has real facility."[27]

When Alice joined the group on a permanent basis the volume from the drummers was still present. Elvin soon left. Elvin felt that the time had come for him to leave the group. Since first joining the band he had an understanding with John that he would one day have to leave to further explore his own musical direction. Elvin felt that Rashied had matured to the point of being capable of carrying on the work and that his leaving would not cause irreparable harm. The differing concepts of the two drummers may also have prompted Elvin's decision as he said, "The other drummer had a different sense of time from mine, so it didn't feel right."[28]

John continued exploring his feeling for rhythm, stating this and other goals: "I'm trying to work out a kind of writing that will allow for more plasticity, more viability, more room for improvisation in the statement of the melody itself before we go into the solos. And I'd like that point of departure to be freer rhythmically. Also I've got drum fever. I'd like to continue exploring the use of more than one drummer . . . And I'd like more horns."[29]

Speaking to critic Leonard Feather, John spoke of his interminable search: "I've had a strange career. I haven't yet quite found out how I want to play music. Most of what's happened these past few years has been questions. Someday we'll find the answers."[30]

When asked if there was a stopping point for him in music, he answered emphatically: "No. You just keep going all the way, as deep as you can. You keep trying to get right down to the crux."[31] "There is never any end. There are always new sounds to imagine, new feelings to get at, and always there is the need to keep purifying these feelings and sounds, so we can really see more and more clearly what we are. In that way, we can give to those listening the essence, the best of what we are. But to do that at each stage, we have to keep on cleaning the mirror."[32]

Wherever the group played, John frequently would call a local drummer to join Rashied. In Philadelphia, he called Warren McLennon. John liked his work, but Alice did not like the volume of his playing which, being a beginning player, he could not control. The audience again reacted unfavorably, probably not only to the drummers but to the whole concept of the music which had departed even farther from the commonly accepted.

Throughout the evening, John was receiving slipped pieces of paper from the audience with requests for *My Favorite Things*, and other previous works.

At one point he only shook his head, saying: "Everybody wants to hear what I've done. Nobody wants to hear what I'm doing."

After the set a large man placed himself in the path John had to take to leave the bandstand, saying with violence, "What is this you're playing. Who do you think you're fooling with this bullshit?" Jimmy Garrison jumped up, "Wait a minute!" John restrained him, looked straight at the man, and walked past him as if he weren't there.

But not all audiences, not even those within the same audience, were the same. The usual pattern was that first those who didn't appreciate the music left. For those who stayed, the music was affecting them in some way. There were those who jumped straight up in the air, shouting 'arrghhhh!' with their hands over their ears and running out of the club. The music would be bringing out all the bad parts of themselves and confronting them with it. They would come back inside to receive more exorcism. Some people who began by patting their feet found that they couldn't, and snapped their fingers quickly. Some just held their heads over to the side, letting the music carry them to paradise. Still others frantically danced and tapped along with the music on improvised instruments of tables and glasses. It was a religious experience for many, and the lines to the door of the clubs were always long.

Folks was ill in the hospital (in 1966) and John went to see him wearing sandals and short pants because of the heat of summer. He gave Folks $20 in change to buy items from the coin machines and a carton of cigarettes. He asked Folks if he should go to Japan. The Japanese had been trying to have him play in their country for years, but he was hesitant to go. Folks advised: "Shit, yeah. But be careful."

But Folks noticed that his friend didn't look too well either. John confided that he was tired. Folks told him: "John, goddammit, check in the hospital and don't let nobody know where in the fuck you at man, 'cept your wife. You got money to do it, man. Do like them whiteys do. Don't let nobody know where you is." John agreed, but did not take his advice to enter the hospital.

When the group arrived in Japan, in July, 1966, the reception was most gracious and overwhelmingly enthusiastic. There was a red carpet from the last step on the plane to a limousine that was to take them to their hotel. As they walked on the carpet, a band played, people carried life-sized posters of each of them and others gave them bouquets of flowers. Soon they met their assistants who were Japanese and assigned to each of them as interpreters, errand runners, and guides during their stay in Japan. Throughout the two-week tour the same excitement and respect greeted them. One restaurant owner gave them paint and brushes and had them sign their names on his wall. If a member of the group were recognized on the street, he would be asked for an autograph written on paper, a shirt, skin, anywhere.

John enjoyed the tour, seeing what he could in the available time, and trying out Japanese instruments such as the Kyoto. Both John and Pharoah received gifts from a factory of their product, plastic saxophones. Still there was little time to really meet the Japanese people. Within the two weeks seventeen concerts had to be given. The schedule was much like the arduous European tours – up at six, out at eight, arrive in the afternoon, rest or eat, perform, sleep, awake the next day to the same routine. When they performed, they played so hard it was like driving one's self to suicide. The group gave all its energies to capacity audiences of up to 7,000.

John would sometimes say that he was tired. Rashied, young, on his first international tour, and excited about playing in clubs, was ready to run around late at night. He thought that John was so accustomed to these things that they had become a bore. Unnoticed but consistently, John held his hand over his right side. He told no one, not even Alice, of his pain. Also within the group, several frictions came to the surface.

The group had developed a practice of playing cowbells, tambourines and other percussion instruments while others were soloing. Rashied, feeling that they didn't really know how to play these instruments, would shout: "Put that motherfuckin' bell down." The situation came to a head when he told John with Pharoah nearby: "Look, when you play a tambourine or when you play a bell, a drum or something, it takes cats a long time to learn to play the instruments correctly. I feel like you can play your horn, but when it comes to playing these percussion instruments, if you ain't got at least that much time on it as you got on your horn, don't be fuckin' with 'em – look, don't play that shit when I'm playing my solo. Just cut that shit loose and let me play my own solo by myself."

HEAT

SILENCE

Pharoah jumped up: "Goddam, man, you tellin' Chief what to do? This is Trane's group, man. I don't see how you can tell Trane what to do!"

Rashied reiterated, "Well, look, man, don't be playing them motherfuckin' tambourines cause first of all, you puttin' your fist through them tambourines, man." He turned to John: "Trane, I know some cats – bad brothers, man – that can play all the tambourines and bells, congas, and shit that you want."

John finally spoke − to the whole group which had gathered around. "Look, I don't care what you do when I'm playing. If you want to play tambourines or bells or whatever you want to do you can do that. But when Shied is playing just cut everything, don't play nothin'. Just let him play his solo and we'll all come back and you can play anything you wanna play." The issue was settled. However, during the same tour, Jimmy Garrison expressed his dissatisfaction.

Jimmy still had not come to terms with the change in the music. He was the only member of the old quartet left. His pride as a professional and an artist were challenged. He felt that he should be able to play in any context, but was frustrated in trying to deal with the direction the music had taken.

One night before an audience of 2,000, in the middle of a performance, he picked up his bass and walked off the stage. The rest of the group continued without him, ending a nearly 3-hour uninterrupted form, ten or fifteen minutes later. John told him backstage: "You know, that's gonna cost you a hundred dollars." Jimmy answered, "Okay, John, but after San Francisco, I don't want to make anymore." John explained: "Man, I understand. It's difficult for me, too, James. But I can't do anymore than what I'm doing."

Before leaving Japan, John prayed at the memorials on the bomb sites in Nagasaki and in Hiroshima. He admired the Japanese for many reasons, one of which was the respect one person showed for another. He found this personal respect lacking in the United States. Much money went down at the end of the tour for everyone in the group. When they left the limousine to board the plane, another red carpet kept their feet from the ground all the way to the first step of the plane.

Jimmy Garrison left the group in San Francisco, and was replaced by Sonny Johnson. In New York the group played the Vanguard. John hired a multitude of percussionists, Bobby Crowder, Omar Ali, who was Rashied's brother, Rogey, Algee Dewitt, and others. They brought their bells, congas, triangles, tambourines and a wide range of other percussion instruments. Rashied was happy.

John had a deep interest in the capabilities of his drummer. The fact that John was involved with concepts similar to his own gave Rashied confidence in pursuing his discoveries about music. En route to gigs, he would discuss rhythmic and polyrhythmic ideas with him. John would write out rhythmic patterns for him, and ask Rashied: "What do you think about this? Do you think maybe I should keep this dotted note over here or change it to a whole note?" or, "How do you like this phrase? Do you think you would like to play it like this?" Rashied would answer: "Man, if you wrote it, it must be alright. I can't tell you to change the whole composition. If you wrote it, I'm gonna have to learn to play it that way."

John was not satisfied with this, and asked directly: "Well, if you don't want to do it like this, can you think of a better way to do it?" Then he handed Rashied the pencil and paper.

Usually John would accept his suggestions. Their personal relationship was that of master and student. Rashied was always asking questions, and John was always giving information. Rashied also learned much about life from John. He and many others felt that John was the baddest thing that happened to the music since Charlie Parker. Yet he never saw him brag or with his chest stuck out. Instead he was always very peaceful, very passionate, and always trying to learn from and be open with people. He would say: "I get something out of everyone who plays. I don't care what they're playing, how good they're playing, how bad. There's something good in it. Everybody has some good quality."

His dress was not flashy, and he didn't interfere with anyone else's dress on the bandstand. He explained things carefully and thoroughly. One didn't walk away from him without understanding what he was saying. Rashied noticed the spiritual books he read. John and Alice gave him a book entitled, *Light On The Path*, which was about ways toward self-improvement. Rashied felt that he was becoming a better person by being around him.

John was merging more and more with the music. The sounds were heavy, and had filled the club almost to the point that it would fly. John was wailing, screaming out feelings, weaving lines of notes. It got so mean that he walked up to the mike, expanded his chest and beat on it, screaming: "Aaaaooooaa!!!" Some in the audience walked out: "Oh no, oh no, Trane done went mad now!"

Rashied looked up from the drums and couldn't continue. He didn't know what to do. Whenever anything new occurred, however, he would ask about it. John explained that it was a type of singing that is done in Tibet. There were musicians there who when they could release no more energy through their instruments, put them down and yodeled: "Man, cause a lot of times, I can't get it all out. So I just have to beat it out of me."

Rashied simply said an understanding:

"Oh."

The yodeling was not done frequently. It was only in those rare instances when it was the natural thing to occur. Sometimes the sound would be high and screaming. Other times it would be deep and thudding, with him striking his chest as though it were a resonant drum.

Two critics collaborated on a story, and attempted to explain it. They wrote that Rashied had something like witchcraft or voodoo powers over John that made him scream. They concluded that the only way Rashied was allowed to play in the group was by keeping a hex on him. Rashied showed him the article. John just laughed, "They don't really know what's happening."

In Philadelphia the group played a benefit for community groups at the Church of the Advocate. This church had a tradition of being available for community meetings and events. It was a relaxing Sunday afternoon. Most in the audience didn't know that McCoy had left. When the master of ceremonies asked John who the pianist was and he answered, "My wife," a wave of surprise went through the audience.

A young Philadelphia saxophonist, Sonny Fortune, asked to sit in. John welcomed him and said that they were going to play *Afro Blue*. Sonny asked for the chords, and John told him: "You'll hear it." Sonny persisted, "Well, give me the chords anyway." John answered, but still gave him all the information he was going to give: "Well, I'm going to just play a medley of things. Then I'm going to do a segment of *Afro Blue*."

The music went on, and came in strong on the beginning of *Afro Blue*, which Sonny followed. The music was vigorous, and the audience receptive. When John put down his horn, the audience, who had never heard him utter a word in previous performances, was shocked when he walked to the mike, moved to make a speech.

Everyone's attention was fixed on him. First he commented on the many fine musicians who came from Philadelphia, and that Philadelphia's music was represented all over the world. In his world travels, he said, this music was favorably received. Then he went on to say what was, in gist, that it was time for Black people to get themselves together and UNITE.

The speech was brief, to the point, and natural. The audience was pleased, many of them thinking that not only is he mean on the horn, but he can speak too. The mood bounced gently on this relaxing Sunday afternoon with everyone feeling good.

His interest in drums had reached the point where he studied the conga himself. Alice and John would practice, with her on piano and John on conga. At times there would be as many as twelve musicians, many of them drummers, on the bandstand, who were hired so openly that he wouldn't know who to pay at the end of the night. He carried a drum ensemble with him into Newark's Front Room.

John and Pharoah were screaming. The drummers were slapping fits all over the skins. The band was at its most intense. The audience was totally confused. Most were familiar only with John's music from the late fifties. They kept turning to Jose, the man-in-charge:

"What's happening, Jose? What's he doing?"
Jose didn't know what to tell them. This was on Monday night. Tuesday was an off-day. Wednesday, the audience still complained. Jose went to the table where Alice, John, Big George, Khalid and his wife were sitting and asked:

"Coltrane, do you think you can bring the music in a little bit, man?"
John looked back at him: "Man, I can't do nothing with it, but play." The conversation was over.

The next day, John was beating on his chest, and chanting. Pharoah was hollering. John was bearing down. Pharoah was bearing down. After the set Jose came to the table again, this time with a list of requests from the audience – *Soultrane, Moments Notice*, etc. John told him: "Look, man, we're not playing that kind of thing anymore." They both got up and went into a back room.

After a few minutes Rashied, sensing that John was at least slightly upset, walked to the door. He calmly opened it, and there was Chief, standing in the middle of the floor, his chest out, and with anger rising through him. He and Jose looked like they were about to fight. Shocked, Rashied thought to himself, "I ain't never seen Chief like this before." John turned to him: "Man, just go out there and pack up! Tell everybody out there to get all their shit off the stage and pack up. We're splittin'." Then he slammed the door – Blamm!!

Before Rashied could tell anybody anything, Jose came running out with John chasing behind him. The argument had gotten to whether or not the group would get paid. John reached into his pocket and gave the money he had to everyone saying: "The gig's off. We're going to Baltimore next week; so you got transportation and everything?

Everything is cool?" Then he got Jose into a corner and cursed him out. He was running it down and no one thought they would ever see him angry.

Around this time there were many jobs that ended prematurely because of John's uncompromising stand on *the music*. He was now impervious to criticism. But there were also those who worshipped the music, and for whom each note was a blessing. One such listener was Frank Kofsky who had previously written praise-filled reviews in *Jazz and Pop* magazine.

During the summer of 1966 he interviewed John in researching his book: *Black Nationalism and the Revolution in Music*. In doing this interview, Kofsky had a particular stereotype of a progressive Black musician in mind, and posed questions that aimed at fitting John into his mold. John's answers, however, gave testimony to his broadness. Also there is considerable information on events that had occurred in his career, and a restatement of his goals:

Kofsky: What do you think about the phrase, *the new Black music*, as a description of some of the newer styles in jazz?

Coltrane: Phrases, I don't know. They don't mean much to me, because usually I don't make the phrases, so I don't react too much. It makes no difference to me one way or the other what it's called.

Kofsky: If you did make the phrases, could you think of one?

Coltrane: I don't think there's a phrase for it, that I could make.

Kofsky: The people who use *that* phrase argue that jazz is particularly closely related to the Black community and it's an expression of what's happening there. That's why I asked you about your reaction to Malcolm X.

Coltrane: Well, I think it's up to the individual musician, call it what you may, for any reason you may. Myself, I recognize the artist. I recognize an individual when I see his contribution; and when I know a man's sound, well, to me that's him, that's this man. That's the way I look at it. Labels, I don't bother with.

Kofsky: But it does seem to be a fact that most of the *changes* in the music — the innovations — have come from Black musicians.

Coltrane: Yes, well this is how it is.

Kofsky: Have you ever noticed — since you've played all over the United States and in all kinds of circumstances — have you ever noticed that the reaction of an audience varies or changes if it's a Black audience or a white audience or a mixed audience? Have you ever noticed that the racial composition of the audience seems to determine how the people respond?

Coltrane: Well, sometimes, yes, and sometimes, no.

Kofsky: Any examples?

Coltrane: Sometimes it might appear to be one; you might say . . . it's hard to say, man. Sometimes people like it or don't like it, no matter what color they are.

Kofsky: You don't have any preferences yourself about what kind of an audience you play for?

Coltrane: Well, to me, it doesn't matter. I only hope that whoever is out there listening, they enjoy it; and if they're not enjoying it, I'd rather not hear.

Kofsky: If people do enjoy the music, how would you like them to demonstrate it? Do you like an audience that's perfectly still and unresponsive, or do you like an audience that reacts more visibly to the music?

Coltrane: Well, I guess I like an audience that does show what they feel; to respond.

Kofsky: I remember when you played at the Jazz Workshop in San Francisco, you sometimes got that kind of an audience, which you didn't get when you played at Shelly's Manne-Hole in Los Angeles; and it seemed to me that that had some effect on the music.

Coltrane: Yes, because it seems to me that the audience, in listening, is in an act of participation, you know. And when you know that somebody is maybe moved the same way you are, to such a degree or approaching the degree, it's just like having another member in the group.

Kofsky: Is that what happened at the *Ascension* date? The people that were there – did they get that involved?

Coltrane: I don't know. I was so doggone busy; I was worried to death. I couldn't really enjoy the date. If it hadn't been a date, then, I would have really enjoyed it. You know, I was trying to get the time and everything, and I was busy. I hope they felt something. To hear the record, I enjoyed it; I enjoyed all of the individual contributions.

Kofsky: What do you think, then, about playing concerts? Does that seem to inhibit the interaction between yourself, your group, and the audience?

Coltrane: Well, on concerts, the only thing that bugs me might be a hall with poor acoustics, where we can't quite get the unit sound. But as far as the audience goes, it's about the same.

Kofsky: Another reason I asked you about Malcolm was because I've interviewed a number of musicians and the consensus seems to be that the younger musicians talk about the political issues and social issues that Malcolm talked about, when they're with each other. And some of them say that they try to express this in the music. Do you find in your own groups or among musicians you're friendly with that these issues are important and that you do talk about them?

Coltrane: Oh, they're definitely important; and as I said, the issues are part of what *is* at this time. So naturally, as musicians, we express whatever is.

Kofsky: Do you make a *conscious* attempt to express these things?

Coltrane: Well, I tell you for myself, I make a conscious attempt, I think I can truthfully say that in music I make or I have tried to make a conscious attempt to change what I've found, in music. In other words, I've tried to say, "Well, *this* I feel, could be better, in my opinion, so I will try to do this to make it better." This is what I feel that we feel in any situation that we find in our lives, when there's something we think could be better, we must make an effort to try and make it better. So it's the same socially, musically, politically, and in any department of our lives.

Kofsky: Most of the musicians I have talked to are very concerned about changing society and they do see their music as an instrument by which society can be changed.

Coltrane: Well, I think so. I think music is an instrument. It can create the initial thought patterns that can change the thinking of the people.

Kofsky: In particular, some of the people have said that jazz is opposed to poverty, to suffering, and to oppression; and therefore, that jazz is opposed to what the United States is doing in Vietnam. Do you have any comments on that subject?

Coltrane: On the Vietnam situation?

Kofsky: Well, you can divide it into two parts. The first part was whether you think jazz is opposed to poverty and suffering and oppression; and the second part is whether you think, if so, jazz is therefore opposed to the United States' involvement in Vietnam?

Coltrane: In my opinion I would say yes, because jazz — if you want to call it that; we'll talk about that later — to me, it is an expression of music; and this music is an expression of higher ideals, to me. So therefore, brotherhood is there; and I believe with brotherhood, there would be no poverty. And also, with brotherhood, there would be no war.

Kofsky: That also seems to be what most of the musicians feel. David Izenson for example, said almost the same thing when I talked with him. He said, well, we're saying in our music we want a society without classes, without these frictions, without the wastes, and without the warfare.

Would you care to comment on working conditions for "jazz" musicians? Do you think that jazz artists are treated as they deserve to be treated; and if not, can you see any reason why they wouldn't be?

Coltrane: I don't know. It's according to the individual. Well, you find many times that a man may feel that the situation is all right with him, where another man might say, that situation is no good for you. So it's a matter of a man knowing himself, just what he wants, and that way, it's according to his value. If he doesn't mind a certain sort of treatment, I'm sure he can find it elsewhere. If he does mind it, then he doesn't have to put up with it. In my opinion, at this stage of the game, I don't care too much for playing clubs, particularly. Now there was a time when it felt all right to play clubs, because with my music, I felt I had to play a lot to work it out, you see. But now I don't think that that was absolutely where it was at; but I had to find it out myself. It is a matter of being able to be at home and be able to go into yourself. In other words, I don't feel the situation in clubs is ideal for me.

Kofsky: What is it about clubs that you don't like?

Coltrane: Well, actually, we don't play the set forty-minute kind of thing anymore, and it's difficult to always do this kind of thing now. The music, changing as it is, there are a lot of times when it doesn't make sense, man, to have somebody

	drop a glass, or somebody ask for some money right in the middle of Jimmy Garrison's solo. Do you know what I mean?
Kofsky:	I know *exactly*.
Coltrane:	And these kind of things are calling for some other kind of presentation.
Kofsky:	In other words, these really are artists who are playing, yet they're really not being treated as artists, but as part of the cash register.
Coltrane:	Yes, I think the music is rising, in my estimation, it's rising into something else, and so we'll have to find this kind of place to be played in.
Kofsky:	Why do you think conditions have been so bad for producing art by the musicians? What do you think causes these poor conditions that you've spoken of?
Coltrane:	Well, I don't know; I don't really know how it came about. Because I do know there was one time when the musicians played more dances, and they used to play theatres and all; and this took away one element, you know, but still it was hard work. I remember some of those one-nighters, it was pretty difficult.
	But it just seems that the music has been directed by businessmen, I would suppose, who know how to arrange the making of a dollar, and so forth. And maybe often the artist hasn't really taken the time himself to figure out just what he wants. Or if he does feel it should be in some other way. I think these are the things which are being thought about more now.
Kofsky:	Do you think the fact that almost all of the original jazz musicians were Black men and have continued to be throughout the generations, do you think this has encouraged the businessmen to take advantage of them and to treat their art with this contempt — ringing up of the cash register in the middle of a bass solo?
Coltrane:	Well, I don't know.
Kofsky:	Most of the owners, I've noticed, are white.
Coltrane:	Well, it could be, Frank, it could be.
Kofsky:	How do you think conditions are going to be improved for the musicians?
Coltrane:	There has to be a lot of self-help, I believe. They have to

work out their own problems in this area.

Kofsky: You mean, for example, what the Jazz Composers Guild was trying to do?

Coltrane: Yes I *do* think that was a good idea, I really do; and I don't think it's dead. It was just something that couldn't be born at that time, but I still think it's a good idea.

Kofsky: This is true in the history of all kinds of organizations in this country — they're not always successful the first time. But I think it's inevitable that musicians are going to try and organize to protect themselves.

Coltrane: Yes.

Kofsky: For example, I was at the Five Spot Monday night, and I figure that there are about a hundred tables in there; and with two people at a table, it comes to about $7.50 a set, at three drinks a set. That means the owner's making $750, say, a set and he has five sets. And I know the musicians for that night aren't getting anywhere *near* five times $750, or even two times $750. So actually it turns out that these businessmen are not only damaging the art, but they're even keeping people away.

Coltrane: Yes, it's putting them up tight, lots of people, man. I feel so *bad* sometimes about people coming to the club and I can't play long enough for them, because, you know, they're hustling you. They come to hear you play and you get up, you have to play a little bit, then split. Something has to be done about it.

Kofsky: Do the musicians who play in these newer styles look to Africa and Asia for some of their musicial inspiration?

Coltrane: I think so; I think they look all over. And inside.

Kofsky: Do they look some places more than others? I heard you, for example, talking about making a trip to Africa, to gather musical sources. Is that the idea?

Coltrane: Well, I intend to make a trip to Africa to gather whatever I can find, particularly the musical sources.

Kofsky: Do you think that the musicians are more interested in Africa and Asia than in Europe, as far as the music goes?

Coltrane: Well, the musicians have been exposed to Europe, you see. So it's the other parts that they haven't been exposed to. Speaking for myself, at least, I'm trying to have a rounded education.

Kofsky: Is that the significance of those rhythmic instruments that
             you've incorporated into your group — to give it a sort of
             Middle Eastern or African flavor?

Coltrane: Maybe so, it's just something I feel.

Kofsky: Why do you think that the interest in Africa and Asia is
             growing at this particular time?

Coltrane: Well, it's just time for this to come about, that's all. It's a
             thing of the times.

Kofsky: Bill Dixon suggested to me that it might have something to
             do with the fact that many African nations became
             independent in the 1950s and changed the way Negroes in
             this country looked at themselves; it made them more aware
             of the African heritage and made them more interested in
             going back and looking for it. Do you think there's anything
             to that line of thought?

Coltrane: Yes, yes, that's part of it.

Kofsky: Another question along the same lines is: it seems that group
             improvisation is growing in importance — for example, what
             you do with Pharoah [Sanders] when you're playing
             simultaneously. And also, of course, *Ascension*. Do you
             think that this is a new trend now, or not a new trend, but
             do you think this is growing in importance now?

Coltrane: Well, maybe. It seems to be happening at this time; I don't
             know how long it's going to last.

Kofsky: Why do you think that's taking place now?

Coltrane: I don't know *why*; it just *is*, that's all.

Kofsky: But it is there — I'm not making something up when I say
             that?

Coltrane: No, no, I feel it, it's there, but I don't know why.

Kofsky: And another question about the new music: I've noticed that
             a lot of the new groups are pianoless; or even in your case,
             where you have a piano, sometimes you'll have the piano lay
             out during a solo, or during parts of a solo. Why is this
             coming about at this particular time? Why the desire to
             deemphasize the piano or to give it another kind of role in
             the group?

Coltrane: I still use the piano, and I haven't reached the point where I
             feel I don't need it. I might, but . . . maybe it's
             because . . . well, when you're not playing on a given

progression, you don't really need it to state these things. And it would get in your way to have somebody going in another direction and you trying to go in another, there it would be better for you not to have it.

Kofsky: It seems that the direction the horns are going in, too, is to get away from the twelve-tone scale — to play notes that really aren't on the piano: the high-pitched notes, the shrieks and screams. I don't know what words you use to describe those sounds, but I think you know what I mean. Sounds that were considered "wrong" — well, still are considered wrong by some people.

Now, if you play those notes that really aren't on the piano, and you have the piano there stating notes, do you feel that this gives some kind of a clash that you'd rather avoid?

Coltrane: I suppose that's the way some men feel about it. As I say, I still use the piano. I haven't reached the point yet, where the piano is a drag to me. The only thing is, I don't, we don't *follow* what the piano does any more, because we all move in our own directions. I like it for a backdrop, you know, for its sound.

Kofsky: You do have the piano, though, lay out for a fairly large part of the time.

Coltrane: Well, I always instruct the piano players that whenever they wish they can just lay out and let it go on as it is. Because after a while, lots of times, the pianists, well, they get tired. If you can't think of anything else to play — stroll!

Kofsky: When I talked to you a couple of years ago in Los Angeles and I asked you if you would ever consider adding another horn to the group, you said probably the thing you would do is, if you added anything you would add drums. [Laughter.] Did you have in mind then these kind of things that . . . ?

Coltrane: I don't even know, man, but I guess so. I still feel so strongly about drums, I really do. I feel very strongly about these drums. I experimented in it, but we didn't have too much success. I believe it would have worked, but, Elvin and McCoy [unintelligible].

Kofsky: It doesn't necessarily have to be two drums. It could be drums and another rhythm instrument. That's what I was really referring to.

Coltrane: I think so too. It could come in different forms, shapes; I just don't know how to do it, though.

Kofsky: After all, the things that you're using in the group now — shakers, bells, maracas — are rhythm instruments too. Not all rhythm instruments are drums.

Coltrane: Oh, that's true.

Kofsky: That's what I meant, when I asked you if that's what you had in mind.

Coltrane: Yes.

Kofsky: Speaking of Elvin and McCoy reminds me of something Sun Ra said, and I'll repeat it. I'll make it clear that I don't put any faith in it, but since he said it, and he told me to tell you, I'll pass it along.

He says that you hired Rashied Ali as a means of driving Elvin and McCoy out of the band, because you didn't want them in the band in the first place, and that was your way of doing it. Do you want to answer that?

Coltrane: No, I don't. I was trying to do something . . . There was a thing I wanted to do in music, see, and I figured I could do *two* things: I could have a band that played like the way we used to play, and a band that was going in the direction that the one I have now is going in — I could combine these two, with these two concepts going. And it could have been done.

Kofsky: Yes. Sun Ra is quite bitter, and claims that you've stolen all of your ideas from him, and in fact that everybody has stolen all of their ideas from him. [Laughter.]

Coltrane: There may be something to that. I've heard him and I know that he's doing some of the things that I've wanted to do.

Kofsky: How do you feel about having another horn in the group, another saxophone? Do you feel that it in any way competes with you or that it enhances what you're doing?

Coltrane: Well, it helps me. It helps me stay alive sometimes, because physically, man, the pace I've been leading has been so hard and I've gained so much weight, that sometimes it's been a little hard physically. I feel that I like to have somebody there in case I can't get that strength. I like to have that strength in that band, somewhere. And Pharoah is very strong in spirit and will, see, and these are the things that I like to have up there.

Kofsky: Do you feel that spurs you on, the presence especially of a man as powerful as Pharoah?

Coltrane: Yes, all the time, there's always got to be somebody with a lot of power. In the old band, Elvin had this power. I always have to have somebody there, with it, you know?

Rashied has it, but it hasn't quite unfolded completely; all he needs to do is play.

Kofsky: That was my impression, too, that he really was feeling his way ahead in the music and didn't have the confidence Elvin had. But then, of course, look how long Elvin was with you before —

Coltrane: He was there, Elvin was there for a couple of years — although Elvin was ready from the first time I heard him, you know, I could hear the genius there — but he had to start playing steadily, steadily, every night . . . With Miles [Davis] it took me around two and a half years, I think, before it started developing, taking the shape that it was going to take.

Kofsky: That's what's so tragic about the situation of the younger musicians now: they don't have that opportunity to play together.

Coltrane: Yes, it certainly needs to be done. It should be happening all the time and the men would develop sooner.

Kofsky: Don Cherry has a record out, *Complete Communion*. I think it's a beautiful record, and one of the reasons I think it's so good is because here he has a group that's worked together for a few months.

Coltrane: Yeah!

Kofsky: And so he knows how to put something together for all the men — it isn't just a "date."

Have you listened to many of the other younger saxophonists besides Pharoah?

Coltrane: Yes, Albert Ayler first. I've listened very closely to him. He's something else.

Kofsky: Could you see any relationship between what you were doing and what he was doing? In other words, do you think he has developed out of some of your ideas?

Coltrane: Not necessarily; I think what he's doing, it seems to be moving music into even higher frequencies. Maybe where I left off, maybe where he started, or something.

Kofsky: Well, in a sense, that's what I meant.
Coltrane: Yes. Not to say that he would copy bits and that, but just
            that he filled an area that it seems I hadn't gotten to.
Kofsky: It seems to me, that your solo on *Chasin' the Trane*, that
            Albert developed some of the ideas that you had put out
            there and he had expressed some of them in his own ways,
            and that this was one of the points from which he had
            begun. Had you ever thought of it in that light?
Coltrane: No. I hadn't.
Kofsky: Did you ever listen to that selection much?
Coltrane: Only at the time it came out, I used to listen to it and
            wonder what happened to me.
Kofsky: What do you mean?
Coltrane: Well, it's a sort of surprising thing to hear this back, because
            — I don't know, it came back another way.
                It was a little longer than I thought it was and it had a
            fairly good amount of intensity in it, which I hadn't quite
            gotten into a recording before.
Kofsky: You were pleased with it?
Coltrane: To a degree, not that I could sit there with it and love it
            forever.
Kofsky: Well, no, you'd never be pleased with anything that you did
            for longer than a week!
Coltrane: I realized that I'd have to do that or better, you see, and
            then I —
Kofsky: I think it's a remarkable record and I also think you ought to
            go back and listen to it.
Coltrane: Maybe so.
Kofsky: Because I don't see any saxophonist now who isn't playing
            something that you haven't at least sketched out before. But
            maybe you would rather not think about that.
Coltrane: No, because like it's a big reservoir, that we all dip out of.
            And a lot of times, you'll find that a lot of those
            things . . . I listened to John Gilmore kind of closely before
            I made *Chasin' the Trane*, too. So some of those things on
            there are really direct influences of listening to this cat, you
            see. But then I don't know who he'd been listening to,
            so . . .
Kofsky: After *Chasin' the Trane* and then *Impressions* came out, you
            did a sort of change of pace. You remember; you did the

album with Duke Ellington and *Ballads*, and the Johnny Hartman album. Whose idea were these albums? Were they yours, or Bob Thiele's?

Coltrane: Well, I tell you, I had some trouble at that time. I did a foolish thing. I got dissatisfied with my mouthpiece and I had some work done on this thing, and instead of making it better, it ruined it. It really discouraged me a little bit, because there were certain aspects of playing – that certain fast thing that I was reaching for – that I couldn't get because I had damaged this thing, so I just had to curtail it. Actually, I never found another [mouthpiece], but after so much of this laying around and making these kind of things, I said, well what the hell, I might as well go ahead and do the best I can. But at that moment, it was so vivid in my mind – the difference in what I was getting on the horn – it was so vivid that I couldn't do it. Because as soon as I did, I'd hear it; and it just discouraged me. But after a year or so passed, well, I'd forgotten.

Kofsky: That's funny, because I think I know your music as thoroughly as any nonmusician, yet that wouldn't have been apparent to me.

Coltrane: That's a funny thing. That's one of the mysteries. And to me, as soon as I put that horn in my mouth, I could hear it. It feels, you know . . . I just stopped and went into other things.

Kofsky: The reason I asked that was because I recall that was the time you had Eric [Dolphy] in and out of the band.

Coltrane: Yes.

Kofsky: And there was a whole wave of really hostile criticism.

Coltrane: Yes, and all of this was at the same time, so you see how it was. I needed all the strength I could have at that time; and maybe some of these things might have caused me to feel, "Well, man, I can't get what I want out of this mouthpiece, so I'll work on it."

Kofsky: You think this might have undermined your self-confidence?

Coltrane: It could have, it certainly could have.

Kofsky: Why do you think there's been all this hostility to the new music, especially in your case?

Coltrane: Oh, man, I never could figure it out! I couldn't even venture to answer it now. Because as I told them then, I just felt that they didn't understand.

              *   *   *

Kofsky: The perfect wrong time to hit you!

Coltrane: Everything I was doing was like that, it was a hell of a test for me, and it was coming out of it, it was just like I always said, man: when you go through these crises and you come out of them, you're definitely stronger, in a great sense.

Kofsky: Did the reaction of Impulse to these adverse criticisms have anything to do with those records that we talked about?

Coltrane: The ballads and that?

Kofsky: Yes.

Coltrane: Well, I don't know. I think Impulse was interested in having what they might call a balanced sort of thing, a diversified sort of catalog, and I find nothing wrong with this myself. You see, I like — in fact most of the songs that I even write now, the ones that I even consider songs, are ballads. So there's something there, that I mean I really love these things.

And these ballads that came out were definitely ones which I felt at this time. I chose them; it seemed to be something that was laying around in my mind — from my youth, or somewhere — and I just had to do them. They came at this time, when the confidence in what I was doing on the horn had flagged, it seemed to be the time to clean that out. And Johnny Hartman — a man that I had stuck up in my mind somewhere — just felt something about him, I don't know what it was. I liked his sound, I thought there was something there I had to hear, so I looked him up and did that album. Really, I don't regret doing those things at all.

The only thing I regret was not having kept that same attitude, which was: I'm going to do, no matter what. That was the attitude in the beginning, but as I say, there were a whole lot of reasons why these things happened.

Kofsky: Do you think that learning how to play the soprano changed your style?

Coltrane: Definitely, definitely. It certainly did.

Kofsky: How so? Could you spell it out?

Coltrane: Well, the soprano, by being this small instrument, I found that playing the lowest note on it was like playing one of the middle notes on the tenor – so therefore, after I got so that my embouchure would allow me to make the upper notes, I found that I would play *all over* this instrument. On tenor, I hadn't always played all over it, because I was playing certain ideas which just went in certain ranges, octaves. But by playing on the soprano and becoming accustomed to playing on tenor from that low B-flat on up, it soon got so that when I went to tenor, I found myself doing the same thing. It caused the change or the willingness to change and just try to play as much of the instrument as possible.

Kofsky: Did it give you a new rhythmic conception too?

Coltrane: I think so, I think so. A new shape came out of this thing and patterns – the way the patterns – would fall.

Kofsky: It seemed to me that after you started playing soprano, and particularly after *My Favorite Things*, then you started feeling that same kind of a pulse on the tenor that hadn't been there in your work before.

Coltrane: I think that's quite possible. In fact, the patterns started – the patterns were one of the things I started getting dissatisfied with on the tenor mouthpiece, because the sound of the soprano was actually so much closer to me in my ear. There's something about the presence of that sound, that to me – I didn't want to admit it – but to me it would seem like it was better than the tenor – I liked it more. I didn't want to admit this damn thing, because I said the tenor's my horn, it is my favorite. But this soprano, maybe it's just the fact that it's a higher instrument, it started pulling my conception.

Kofsky: How do you feel about the two horns now?

Coltrane: Well, the tenor is the power horn, definitely; but soprano, there's still something there in just the voice of it that's really beautiful, something that I really like.

Kofsky: Do you regard the soprano as an extension of the tenor?

Coltrane: Well, at first I did, but now, it's another voice, it's another sound.

Kofsky: Did you ever use the two horns on the same piece, as you did on *Spiritual*?

Coltrane: I think that's the only time I've done that. Sometimes in clubs, if I feel good, I might do something like this – start on one and end on another – but I think that's the only one on record.

Kofsky: What prompted Pharoah to take up the alto? Was that to get away from – two tenors?

Coltrane: I don't know. This is something he wanted to do, and about the same time I decided I wanted to get one, so we both got one.

Kofsky: I haven't heard you play the alto. Do you play it much?

Coltrane: I played it in Japan. I played it in Frisco a little bit, but I've had a little trouble with the intonation of it. It's a Japanese make, it's a new thing they're trying out, so they gave us these horns to try, and mine has to be adjusted at certain points where it's not quite in tune, so I don't play it, but I like it.

Kofsky: I saw a picture of you with a *flute*! Are you playing that too now?

Coltrane: I'm learning.

Kofsky: You're always learning aren't you?

Coltrane: I hope so. Always trying to learn.

Kofsky: I looked at the *Down Beat* and *Jazz* Critics' Polls two years in a row, and both years, this and last year, I noticed that European critics are much more in favor of the new music than the Americans. Almost 50 percent or 60 percent of them would vote for new musicians, whereas, say only about a quarter of the Americans. Is this what you found in Europe? – or in general, have you found outside the United States that your music is more favorably received by the critics, the power structure, shall we say, than in the U.S.?

Coltrane: I'd say in the new music – and when I say new music, I mean most of the younger musicians that are starting out – I know that they definitely have found a quicker acceptance in Europe than they have here. When I started, it was a little different, because I started through Miles Davis, who was an accepted musician, and they got used to me here in the States. Now when they first heard me with Miles here, they did not like it.

Kofsky: I remember.

Coltrane: So it's just one of those things: everything that they haven't heard yet and that's a little different, they are going to reject it at first. But the time will roll around, the time when they will like it. Now, by being here with Miles and running around the country with him, they heard more of me here, and consequently they began to accept it before they did in Europe, because they hadn't heard me in Europe. When we went to Europe the first time, it was a shock to them there. They booed me and everything in Paris, because they just weren't with it. But now I find, the last time I was in Europe, it seems that the new music — they've really opened up. They can hear it there better than they do here.

Kofsky: I think that part of this is because what's happening in the new music is analogous to what's happened in painting, say, and sculpture and literature; and the people who appreciate jazz in Europe, are much more aware of this. What do you think of this?

Coltrane: Well, I don't know.

Kofsky: In Europe, jazz is regarded as a serious art, whereas here, it's regarded as, well . ...

Coltrane: Whatever it is.

Kofsky: As part of the nightclub business. Otherwise, you couldn't have a magazine like *Down Beat*.

I know Albert [Ayler] is going back to Europe, and I know that there are many of the younger musicians who want to get away from the States because they just don't feel there's any hope for them here.

Do you remember Third Stream Music, what was called Third Stream Music?

Coltrane: Yes.

Kofsky: Did you ever feel, much of an inner urge to play that kind of music?

Coltrane: No.

Kofsky: Why do you think it didn't catch on with the musicians? Was there anything about it that suggests why it was never popular with them?

Coltrane: I think it was an attempt to create something, I think, more with labels, you see than true evolution.

Kofsky: You mean, it didn't evolve naturally out of the desires of the musicians?

Coltrane: Maybe it did; I can't say that. It was an attempt to do something, and evolution is about trying too. But there's something in evolution — it just happens when it's ready, but this thing wasn't really where it was coming from. What was it — an attempt to blend, to wed two musics? That's what it really was.

Kofsky: You said, talking about saxophone players, that there was a common pool that everybody dipped into. Maybe here, there wasn't enough of that pool for the musicians to dip in to.

Coltrane: Well, I just think it wasn't time. It was an attempt to do something at a time when it wasn't time for this to happen, and therefore it wasn't lasting. But there may have been some things that came out of this that have been beneficial in promoting the final change, which is coming. So nothing is really wasted, although it might appear to fail or not succeed the way that men would have desired it to.

Kofsky: Even the mistakes can be instructive if you try to use them.
           Do you make any attempt, or do you feel that you should make any attempt, to educate your audience in ways that aren't strictly musical. That is, it's obvious that you want your audience to understand what you're doing *musically*. But do you feel that you want them to understand other things, too, and that you have some kind of responsibility for it?

Coltrane: Sure, I feel this, and this is one of the things I am concerned about now. I just don't know how to go about this. I want to find out just how I should do it. I think it's going to have to be very subtle; you can't ram philosophies down anybody's throat, and the music is enough! That's philosophy. I think the best thing I can do at this time is to try to get myself in shape and know myself. If I can do that, then I'll just play, you see, and leave it at that. I believe that will do it, if I really can get to myself and be just as I feel I should be and play it. And I think they'll get it, because music goes a long way — it can influence.

Kofsky: That's how I got interested in those things I was talking about earlier, Malcolm X. I might not have come to it, or come to it as fast, if it hadn't been for the music. That was my first introduction to something beyond my own horizons, that would make me think about the world I was living in.

Coltrane: Yes. That's what I'm sure of, man, I'm really sure of this thing. As I say, there are things which as far as spirituality is concerned, which is very important to me at this time, I've got to grow through certain phases of this to other understanding and more consciousness and awareness of just what it is that I'm supposed to understand about it; and I'm sure others will be part of the music. To me, you know, I feel I want to be a force for good.

Kofsky: And the music too?

Coltrane: **Everywhere. You know, I want to be a force for real good. In other words, I know that there are bad forces, forces out here that bring suffering to others and misery to the world, but I want to be the force which is truly for good.**

Kofsky: I don't have any more of my prepared questions to ask you – or my improvised questions to ask you. [Laughter.] I had a lot of questions here that were related just to you. Many of those questions about music I don't ask of the other musicians; but I've always had a very special interest in your work, so I took this opportunity, since I don't know when I'll ever get the chance to get you down on tape again.
            Do you have anything else that you'd like to get on here?

Coltrane: I think we just about covered it, I believe, just about covered it.

[As John drove me back to the station, the tape recorder was left on and we continued to talk. After some humorous exchanges, the conversation turned to the proper function of a jazz writer or critic.]

Kofsky: If you can't play the music, and if you're going to write about, you have, I think, an obligation to do it as conscientiously as possible.

Coltrane: Yes, I believe it, man.

Kofsky: And always when it's a question of your opinion versus the musician's opinion, to give the benefit of the doubt to the musician, because he knows the music far better than you'll ever know it. In other words, you have to be humble. A lot of writers aren't humble; they get arrogant because they think they have some kind of power.

Coltrane: Well, that's one of the main causes of this arrogance – the idea of power. Then you lose your true power, which is to be part of all, and the only way you can be part of all is to understand it. And when there's something you don't understand, you have to go humbly to it. You don't go to school and sit down and say, "I know what you're getting ready to teach me." You sit there and you learn. You open your mind. You absorb. But you have to be quiet, you have to be still to do all of this.

Kofsky: That's what so annoyed me about all of that stuff they were saying about you in '61.

Coltrane: Oh, that was terrible. I couldn't believe it, you know, it just seemed so preposterous. It was so ridiculous, man, that's what bugs me. It was absolutely ridiculous, because they made it appear that we didn't even know the first thing about music — the first thing. And there we were really trying to push things off.

Kofsky: Because they never stand still.

Coltrane: Eric [Dolphy], man, as sweet as this cat was and the musician that he was — it hurt me to see him get hurt in this thing.

Kofsky: Do you think that this possibly contributed to the fact that he died so young?

Coltrane: I don't know, but Eric was a strong cat. Nobody knows what caused it. The way he passed, there was a mystery about it.

Kofsky: I didn't mean that it was directly the cause, but —

Coltrane: Indirectly?

Kofsky: Yes.

Coltrane: Yes. The whole scene, man. He couldn't work . . .

Kofsky: That's what I meant, really.

Coltrane: He always seemed to be a very cheerful young man, so I don't *think* that would put him . . . I don't think so, because he had an outlook on life which was very, very good — optimistic, and he had this sort of thing, friendliness, you know, a real friend to everyone. He was the type of man who could be as much a friend to a guy he'd just met today as he was to one he'd known for ten years. This kind of person, I don't think it would really hurt him to the point where he would do something to hurt himself consciously or unconsciously.

Kofsky: Yes. That friendliness was one of the things that has impressed me about the musicians here. I really didn't expect to be greeted with open arms, because I am an outsider, after all. And yet I have been amazed constantly at how eager the musicians were to cooperate when they decided that I was sincere and that this wasn't a joke or a con or something of that nature.

Coltrane: I think all we need is sincerity, empathy . . .

I think I want to get closer to town. Maybe there's something I can do in music. Get a place, a little room to play in. I don't want a loft, but maybe there's something I can get to play in, just some place to be able to work in.

Kofsky: Where do you play at home?

Coltrane: Anywhere. There's a room over the garage that I'm getting fixed now and I think it's going to be my practice room. You never know. Sometimes you build a little room and it ends up you still going in the toilet. I hope I like it, but . . . I keep a horn on the piano and I have a horn in my bedroom — a flute usually back there, because when I go there I'm tired and I lay down and practice.

Kofsky: About how many hours a day do you play?

Coltrane: Not too much at this time. I find that it's only when something is trying to come through that I really practice. And then I don't even know how many hours — it's all day, on and off. But at this time there's nothing coming out now.

Kofsky: I was very surprised to hear you practicing at all, because I just couldn't conceive of what you could find to practice! But I know it isn't like that.

Coltrane: I *need* to practice. It's just that I want something to practice, and I'm trying to find out what it is that I want, an area that I want to get into.[33]

His search for "something to practice" looked squarely into Africa. Olatunji, the Nigerian drummer, had spoken to him of a Center of African Culture that he sought to establish in Harlem. He was having difficulty because of a lack of funds. Those who promised to contribute didn't. The Board of Education complicated matters by ordering that since the center was to be a school, certain specifications as to distribution of space and lighting had to be met. This required the hiring of an architect and a contractor. Olatunji told John of his difficulties. John sent him three checks for $250 each during 1966, before the school had materialized. They had talked since 1961, when they first met, of making a record together, which never occurred. He tried to get Impulse to give Olatunji a recording contract but they allegedly refused. As funds slowly but surely came in, John expressed his happiness over the blossoming of Olatunji's dream: "That's very good that you're going to start a school. Now I have a place to come. Because right now I don't think I'm making any progress. I should go right ahead and explore new avenues." Olatunji then told him how he had been trying to convince musicians that they should study African languages because of their relationship to the music, rhythmically and tonally.

John agreed, and told him that he wanted to take lessons at the school, but in privacy. Olatunji showed him a backroom of the unfinished interior where he could practice and take lessons and said to him: "I'll give you practice in the language. I'll sing some of the songs."

John wanted a broad spectrum of courses — African religion, Yoruba, African history, music and dance. They spoke of going to the homeland together. John wanted to take his horn with him, not to perform, but to practice whatever he learned. John said to Olatunji: "Next time you go to Africa, I'm going with you. I gotta go over there. I want to go over there with someone like yourself." Olatunji assured him that they would certainly go together, and John spoke of "having to get to the source," feeling that Africa contained the throbbing heart, from which all the music came.

In the Kofsky interview, he hinted at "a place" that he wanted in the city to play in. This would be somewhere that creative musicians could experiment without interference. John also liked the convenience of being able to play there whenever he wanted. It would be opened to the public for the price of a soda or some very small charge. Above it there might be a bookstore. Alice spoke of his plans and reasons for this effort: "He was disturbed because the type of music he played was confined to nightclubs. It was music for listening, not for drinking in all the places where there is so much buying and selling."[34]

Ornette Coleman put it bluntly: "I would like to play for audiences who aren't using my music to stimulate their sex organs. A nightclub is not where jazz gets its best audience because it's still based on getting drunk enough to go after the flesh nearest you."[35] Also there were the cramped spaces of a nightclub and the gangster element.

Alice continued her explanation of their plans: " . . . we had thought of setting up a center that would be like a church, we wouldn't call it a church, because it might frighten people away and they might wonder what kind of church it was, but it would be a church in that it would be a place for music and meditation, and maybe someone would feel like praying. It would bring others a kind of fellowship based on music, because he thought music was a single universal force and that there could be no dividing lines or categories."³ ⁶

These plans were consistent with his life: "My goal is to live the truly religious life and express it in my music. If you live it, when you play there's no problem because the music is part of the whole thing.⟨To be a musician is really something. It goes very, very deep. My music is the spiritual expression of what I am − my faith, my knowledge, my being."³ ⁷⟨

He took great pleasure in family life, and was successful enough to work when he wanted. His children made him happy as shown by an 8mm home-made movie showing him romping in the backyard with his three sons. He enjoyed listening to Albert Ayler, especially the way he was able to play so much in the high register. But he hated to waste time going into the city dealing with the traffic and being taken from his music.

Khalid and his wife would visit often, spending the whole day. John and Khalid talked of Islam, positions for prayer, diet and just casual topics. John told him of a white boy who had been in his group, but that what he had to do was too deep for him. He also told of his feeling that the spirituality of man was more important than the experiences from drugs, and that a man should not be dependent on drugs for these experiences. On liquor, John said that he would rather drink grape juice than wine. He disliked gossip, and those who called him on the phone would try to speak in a positive manner. Whenever John and Khalid spoke of women, it wouldn't be the conversation of most men about how nice it would be to have this one or that one. Instead they spoke of what a distraction they could be when you're trying to remain on a spiritual plane. Once in a club they were standing together when a lady approached them. She was all hip and perfumed: "Hey, John. What's happening?" Both, who were on a high spiritual plane, moved back from this interference. There were times when Khalid visited that they didn't talk at all, or very little. Both were very quiet men. Khalid would knock on the door. John would answer and greet him warmly. Then there would be a lull which John would break by saying: "Well, I guess we'd better play." At another time Khalid told John of a dream he had of Thelonious Monk. Monk was riding in a car, then he was floating above it. John told him that he had the same dream recently.

Electronic instruments were coming into extensive use in the middle sixties. But John was wary of them, feeling that they might turn out to be just another gimmick. He ate mostly vegetables, fruits and juices, especially carrot juice. Occasionally he would break down and eat meat. He told Khalid of his dilemma when a friend from down south called and told him that he was bringing some pig's feet for him. He didn't want to be rude and not accept it, but he did not want to eat the pork either. Once when Khalid called before visiting John asked him to bring a watermelon. He told Khalid of his fasting for seven days once, and how this made him more conscious of his spiritual self. When he ate meat again he said that he could feel the vibrations in the food of the personalities of the people who handled it, and the fear of the animals when they were slaughtered.

On a visit to Khalid's house John brought his oldest son, John Jr. After he and Khalid played for a while, John put the saxophone in his son's mouth, who was able to produce a definite sound. Khalid struck the same note simultaneously, and little John Jr. jumped with excitement.

Folks would call, adding many dollars to his telephone bill from their hours of long conversation. They would discuss material for albums as well as social issues. John spoke of his admiration for the younger generation: "The young cats today are together, man. They ain't gettin' high and fuckin' up like they used to."

Another friend came to visit. John first met George Braithe at a jam session in the Village, where he was impressed with George's ability to play two horns at the same time. They had met again in California where George was stranded, and John gave him a small loan to help him return to the East Coast.

George parked the bus he drove to John's house between two trees near the driveway. He took out his horn and practiced a few minutes before knocking on the door. John answered. He had his saxophone in his hand and a tape recorder strapped to his back blaring out a new music he was developing. He called Alice and welcomed George: "Come right in. – Do you have your horn? I'd like you to show me about the two horns." George took out his horns and played, causing John to say: "Oh, man, that's really fantastic. Maybe we can play something together. And maybe we can write something down." He thought a moment: "That's what I'll do. Let me get my wife so we can play something." The three of them played for an hour. Alice left and the two men sat on the couch.

George asked how he obtained the percussive character of his notes. John explained that it was done by a definitive way of closing the keys rather than by rapid movement of the tongue, as George had thought. John taught, and they played for another hour – completely engrossed. Finally John broke in: "Man, this could go on for days." He explained that many household events were about to occur together. John's mother was due to arrive at the train station and needed a ride.

Later in the year, during October, George visited again. This time the tape recorder on John's back was screaming. He was developing another advance in his music and gave George a written part of a form to be played at some future time.

Customarily, at performances, John would walk around the club after playing. Now, however, he would be exhausted, spreading his large body across a chair. He was telling friends that he was going to take fewer engagements, stay home, rest and study, because his health wasn't good. On October 15th, an article appeared in *Melody Maker* which speculated on his new moves:

> Has John Coltrane "done a Sonny Rollins" and temporarily retired from the jazz scene to "rethink" his music?
>
> It seems a reasonable inference from reports and rumours circulating in New York. One musician, close to the tenorist, has said that Coltrane was fed up with the whole current scene and had reached the point where he feels he is musically lost.
>
> Recently, too, Coltrane – a most gentle and courteous man – has refused to see visitors.
>
> He has also cancelled his trip to Europe including a concert and TV in Britain scheduled for next month.[38]

He was universally acclaimed as the leader and father figure of the new music. He was at the pinnacle of his career, and admired by the young musicians. His role as summarizer of all the schools of Black music, past and present, his deep emotionality, and the clean way of life he represented were inspiring to them.

Marion Brown, a prominent member of this group, was undergoing a difficult period in his life. He had made records but received little money from them. He had suffered through a bout of pneumonia and was confronted with the reality of poverty: "I was playing this concert, and when I finished a solo, I backed off-stage. There was Coltrane with the lights behind him, beatified. He held out his arms and took me in and I wept like a child. I'd been through so much, and held so much in, but I didn't cry until Coltrane told me it was alright."[3][9]

XV

Embrace

"Man, I finally got me one of these shorts. I got the money — so I treated myself," John said to Rashied as they drove around the city. Their relationship had just gotten to the point where they would hang out together, going from club to club, fruit stands and other places in New York. Folks heard about the new car: "Man, they tell me you got a Jaguar."

John: "Yea, man, this thing is like a toy to me. I just ride, man — like you do a new bicycle." Still John complained of the long ride from Huntington to the city and back. He planned to give his mother the house in Huntington, and to move to northern New Jersey, where it was easier to get to Manhattan.

It was early 1967. The group was playing the Vanguard. Among the friends John saw there were Rocky Boyd and Big George. He told Big George that he had "stomach trouble." George reassured him: "Aw, man — stomach trouble? You can get over that."

He told Rocky that he had to have an operation, adding mildly: "I'm afraid of it. I'm really afraid."

Rocky advised, "Get it out right away," and tried to console: "It won't hurt you, man. You got to have something done to it."

Khalid also noticed some changes in John. He was more distant and his eyes were wide open, as if with wonder. He wanted to talk even less than before. Khalid began speaking of colors he saw in the music, but John was insistent on speaking only of God. He was at one with the music which reflected the grace and expansiveness of his spirit.

With the help of his lawyer, Harold Lovette, John formed his own record company named Jowcol Recording Corporation. Under this label he recorded four forms: *Manifestation, Reverend King, Lord Help*

Me To Be, and *The Sun.* John played tenor sax and bass clarinet. Alice played piano; Jimmy Garrison was on bass. Pharoah Saunders was on tenor sax and flute. On drums were Rashied Ali and Ben Riley.

Manifestation is a highly energetic form which begins on a forcefully gyrating plane. With the rest of the band rising collectively, John shapes the energy with repeated low honks from his horn. On this record he creates a spatial effect in which one sound seems to be shallower, another deeper and still another purpled into an arch.

Alice plays a solo that is energetic, but relatively quieter. On the crest of her last note, John enters with a shock wave, a low maddening sound that sets off the freest excursions of the brain. *Manifestation* is a form that is overwhelming in its energy. Alice explained the title which was placed on the music: *"Manifestation* is God manifesting as strength and force throughout the Universe: cosmic energy – atomic, the primary substances composing matter and spirit."

Reverend King begins with tranquillity, and builds up to another form of tremendous energy. It begins with the incantation,

> A – um – ma – ni – pad – me – hum
> A – um – ma – ni – pad – me – hum
> A – um – ma – ni – pad – me – hum[1]

These sounds represent the seven breaths of man. John was inspired to create the form after reading an article on the great leader.

Alice created the two forms, *Lord Help Me To Be* and *The Sun*, on which John and Pharoah chant with feeling:

> May there be love and peace and perfection
> throughout all creation, oh God.[2]

Each time the incantation is said differently with emphasis on different words. The last time it is spoken softly, and John's voice breaks slightly on the last word, "God," in an expression of earnest prayer.

Recording at this time was also done on the Impulse label. John took the group into the studio more frequently than before, seemingly almost at whim. Four of these tapes are representative of a new phase of creativity that he was fashioning. February 15th *To Be* and *Offering* were recorded.

To Be is a widely spaced form which seems like rapidly moving but gentle winds and spirits slowly dancing. Pharoah plays piccolo; and there may be a Japanese influence in the tone John obtains from the flute. *Offering* begins with a plush sound of grace. It soars upward into lavish shapes.

On March 7th *Expression* and *Ogunde* were taped. *Ogunde* was named after a Nigerian musician who began a movement in that country of returning to the traditional African music. This was in contrast to the music which was directly from, or influenced by, Europe. The form *Ogunde* was lyrical and free. A true elasticity had been attained in the group. John could improvise in any direction with the others being flexible enough to move in the same direction. Often the others didn't know what he was going to play before he began.

Like a liquid molding around a turn, they would follow the strong feeling he set.

Expression is like obtaining entry into a garden of peace with green, thick ivy growing luxuriantly along the trees. The form has heavy wide sweeping gestures, twisted contortions, mixed with a brief falling into a high energy sphere. Alice solos like cascading waterfalls breaking into jewels   at   the   bottom;   after   which   John   reenters bizarre-scream-yelp-splitting wails with trembling like the wonderful confusion after being touched by the Creator.

On a trip into the city John ran into Big George, asking him:

"Do you know where Monk lives?"

"Yeah."

John: "Well, let's go up to Monk's house. I want to see him get dressed. Man, that's the funniest shit you've ever seen in your life, seeing that cat get ready to go to work."

They got to the door of the apartment where Monk lived, and rang the bell.

"Who is it?"

Answer: "Coltrane."

The buzzer made a loud noise, Braaannnng! and they walked in.

Monk wasn't home so his wife sent Thelonious Jr. to look for him. Usually Monk would be somewhere with a lot of people around him. He seemed to attract people the way Big Brown, a poet who frequented the nightclubs, and with a never-ending rap, would. Finally, John noticed that they had been waiting for an hour. He and George were about to walk out when the bell rang. Monk opened the door, saw John, and greeted him with:

"Coltrane!"

They grabbed and hugged each other. Monk, now happy, said to him: "Man, I got your picture on my piano. I was just looking at it today!" He took John over to the piano and showed him a vivid photograph of him and Alice from a Japanese magazine. Then, with Big George, the three went out on the terrace where a fog blanketed the air. John told Monk: "Man, I was just thinking about this music." Monk interrupted: "Aw, man, bad motherfucker like you. You shouldn't think – just play."

After conversing for a while, they returned to the apartment. It was time for Monk to get ready to go to work. As expected there was confusion before he left. He couldn't find his hat. Everyone looked frantically in the kitchen, the closets, the bedrooms. His wife was worried. Finally it was found – on the living room couch. Everyone sighed with relief.

After leaving Monk's apartment, Big George and John went to the Five Spot where Elvin was playing. It was a Thursday night, and the crowd and musicians were nonchalant. After John took a seat, whispers passed from mouth to ear to mouth – "Trane's in the audience." "Trane's in the audience." "Look, there's Trane sitting over there." Some who couldn't restrain themselves got up and walked across the room to get a better, though less discreet, look. The livened spirit of the audience began to show in the musicians. Elvin looked up and began bashing on the drums. More people began coming into the club and soon it was like a Saturday night in full swing.

Next they went to the Vanguard to see Monk. From there they went to the Pookie's Pub to see the bassist Charles Mingus and ended their tour at the Half Note where Max Roach was performing. That night, just as they were about to part, John said:

"Thanks, Big George."

"Thanks for what?"

He explained that he was thankful that George had encouraged him to go to the clubs and hear other musicians. He had been practicing at home so much that he rarely got to see others.

Olatunji, struggling with several factors that opposed his project, was finally at the point of opening his Center of African Culture on 125th Street in Harlem. He, John, and another musician, Yusef Lateef, had been discussing the promotion of their own concerts. They were dissatisfied with the flat rate they received while the promoter's earnings rose as the audience got larger.

Each agreed to jointly promote a concert. Olatunji was to be responsible for obtaining the concert hall and publicity. The program was to show the development of Black music from its roots in Africa to its present point. There was to be scenery, and the program was to be educational. Olatunji obtained Philharmonic Hall at Lincoln Center for March, 1968. It was booked up to that time. With money gained from this concert they planned to proceed with a continuing series in cities around the country. Also they agreed to accept the risks inherent in promotion, resolving not to stop if their concert was not successful financially.

The Center of African Culture opened in April. Olatunji asked John to play at the opening, which he did for scale, from $40 to $80 per man, donating the remainder to the school. April 23rd, the day of the opening, people were lined out into the street waiting for seats in the small space that the school had. Three hundred dollars was left over after the scale payment, which was donated to the school. On May 7th the group, with John, Alice, James Garrison, Rashied Ali and Donald Garrett on bass performed at the Left Bank Jazz Society in Baltimore. Time continued.

In June, 1967, Max Gordon, owner of the Village Vanguard, called John, asking if he were interested in playing there. He told Gordon that he was sorry, but that he was practicing new material which he didn't feel was ready for the public.

Word had filtered out to a few people that John was ill. Max Roach got the news and called John, suggesting that he see a Hindu healer named Majumdar. Majumdar had healed Abbey Lincoln, then Roach's wife, of an ovarian disease. Early in July Alice and John went to Majumdar's Manhattan apartment. John's mood was very low and Alice was alarmed. The meeting was only about 15 minutes. Majumdar, not realizing the gravity of the situation, advised breathing exercises, restriction to certain foods, and a return appointment, which was never kept.

Big George called, not having seen John for some weeks after their tour of the clubs in the city. Alice answered saying that he couldn't come to the phone but would call back. A few days later he called again. John picked up the phone.

His voice was different. It was obvious that he was in great pain. John said to him: "Yeah, man, the other day I was going to the doctor and the pain got so mean I had to come back in the house." John went on to speak of his plans to move to New Jersey so he could be closer to Manhattan. He wanted to give his mother the house in Huntington.

George offered to help him move. Then the conversation changed with John speaking with an edge to his voice: "Yeah, they're gone now, but they'll be back later on. They come and go." George thought he was speaking of Alice and the children, coming and going from the house.

The next day George called again. John sounded his usual self, relaxed. They spoke of health foods, with John suggesting: "If you want something to munch on, there's some stuff called soy beans. Man, it's like chicken, roast beef and all of them!"

At home he would lie for hours on the couch, listening to tapes of the music he recently created. He made furtive business calls concerning insurance and occasionally prefaced his conversations with Alice with phrases like, "If I ever play again . . . " and "If I have to leave you . . . "

He complained of being tired of working nightclubs and all the travels and discomfort involved with playing on the "circuit." His physician advised hospitalization for at least a year, but he refused. He had been ill for at least a year. No one knew why John had his hand over his right side in many of the photos Rashied took in Japan. By the next year, on Sunday June 16th, the symptoms from the liver cancer with which he suffered prevented him from even ingesting a bowl of soup. He walked in pain out the door of the house, got into the car with Alice and the children and drove in spite of his illness to the hospital. While lying in the hospital bed, he held Alice's hand, and asked:

"Are you ready for this?"

Newark was in turmoil. Riots, anger and death hung over the crying air. Imamu Baraka was taken off to jail, with his wife beside him carrying their child in her arms. The fog spread its cool blanket over the early morning. July 17th, 1967, John Coltrane was dead.

"I want to be the force which is truly for good."

Glass tunnels closed again while through them howled the stench of time. An evil spirit descended upon us. Crystal tapestry exploded into small daggers. Newark was aflame. Repression of our people was in Full Terror.

" . . . it is all with God. He is gracious and
merciful. His way is love."

Little children, reach for him.   They cannot. He is taken.

Pyramids, block the path.   Even we are powerless
                                             before the demon time.

His fingers barely touch ours.   His life struggles
                                                  within my water

We grasp, crying to caress his
love

            Our bodies shake for lack of hope

            Broken tears fall upon mercy's dry desert.

    Snakes and leopards peel from the ghetto walls. The sound of the
lash cracks in the countryside.

John, watch over us.   My love will always be with you.

Stars and planets feed him well.   We will. He is among
                                                    us now.

            But we see his body here, still too much asleep.
            He does not smile when our warmth touches him.
            We imagine that his lips, his eyelashes move,

                        we touch
                        we crumble.

FOOTNOTES

Chapter II

1. Simpkins, Alicia, "Little Boy on His Sailing Red Bike," copyright © 1975 Alicia Simpkins

Chapter III

1. Hines-Eckstine, "Jelly, Jelly" Advance Music Corp.

2. Dan, Barrelhouse, "No Place for Drum Solos in Jazz, Critic Claims" 9/15/40, page 11, copyright © *Down Beat.* Reprinted from *Down Beat* by special permission.

3. Cartoon with caption, "My Lips Still Giving Me Trouble," copyright © by *Down Beat.* Reprinted by special permission.

4. "The Golden Gates" gospel group "Religion Is A Fortune."

5. Much dissatisfaction exists with the term "Jazz" which originally was an obscenity used by whites in the 1890's for sperm. Those who created the music did not make the label it has gone by. Hence, this word is used only when absolutely necessary for historical clarity and in quotations of others.

Chapter IV

1. From "The Mananan" special issue of a Navy newspaper issued sometime between 1945 and 1946. Edwin Simmons, Editor-in-Chief.

2. "I'm A Big Fat Mama" *Negro Workaday Songs*, North Carolina Press, Chapel Hill, North Carolina.

3. Dizzie Gillespie Quartet, singer, "Rubber Legs" Williams; Dizzy Gillespie, trumpet; Charlie Parker, alto saxophone; Lucky Thompson, tenor saxophone; Tiny Grimes, guitar; Red Callender, bass; Sid Catlett or Kenny Clarke, drums. Dial records, later Savoy records, 1945. Thanks to Richard Freniere for making me aware of this record.

4. Russell, Ross, "Jazz Style in Kansas City and the Southwest," University of California Press, Berkeley, Los Angeles, London 1971, p. 32.

5. Ibid, p. 40.

6. Shapiro and Hentoff, "Hear Me Talkin' to Ya," Holt, Rinehart, and Winston, Inc. New York hardbound edition, p. 355.

7. Reisner, Robert, "The Legend of Charlie Parker" interview with Tommy Douglass Citadel Press New York 1962.

8. Ibid. Interview with Gene Ramey.

9. Gazzaway, Don, "Butler and Bird," *Jazz Review*, 2/60.

10. The term "changes" refers to a sequence of chords such as E-minor seventh, to G-flat major, to B-flat major, etc.

11. Ellison, Ralph, "Shadow and Hot" Random House Inc. Alfred A. Knopf Inc. New York, p. 225.

12. Gitler, Ira, "Jazz Masters of the Forties," MacMillan Co., 1966, p. 20.

13. See Appendix for the characteristics of this change in the music. I am deeply indebted to the material in *Jazz Style in Kansas City and the Southwest* and *Music: Black, White and Blue* by Ross Russell and Ortiz M. Walton, respectively, for this analysis. I am also thankful to pianist-composer Bob Neloms for writing the example shown of codified chord progressions.

14. This arrangement of words is intended to liberate each word in space so that they may be read in a variety of ways — horizontally, zig zag, vertically, circularly, etc. By this means, a variety of emotional amplifications of the conscious emotional input can be obtained. These amplifications are also dependent upon the feelings of the reader.

15. Coltrane, John, "Coltrane on Coltrane," 9/29/60, pp. 26-27, copyright © by *Down Beat*. Reprinted by special permission.

16. Ibid. There are slight differences from the published version due to the fact that this material was taken from the rough draft used courtesy of Naima Coltrane.

Chapter V

1. Coltrane, John, *Down Beat* version, op. cit.

2. The double diminished scale consists of alternating whole and half steps. For example, beginning with C one goes up a whole step to D then a half step to E-flat, a whole step to F, a half step to F-sharp, etc. until you reach C an octave higher.

3. Article probably from the *Philadelphia Tribune* late 1940's.

4. Shapiro and Hentoff (eds.) "The Jazz Makers," Holt, Rinehart, and Winston Inc. 1957, p. 208.

5. Lomax, Alan and Abdul, Raoul (eds.) "3,000 years of Black Poetry" Fawcett Publications Inc. Greenwich, Conn. 1970, pp. 61-62. Permission graciously granted by Abdul Raoul.

6. Blume, August, "An Interview with John Coltrane," *Jazz Review*, 1/59, p. 25.

7. Gardner, Barbara "Jazzman of the Year: John Coltrane" *Music*. A special issue of *Down Beat* 1962, pp. 66-69. Copyright © by *Down Beat*.

8. Gitler, Ira, "Trane on the Track," *Down Beat*, 10/16/58, pp. 16, 17, copyright © by *Down Beat*.

9. Ibid.

10. Ibid.

11. Ibid.

12. Ibid.

13. These women's names have been changed.

Chapter VI

1. Gitler, Ira, "Trane on the Track," op. cit.

2. Coltrane, John, *Down Beat* version op. cit.

3. Hentoff, Nat, record review, *Down Beat* 10/6/54, p. 12, copyright © by *Down Beat*. Reprinted by special permission.

4. Gitler, Ira, "Trane on the Track," op. cit.

5. Blume, August, op. cit.

6. Gitler, Ira, op. cit.

7. Gardner, Barbara, *Music*, op. cit.

8. Hentoff, Nat, record review, *Down Beat*, 5/16/56, p. 26, copyright © by *Down Beat*. Reprinted by special permission.

9. Gleason, Ralph, record review, *Down Beat*, 1/14/56, p. 26, copyright © by *Down Beat*. Reprinted by special permission.

10. Hentoff, Nat, record review, *Down Beat*, 11/14/56, p. 28, copyright © by *Down Beat*.

11. Hentoff, Nat, record review, *Down Beat,* 12/12/56, p. 39, copyright © by *Down Beat*.

Chapter VII

1. Coltrane, John, rough draft, op. cit.

2. One of the devices that came from investigation of chord progressions was used to create the later composition, *Countdown*, in which a formula was superimposed on the Miles Davis composition, *Tune Up*. *Tune Up* is essentially a series of II-V-I changes.

$$/ E^{-7} / A^7 / D^\triangle /$$
$$/ D^{-7} / G^7 / C^\triangle /$$
$$/ C^{-7} / F^7 / B^{b\triangle} /$$

The formula consisted of starting at, for example, E going up a halftone to F, then proceeding in alternating 2½ and 1½ steps until you get to A and then to D. Hence, E-diminished 7th to A-seventh to D becomes,

$$E^{-7} \ F^7 / B^{b\triangle} \ D^{b7} / G^{b\triangle} \ A^7 / D^\triangle /$$

and the remainder becomes,

$$D^{-7} E^{b7} / A^{b\triangle} B^7 / E^\triangle G^7 / C^\triangle /$$
$$C^{-7} D^{b7} / G^{b\triangle} \ A^7 / D^\triangle \ F^7 / B^{b\triangle} /$$

At the end of this sequence John added,

$$E^{-7} / F^7 / B^{b\triangle} / E^{b7} /$$

Putting it all together *Tune Up* with few chords becomes the structure below with four chords added to each set of III-V-I's.

$$E^{-7} F^7 / B^{b\triangle} \ D^{b7} / G^{b\triangle} \ A^7 / D^\triangle /$$
$$D^{-7} E^{b7} / A^{b\triangle} B^7 / E^\triangle G^7 / C^\triangle /$$
$$C^{-7} D^{b7} / G^{b\triangle} \ A^7 / D^\triangle \ F^7 / B^{b\triangle} /$$
$$E^{-7} / F^7 / B^{b\triangle} / E^{b7} /$$

This formula can fit onto any set of II-V-I changes. This is one of three such devices known to this author which John developed for going from one harmonic point to another. A concentrated search should be made for other such formulae.

3. Hentoff, Nat, record review 4/18/57, p. 28 copyright © by *Down Beat*. Reprinted by special permission.

4. Ibid. P. 30.

5. Gleason, Ralph, record review, 5/16/57, p. 22, copyright © by *Down Beat*.

6. Blume, August, op. cit.

7. Al Heath's name is now Kuumba, which in Swahili means creativity.

8. Blume, August, op. cit.

9. Ibid.

10. Coltrane, John, *Down Beat*, op. cit.

11. This name has been changed.

12. Coltrane, John, *Down Beat*, op. cit.

13. Ceruli, Dom, record review, 12/26/57, p. 39. Copyright © *Down Beat*. Reprinted from *Down Beat* by special permission.

Chapter VIII

1. Coltrane, John, *Down Beat*, op. cit.

2. Coltrane, John, rough draft, op. cit.

3. Ibid.

4. From Liner Notes *Giant Steps* by permission Atlantic Records.

5. Record Review, *Metronome*, 1/58, p. 20.

6. Record Review, *Metronome*, 2/58, p. 34.

7. Gold, Don, record review *Down Beat*, 1/23/58, p. 20, copyright © by *Down Beat*. Reprinted from *Down Beat* by special permission.

8. Tynan, John, record review, *Down Beat*, 4/3/58, p. 24, copyright © by *Down Beat*.

9. Gold, Don, record review, *Down Beat*, 5/15/58, p. 24, copyright ©by *Down Beat*.

10. Review of Newport Jazz Festival, *Down Beat*, 8/7/58, p. 16, copyright © by *Down Beat*.

11. Ceruli, Dom, record review, *Down Beat*, 1/11/58, p. 36, copyright © *Down Beat*. Reprinted from *Down Beat* by special permission.

12. ? Cleveland ? newspaper, 12/27/58.

13. Gitler, Ira, "Trane on the Track," op. cit.

Chapter IX

1. From liner notes *Giant Steps* by permission Atlantic Records.

2. Ibid.

3. From original workbook of John Coltrane. Many thanks to Naima Coltrane.

4. Structure of *Countdown* explained in previous footnote, Chapter 7, no. 2.

5. From liner notes of *Giant Steps* used by permission Atlantic Records.

6. Ibid.

7. Ibid.

8. Oakland *Tribune* 6/4/59.

9. Ibid. 6/14/59.

10. "Caught in the Act," *Down Beat*, 8/6/59, p. 14, *Down Beat*, copyright © by *Down Beat*.

11. Carno, Zita, "The Style of John Coltrane," Part I, 10/59, pp. 17-21. Part II, 11/59, pp. 13-17 *Jazz Review* used with the gracious permission of Miss Zita Carno.

12. Carno, Zita, "The Style of John Coltrane, Part I, 10/59, pp. 17-21. Part II, 11/59, pp. 13-17, *Jazz Review* used with the gracious permission of Miss Zita Carno.

13. Ra, Sun, "The Potential," from liner notes of album "Sun Ra" used courtesy Sun Ra and kind permission of Saturn Records, copyright © 1965.

14. *Solaristic Precepts*, courtesy Sun Ra and with the help of Pat Patrick.

15. "Finally Made," *Newsweek* magazine, 7/24/61, p. 64, copyright © Newsweek, Inc. 1961. Reprinted by permission.

16. Actual signature of Ornette Coleman used with his kind permission.

17. Spellman, A. B., "Black Music," Schoeken Books, New York, p. 84.

18. Ibid, p. 123-124.

19. Ibid, p. 81.

20. Interview with George Russell, *Down Beat*, 5/29/58, p. 15, copyright © by *Down Beat*.

Chapter X

1. Record review of *Giant Steps*, Oakland *Tribune*.

2. "Trane Stops in the Gallery," *Sunday News*, 5/15/60.

3. Dance, Stanley, "Tyner Talk," *Down Beat*, 10/24/63, pp. 18-19, copyright © *Down Beat*. Reprinted by special permission.

4. From liner notes of *Coltrane Live at Birdland*, Impulse Records.

5. Pages from workbook of John Coltrane with gracious permission of Naima Coltrane.

6. Coltrane, John, rough draft, op. cit.

7. Dance, Stanley, op. cit.

8. Liner notes, *Coltrane Live at the Village Vanguard*, Impulse Records.

9. Coltrane, John, *Down Beat*, op. cit.

10. Coltrane, John, rough draft, op. cit.

11. Ibid.

12. Ibid.

13. Ibid.

14. Coltrane, John, *Down Beat*, op. cit.

15. Coltrane, John, rough draft, op. cit.

16. Letter, courtesy Naima Coltrane.

17. Postcard, courtesy Naima Coltrane.

18. From liner notes *Live at the Village Vanguard*, Impulse Records.

Chapter XI

1. Dance, Stanley, op. cit.

2. Liner notes *Ole Coltrane*, permission Atlantic Records.

3. Gardner, Barbara, op. cit.

4. Liner notes *Africa Brass*, Impulse Records.

5. Ibid.

6. Ibid.

7. Ibid.

8. Ibid.

9. "Finally Made," *Newsweek* magazine, 7/24/61, p. 64, copyright ©
   Newsweek, Inc. 1961. Reprinted by permission.

10. *Black Creation*, Fall 1972, p. 23 [Institute of Afro-American Affairs at
    N.Y.U., N.Y., N.Y.].

11. *Variety Magazine*, 7/26/61, p. 55. Used by permission *Variety Magazine*.

12. DeMicheal, Don, "John Coltrane and Eric Dolphy Answer the Jazz Critics,"
    Down Beat, 4/12/62, p. 20, copyright © *Down Beat* 1962. Reprinted by
    special permission.

13. Ibid.

14. Liner notes, *Live at the Village Vanguard*, Impulse Records.

15. Ibid.

16. Ibid.

17. Ibid.

18. Tynan, John, *Down Beat*, 11/23/61, p. 40, copyright © by *Down Beat.*

19. Dawbarn, Bob, *Melody Maker*, 11/18/61, p. 15.

20. Ibid.

21. From liner notes, *Live at the Village Vanguard Again*, Impulse Records.

22. Garland, Phyl, "The Sound of Soul," p. 188, H. Regenery Co.

23. Williams, Martin, record review, p. 30, *Down Beat*, 1/18/62, copyright © by
    Down Beat.

24. Courtesy Naima Coltrane.

25. ? *The News* ?, a California paper, 3/29/62.

26. DeMicheal, Don, *Down Beat*, op. cit.

27. Rough draft of above *Down Beat* article courtesy Naima Coltrane.

28. Letter courtesy George Russell "Big George" (not the musician) and Naima
    Coltrane.

29. Gitler, Ira and Welding, Pete, record reviews, *Down Beat*, p. 29.

30. Courtesy Naima Coltrane.

31. "Bob Thiele Talks to Frank Kofsky about John Coltrane," CODA
    Publications, 5/68, pp. 3-10, Canada. Reprinted permission CODA
    Publications.

32. Ibid.

33. Kofsky, Frank "Interviews with John Coltrane," p. 224-243, copyright © 1970 by Pathfinder Press, Inc., reprinted by permission of Pathfinder Press, Inc.

34. "Bob Thiele Talks to Frank Kofsky about John Coltrane," CODA, op. cit.

35. Kofsky, Frank, op. cit.

Chapter XII

1. From postcard containing this quotation courtesy Naima Coltrane.

2. Source not known.

3. *The Digo Wedding Dance* recorded late 30's before **WW II** by Arch Oboler in Kenya. Many thanks to Richard Freniere who has this record in his private collection.

4. *Melody Maker*, 9/28/63, p. 11.

5. Interview with Albert Ayler, *Down Beat*, 11/17/66, p. 17, copyright © by *Down Beat*. Reprinted by special permission.

6. Ibid.

7. CODA, op. cit.

8. Kofsky, Frank, op. cit.

9. *Down Beat*, 8/27/64, p. 13, copyright © by *Down Beat*.

10. *Melody Maker*, 7/11/64, p. 6.

11. Liner notes *Love Supreme*, Impulse Records.

Chapter XIV

1. *Melody Maker*, 12/19/64, p. 6.

2. Mathieu, Bill, record review, p. 25, *Down Beat*, 4/9/64, copyright © by *Down Beat*.

3. Sinclair, John, record review, *Jazz*, 9/64, pp. 16, 17.

4. From liner notes of *Infinity*, Impulse Records.

5. Liner notes of *Kula Se Mama*, Impulse Records.

6. Ibid.

7.   Liner notes from *Ascension*, Impulse Records.

8.   `Ielody Maker*, 7/31/65, p. 10.

9.   Ibid. 8/14/65, p. 6.

10.   Liner notes, *Om*, Impulse Records.

11.   Liner notes *Live at the Village Vanguard Again*, Impulse Records.

12.   Liner notes *Meditations*, Impulse Records.

13.   Part of incantation from the recording of *Om*, Impulse Records.

14.   Liner notes *Om*, Impulse Records.

15.   Ibid.

16.   Liner notes *Kulu Se Mama*, Impulse Records.

17.   Spellman, A. B., "Trane — A Wild Night at the Gate," *Down Beat*, 12/30/65, pp. 15, 44, copyright © *Down Beat*. Reprinted by special permission.

18.   Liner notes *Live at the Village Vanguard Again*, Impulse Records.

19.   Liner notes *Meditations*, Impulse Records.

20.   Ibid.

21.   *Variety Magazine*, 3/16/66, p. 65. Reprinted permission *Variety Magazine*.

22.   Garland, Phyl, op. cit.

23.   "Jazz and Pop," 9/68, pp. 123-124.

24.   *Essence* magazine, 12/71, p. 42.

25.   Garland, Phyl, op. cit.

26.   "Jazz and Pop," 9/68, pp. 123-124.

27.   *Live at the Village Vanguard Again*, op. cit.

28.   *Melody Maker*, 4/16/66, p. 6.

29.   *Meditations*, op. cit.

30.   *Melody Maker*, 4/16/66, p. 6.

31.   *Live at the Village Vanguard Again*, op. cit.

32.   *Live at the Village Vanguard Again*, op. cit.

33. Kofsky, Frank, op. cit.

34. Garland, Phyl, op. cit.

35. *Newsweek*, 12/12/66, p. 108, copyright © Newsweek, Inc., 1966. Reprinted by permission.

36. Garland, Phyl, op. cit.

37. *Newsweek*, 12/12/66, p. 108, copyright © Newsweek, Inc. 1966. Reprinted by permission.

38. *Melody Maker*, 11/15/66, p. 8.

39. *Newsweek*, 12/12/66, p. 108, copyright © Newsweek, Inc., 1966. Reprinted by permission.

Chapter XV

1. Liner notes *Cosmic Music*, Impulse Records.

2. Liner notes *Cosmic Music*, Impulse Records.

INDEPENDENT PRODUCERS

This page is dedicated to informing the public of some of the organizations which make products that are of benefit to the spiritual health of people.

African Economic Council, 1 West 131st Street, Harlem, New York 10037, Telephone: 368-1283

    Products: 1. Im-Hotep Records — Titles include: "The Sahel Concert" at Town Hall; "The Black Bill of Rights"; "Ethnic Expressions" - Roy Brooks and the Artistic Truth live at Small's Paradise, New York City, featuring Eddie Jefferson and Black Rose; "The Black Queen of Beauty"; "The Black Soldiers."

    2. Black Glory Publishing and Printing Corp. — 16 books and magazines of suppressed and long-forgotten research on the African world.

    3. Carver Food Association

    4. Grandassa Food Market Inc.

Directors: James E. Davis, Robert Harris

Cosmic Music: A Black Music Magazine, 1944 Madison Ave., Harlem 10035
(First issue devoted to John Coltrane.)

George Edward Tait - Publisher and Editor

Cynthia Hackette - Executive Secretary

Impressions Magazine: A Black Arts and Culture Magazine, Lincolnton Station Drawer Z, 2266 Fifth Ave., New York, N.Y. 10037, Telephone: 862-2326.

Robert Bryan, Publisher

B. J. Ashanti, Literary Editor

Musical Dimensions, 289 Utica Ave., Brooklyn, N.Y. Telephone: 773-8423
    Purpose: to develop the talents of our young in the arts.
    Credo: "Music is the best tool to educate our young and to fight our enemies."

Don Echoles, Director

Nok Publishers, 150 Fifth Ave., Suite 1103, New York, N.Y. 10011. Telephone: 989-2506
    Titles: "Anatomy of An African Kingdom"; "British Administration in Nigeria"; "Guardians of the Sacred Word" (poetry); "King JaJa of the Niger Delta."

Che Ude, Editorial Director

Triumph Record Company, 772 West End Avenue, New York, N.Y. 10025.
    "Sounds of Togetherness" music group

Jothin Collins, Director

Ujamaa Records, Box 5048, FDR Station, New York, N.Y. 10022. Telephone: 427-8811
    Album Title: "Ted Daniel Sextet"

Ted Daniel, Director

Olatunji's Center for African Culture, 43 E. 125th Street, New York, N.Y. 10027. Telephone: 427-5757
    Instruction in African music, languages, dance.

Michael Olatunji, Director

Appendices

Developments in Music
Brought About in the 40's

1.   On every instrument, a lighter and more luminous sound than before, with less vibrato (letting a note waver as a singer's voice will often do).

2.   More complex rhythms (polyrhythms) — in part a product of the Kansas City idea of setting riffs (melodic or rhythmic figures) behind jazz solos. Instead of a big bass drum, a smaller one with a tighter well defined sound same into use. The feeling of the drums was more up as if the beat were rising under a soloist instead of pushing along with him. This use of rhythm was present in the Basie and other Kansas City bands. In its final development the basic beat was maintained on the cymbals and the bass drum was used freely to accentuate emotional high points.

3.   A new approach to harmony with free use of passing tones; experiments in modulation to unrelated keys and the establishment of the flatted fifth.

4.   Substantially extended solo lines that dispensed with the well defined sections of time to which phrases had previously been confined.

5.   New levels of instrumental virtuosity.

6.   Use of only five to seven pieces instead of the previous large orchestra.

7.   Utilization of progressions from already existing compositions to derive a melody different from the original. Thus a popular song of the forties such as *How High the Moon* became *Ornithology* and *What Is This Thing Called Love?* became *Hot House*.

8.   Development of an ingenious code system in which an entire composition occupied only a few lines of paper. This code consisted of symbols representing chords along with symbols for the amount of time to be given each chord. The system replaced the long arrangements or sheet music that had been used previously. Below is an example of this code written by Bob Neloms, pianist-composer.

[Points 1 - 6 above from "Jazz Style in Kansas City in the Southwest" by Ross Russell, University of California Press, Berkeley, Los Angeles, London, 1971. Points 7 - 8 from "Music: Black White and Blue" by Ortiz Walton, W. Manor, N.Y., 1972.

Dear "Nut",

I hope you like
These Photos.
This one is was
Taken From The American
Side about 2 Blocks
From The Club we
are working in.

John

GENUINE REPRODUCTION FROM KODACHROME ORIGINAL IN CURTEICHCOLOR

PROSPECT POINT

GENUINE CURTEICH-CHICAGO "CURTEICHCOLOR" GIANT POST CARD (REG. U. S. PAT. OFF.)

PANORAMIC
POST CARD
OF NIAGARA FALLS

Miss Juanita Austin
1816 N. 7th St.
Phila. Pa.

From *Jazz Review*
Jan. 1959, p. 34

Good Bait finds Trane rocking and bouncing in a dancer's groove. He is a shouter, indeed at times a screamer. The intensity of feeling is hot and one's foot is apt to start tapping. Red Garland lays down some petunia-scented chords loaded with tension, heat and song which have the effect of bringing everyone closer together and in his solo he delights the ears with a few dazzling figures employing most of the keyboard, lines that contain a rhythmic vitality and a blinked slyness. After Paul's solo we have a section of fours, notable for Trane's hot return, making two statements which are happy hair raisers.

The ballad, *I Want to Talk About You*, is realized in Trane's particularly haunted way. His ballad approach in general is one in which the realities of the day assert themselves — he is detached, dry, melancholy, fearful and yearning.

Devices such as tremolo and rubato can be interesting depending on the ingenuity of the person playing. If the tremolos lack interesting harmonic implications, the result is a throwback to silent movie days or the piano roll. If the rubatos are pompous and devoid of all musical life (which would come from interesting sounds and rhythms culminating in a logical musical thought) then they are lies because they have no basis in reality.

During the second and third chorus of Coltrane's improvisations on the attractive *You Say You Care*, the group attains a good group feeling (all the players support Trane, attaining an intensity that complements his playing.). The selection of this tune demonstrates another facet of Trane's ability, the ability to see unfamiliar material and turn it into a forceful jazz expression. This is one way of gauging his musical ability and is also additional evidence of his stature in relation to the rest of the field. *Russian Lullaby* is taken at a jet's tempo with Paul Chambers playing in an even rockbottom way which anchors the rhythm section and makes it easier for Coltrane to fly.

Coltrane at times seems to play away from everyone rhythmically, and yet his line has a time that is angular and evil and laden with its own rhythm. His playing sometimes becomes a mirror of the past reminding one of the precision of Benny Carter, Stitt, and Gordon of the late 40s, with the texture of Pres. His interval conception is a whole one as he utilizes large and small intervals. He used the entire range of his horn. In ballads, he ventures into areas of sound that are uncommon. One is reminded of Hodges, his security of tone in the higher registers. Also, the vocal feeling of Eckstine and Sarah. In his blues playing there is Bird as well as Rollins. In short his expression is a beautiful and meaningful one. His education and experience come out of his associations with men like Hodges, Gillespie, Miles and Monk.

His own ability, his perception and wisdom show themselves in his own compositions, the organization sound-wise in such pieces as *Training In, Straight*

Street, etc. In short, his tone is beautiful because it is functional. In other words, it is always involved in saying something. You can't separate the means that a man uses to say something from what he ultimately says. Technique is not separate from its content in a great artist.

—Cecil Taylor

From *Jazz Review*
Jan. 1959, p. 34

Side 1: *Dr. Jekyl*, while not especially melodic, gives the group an excellent opportunity to "stretch out." The eights and fours between Miles and Philly Joe Jones are fiery and invigorating. Paul Chambers, in spite of the fast tempo, takes a soulful solo. The exchange of choruses between Coltrane and Cannonball is the high point of the track, and the rhythm section is very stable throughout.

Sid's Ahead is, in reality, the old, and now classic, *Walkin'*. During his solo, Coltrane is very clever and creative in his handling of the substitute chords. Miles strolls (without piano) beautifully. He is a true musical conversationalist. Cannonball is quite "funky" at times, and Chambers exemplifies his ability to create solo lines in the manner of a trumpeter or saxophonist.

The third track, *Two Bass Hit*, opens with everyone on fire – particularly Philly, whose punctuation and attack are as sharp as a knife. Coltrane enters into his solo moaning, screaming, squeezing, and seemingly projecting his very soul through the bell of his horn. I feel that this man is definitely blazing a new musical trail. Philly and Red Garland back the soloists like a brass section, an effect which always creates excitement.

Side 2: The theme of *Milestones* is unusual, but surprisingly pleasant – particularly the bridge where Miles answers the other horns, achieving an echo effect. Philly's use of sticks on the fourth beat of every bar is quite tasteful. Cannonball cleverly interweaves melodies around the changes. Miles is as graceful as a swan, and Coltrane is, as usual, full of surprises.

Red Garland, who is undoubtedly one of today's great pianists, is spotlighted in *Billy Boy* with Philly and Paul. The arrangement is tightly knit and well played. Red employs his block chord technique on this track and plays a beautiful single line, as well. Philly and Paul do a wonderful job, both soloing and in the section.

Straight No Chaser is a revival of a Thelonious Monk composition of a few years ago – the spasmatic harmony makes it quite interesting. Cannonball is excellent on this track. I may be wrong, but he seems to have been influenced somewhat by Coltrane. Miles paints a beautiful picture, as surely as with an artist's brush. He has a sound psychological approach in that he never plays too much. He leaves me, always, wanting to hear more.

I have heard no one, lately, who creates like Coltrane. On this track, he is almost savage in his apparent desire to play his horn thoroughly.

Red plays a single line solo with his left hand accompanying off the beat. He closes the solo with a beautiful harmonization of Miles' original solo on *Now's The Time*. Here, Philly goes into a subtle 1-2-3-4 beat on the snare drum behind Red's solo, setting it off perfectly. This is the best track of the album.

In closing, I'd like to say – keep one eye on the world and the other on John Coltrane.

– Benny Golson

"The Style of John Coltrane" from *Jazz Review* October and November, 1959, pp. 17 - 21 and pp. 13 - 17, respectively. Written by Zita Carno and used with her kind permission.

Part 1

. . . Benny Golson, and to a lesser extent, Hank Mobley and Junior Cook, have been most strongly affected. Especially interesting is Golson because until recently he sounded like a cross between Lucky Thompson and Coleman Hawkins, with other elements thrown in. Such a complete switch as this is as clear an indication as any of Coltrane's influence. Cannonball Adderley is by now classic proof that you can't play with Coltrane without being influenced by him. Even Miles Davis and Horace Silver have picked up a few things from him and have been working around with them.

Just what is it he's doing that has such an effect?

A lot of people may be moved to think of Charlie Parker as the widespread influence. Everyone tried to imitate him as much as possible, to sound as nearly a carbon copy of him as they could – which was only natural when you consider that he revolutionized jazz.

But what Coltrane has been doing is to get the ones he has influenced into the "hard" groove and then stimulate them to think for themselves, to work out ideas of their own within the framework of this style. For one there's Wayne Shorter, a tenor man from New Jersey whose style is as close to Coltrane's as any, yet doesn't sound like his.

Coltrane's style is many-faceted. There are many things to watch for in his playing, and the fact that he is constantly experimenting, always working out something new – on and off the stand – leads to the conclusion that no matter how well you may think you know what he's doing, he will always surprise you.

To begin my discussion of the various aspects of Coltrane's playing, I would like to elaborate a bit on the remarks I made above concerning the failure of listeners to find anything "familiar" – any cliches – in his solos.

He does have a few pet phrases that he will use in his solos. But you could hardly refer to them as cliches. They are his own, and he never even plays them exactly the same way twice. True, I have heard other instrumentalists – tenor men, trumpeters – pick them up and try to play them, but there is a certain inflection in the way he plays these phrases that no one could ever hope to duplicate.

Perhaps the most familiar of these phrases is the one shown in Example 1a.

But very often he will employ it sequentially in the course of building up a solo (or reaching the climax of one), and he is an expert in the subtle use of sequences for this purpose. Notice what he does with that same phrase towards the end of his solo on *Bass Blues*, Example 1b. Notice how he alters the phrasing. You will find the same sort of thing in tracks like *Straight No Chaser* and *Soft Lights and Sweet Music*.

Another phrase that recurs frequently in his playing is this one, which undergoes even more alterations: Example 2a gives it in a portion of his solo on *Blue Train*. Example 2b shows what happens to that same phrase at the beginning of his second chorus on *Bakai*.

Before I go any further, I would like to discuss a most controversial aspect of Coltrane's playing: his technique. It is an excellent one – one of the finest. His command of the instrument is almost unbelievable. Tempos don't faze him in the least; his control enables him to handle a very slow ballad without having to resort to the double-timing so common among hard blowers, and for him there is no such thing as too fast a tempo. His playing is very clean and accurate, and he almost never misses a note.

His range is something to marvel at: a full three octaves upward from the lowest note obtainable on the horn (concert A-flat). Now, there are a good many tenor players who have an extensive range, but what sets Coltrane apart from the rest of them is the equality of strength in all registers which he has been able to obtain through long, hard practice. His sound is just as clear, full and unforced in the topmost notes as it is down at the bottom.

That tone of his, by the way has been, and doubtless will continue to be, a subject of debate. A result of the particular combination of mouthpiece and reed he uses plus an extremely tight embouchure, it is an incredibly powerful, resonant and sharply penetrating sound with a spine-chilling quality. There are many who argue that it is not a "good" saxophone sound. Exactly what is a good saxophone sound? Are we to go along with those who hold that the only really good sound is of the Lester Young or of the Coleman Hawkins variety and therefore assume that none of the younger "hard" tenor players has a "good" sound? Lester Young's sound suited Lester Young, and Coleman Hawkins' sound is great for Coleman Hawkins. A sound is good if it suits the player's style and conception. So it is with Coltrane.

A word about his intonation. Those listeners who say that he doesn't play in tune have been deceived by that sharp edge in his sound. Of course, I don't mean to imply that his horn is immune to weather changes – no instrument is. And there are days when he has some intonation difficulties. But he plays in tune.

I mention all these things because they have a direct connection with a good

opied by pianist Lillette Jenkins

Note: The division in the first two measures is an arbitrary one. It is almost impossible to divide such a phrase into groups of so many notes here and so many notes there really accurately because of the speed of the playing.

many things that Coltrane does. A technique like his seems essential to his approach, as we shall see.

There is far more to Coltrane's style than "hard drive." Hard drive is only one aspect of it, and even then it is an entirely different kind from that of, say, Sonny Rollins. Coltrane seems to have the power to pull listeners right out of their chairs. I have noticed this terrific impact on the various rhythm sections he has played with; he pulls them right along with him and makes them cook too. An interesting phenomenon is what happens to rhythm sections when Coltrane takes over from another soloist. Say Miles Davis is the first soloist. Notice that the rhythm section doesn't push. They are relaxed behind him. Now Coltrane takes over, and immediately something happens to the group: the rhythm section tightens up and plays harder. The bass becomes stronger and more forceful, as does the ride-cymbal beat; even the pianist comps differently. They can't help it – Coltrane is driving them ahead. This is most noticeable on medium and up tempos where he is most likely to cut loose. (It would be most interesting to see what would happen to a typical West Coast rhythm section should they find themselves having to play behind him.)

Coltrane's kind of "funk" drives, rather than swings. And it is less obvious. Listen carefully to his solos on such tracks as *Blue Train* and *Bass Blues* and you will hear some excellent examples. But listen carefully, because it won't be as easy to spot as Horace Silver's kind. That solo on *Blue Train* is such a revealing example of so many facets of his style and conception that I will transcribe it in its entirety, with accompanying explanatory notes.

Coltrane's harmonic conception is perhaps the most puzzling aspect of his style, inasmuch as it is so advanced. For one thing, he really knows what to do with the changes of the tunes he plays. This is apparent not only in his playing, but also – as we shall see – in his writing. He knows when to stick with the basic changes and when to employ those unusual extensions and alterations that a lot of people refer to as "blowing out of the changes" because they don't quite hear just what he is doing. He is very subtle, often deceptive – but he's always right there.

An excellent insight into these harmonic devices of his can be found in that weird phenomenon which has been variously referred to as "sheets of sound," "ribbons of sound," "a gosh-awful lot of notes" and other things. These are very long phrases played at such an extremely rapid tempo that the notes he plays cease to be mere notes and fuse into a continuous flow of pure sound. Sometimes they do not come off the way he wants them to, and that is when the cry of "just scales" arises. That may be, but I dare anyone to play scales like this, with that irregular, often a-rhythmic phrasing, those variations of dynamics, and that fantastic sense of timing.

But more often they work out the way he wants them to, and then one hears things. There is an unbelievable emotional impact to them, plus a fantastic residual harmonic effect which often is so pronounced that in many instances the piano wouldn't be missed if it weren't playing. A perfect example of this occurs halfway through Coltrane's solo on *Gold Coast.* (Example 3)

The piano plays the changes behind this, but it seems that just drums and bass would be sufficient, because in this section the changes are right there, as you

Copied by pianist Lillette Jenkins

can see.

An example of implied changes occurs in the unaccompanied run he plays in the tag of *Russian Lullaby*. (Example 4) Look at the transcription carefully, and you will be able to pick out a definite chord progression. It is probably the one Coltrane had in mind.

Some fantastic things happen when he plays on blues changes, the most basic ones. Example 5 is his first two choruses on *Straight No Chaser*. The changes are regular blues in F. Keeping that in mind, notice the way Coltrane subtly plays all those extensions and alternations of the chords. It does seem at first as if he were "blowing out of the changes." Actually he is not. That is a very important part of Coltrane's harmonic concept: his awareness of the changes and what to do with them. The same sort of thing occurs with telling effect in the middle of his solo on *Blue Train* as we will see. You will also notice it in certain portions of his solo on *Bass Blues* if you listen carefully.

Coltrane's sense of form is another source of wonderment. He has very few equals at building up a solo, especially on a blues — and building up a good solo on a blues is not easy.

Part 2

There are a number of devices which Coltrane employs in building a solo which are by no means obvious, and which would take repeated hearings to spot. But once you know what they are, you will be able to understand more fully just how he goes about it.

One of them — and it shows up at once on *Blue Train* — is his little trick of building up on a single note (as in this case) or a short phrase, then taking off from there. It is personal with him, like so many of the things he does.

Another is his wonderful use of sequences — which I mentioned earlier in the end of his solo on *Bass Blues* wherein he employs one of his pet phrases this way. Another excellent illustration is his tag on *Locomotion*: (Example 6)

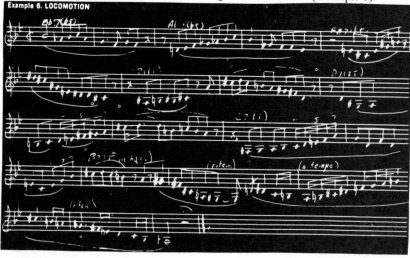

Example 6. LOCOMOTION

Example 7. BLUE TRAIN

C7 chord here
what I mean about harmonic
again building
if this ain't funk, what is it?
easing off in preparation for the entrance of the next soloist
here comes
one of these sequence

Coltrane has a way of starting his solos in the least expected places. What is more, he never does anything exactly the same way twice. He also has a peculiarly individual way of altering the phrasing, unlike anything ever heard before. It is almost impossible to describe it, but if you look back at Example 1b, in part one of this article, you will see something of it. It involves an extremely subtle shifting of accentuation (you'll see this also in Examples 2b, 4 and 5, as well as in the solo on *Blue Train*), which results in previous often a-rhythmic phrasing that will throw the unwary listener off the track.

At this point I am going to do what I said I'd do earlier — quote Coltrane's complete recorded solo on *Blue Train*, inasmuch as it is a perfect example of so many of the previously mentioned aspects of his style and a good blues solo.

The tune itself is a revealing sample of Coltrane's writing, being as direct and straightforward as his playing, and offering a tremendous insight into his overall conception. It is a most powerful blues line, brooding, mysterious, almost like an eerie chant; someone has remarked that it is more than just a blues, that it has other meanings in it. This is true of everything he does.

There are some unusual things about this solo.

For one thing, this recording was done during his tenure with Thelonious Monk, and here and there are isolated flashes of certain aspects of his current work — sort of a preview of things to come, as it were. I refer particularly to the "sheets of sound," which, it is interesting to note, is a spontaneous development.

This solo continues to build up all the way to the last chorus. It reaches its peak at the sixth chorus, where the other two horns come in with a riff (Example 7a) which repeats six times, and adds even more impetus. This constant building-up is a most striking feature of Coltrane's work, and has been apparent even from his earliest days with Miles Davis. Then, too, notice how he tends to stay in the high register of his horn. Well, he can be justly proud of that register. It is strong, clear and — in his hands — full of a terrific emotional impact.

He does one thing that is unusual in that it is difficult to do well: he slurs those long phrases all the way and plays them so clearly. There is ample evidence of how solid his technique is — that fluid, unerring finger action.

Lest you think that Coltrane's playing consists of cooking and more cooking, I'd like to say a few words about the way he handles slower tempos. I mentioned earlier in discussing various aspects of his technique, his fantastic control which enables him to play a ballad without having to double-time on it. But that control isn't all. Except for the fact that he is more intense, his ballad concept could be likened to that of Miles Davis. He has the same straightforward, thoughtful approach. And I'm not just talking about the classic *'Round Midnight* he did with Miles; there are plenty of other tracks which provide a fine demonstration of this kind of lyricism: his unusual interpretation of the seldom-done standard *While My Lady Sleeps*, for instance, or *Slow Dance*, to give two examples. They are object lessons in how to play a ballad without unnecessary "cooking."

That is Coltrane the instrumentalist — powerful, sensitive, ahead, and always experimenting. Now I'd like to talk a bit about Coltrane the jazz composer and arranger, inasmuch as it may throw still further light on certain other aspects of

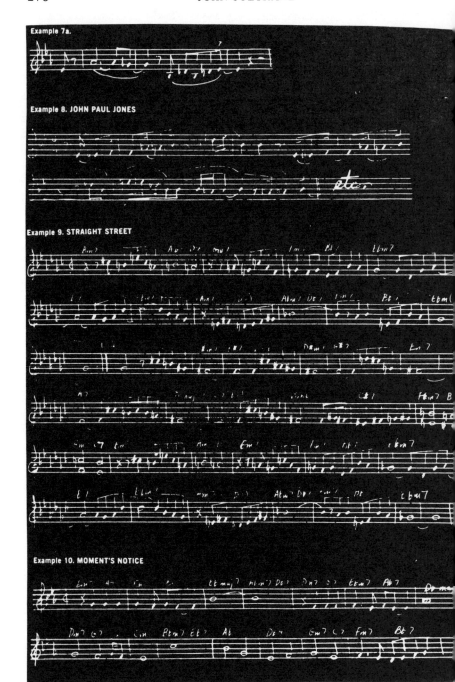

Example 7a.

Example 8. JOHN PAUL JONES

Example 9. STRAIGHT STREET

Example 10. MOMENT'S NOTICE

Example 11. LOCOMOTION

Example 12. WHILE MY LADY SLEEPS

(Tenor)

INTRO.

(Bass)

Notice the ostinato bass --very effective here.

etc.

Example 13. Intro to STAR EYES

Here is how it starts out. (again the ostinato bass.)

(Again the ostinato bass)

Here's what he does with it a descending line scored for three horns

(3 horns)

Unusual harmonic progression, isn't it? That's a fair example of what Coltrane does his conception.

Coltrane's writing may not be quite as familiar as his playing, except to his most avid followers. He is, like Horace Silver and Benny Golson, always experimenting with different structures and unusual chord progressions – but his writing is easily distinguishable from that of the other two.

For one thing, his melodic lines – blues or not – are all very powerful, direct and straightforward, with strong emotional impact. When he gets "funky" (the theme of *Blue Train* is a perfect example) it is, as I said earlier, hard, driving, intense – not like any other kind. Even *John Paul Jones*, which he composed a few years ago, could never be taken for a line by someone like Horace Silver, despite the fact that it is slower and more relaxed. (Example 8)

Among other tunes of this kind is one called *Straight Street*, which, although based on twelve-bar phrases, could never be mistaken for a blues. (Example 9)

The chord progression, by the way, is a characteristic one. If you look closely, you will notice that it is the old familiar II - V changes – with a twist not instantly noticeable. Of course, you know that it's this II - V business, because I told you so, and there it is in front of you. But if you were listening to it for the first time, you might notice only that the changes *seem* out of the ordinary. Coltrane handles this so cleverly that you don't realize just what it is. Another example of this occurs in *Moment's Notice*. Example 10 gives part of the introduction.

The deceptiveness that is part and parcel of Coltrane's writing also shows up in his blues *Locomotion*. The structure of this tune is not too unusual: 12 - 12 - 8 - 12 blues is now almost standard on the East Coast. But even here he has a little twist: he has each succeeding soloist take an unaccompanied eight-bar break before going into his solo.

But it is the rhythm of that eight-bar riff in the line itself that is really confusing. (Example 11)

You hear it on the recording, and it sounds as if the accented E-flat were on the first beat of the measure. As you can see, it isn't. (I was thrown off by it on the first couple of hearings, and I'm supposed to have a good ear!)

His approach to arranging is just as different as everything else he does. Very often what he does amounts to an almost complete reharmonization or reconstruction of a tune or part of it, and right there you get another view of his harmonic conception.

For instance, the first few bars of his arrangement of *While My Lady Sleeps*. (Example 12)

Another illustration of the reconstructive process he uses can be seen in what he does to the familiar Latin-beat introduction so often played on *Star Eyes*. (Example 13)

As I said in the first part of this series, the only thing to expact from John Coltrane is the unexpected.

Honest John
The Blindfold Test

By Leonard Feather

The *Blindfold Test* below is the first interview of its kind with John Coltrane. The reason is simple: though he has been a respected name among fellow musicians for a number of years, it is only in the last year or two that he has reached a substantial segment of the jazz-following public.

It is the general feeling that Coltrane ranks second only to Sonny Rollins as a new and constructive influence on his instrument. Coltrane's solo work is an example of that not uncommon phenomenon, an instrumental style that reflects a personality strikingly different from that of the man who plays it, for his slow, deliberate speaking voice and far-from-intense manner never would lead one to expect from the the cascades of phrases that constitute a typical Coltrane solo.

The records for his *Blindfold Test* were more or less paired off, the first a stereo item by a big band, the next two combo tracks by hard bop groups, the third pair bearing a reminder of two early tenor giants, and the final two sides products of miscellaneous combos. John was given no information before or during the test about the records played.

The Records

1.   Woody Herman. *Crazy Rhythm* (Everest Stereo). Paul Quinichette, tenor; Ralph Burns, arranger.

Well, I would give it three stars on the merit of the arrangement, which I thought was good. The solos were good, and the band played good. As to who it was, I don't know . . . The tenor sounded like Paul Quinichette, and I liked that because I like the melodic way he plays. The sound of the recording was very good. I'd like to make a guess about that arrangement — it sounded like the kind of writing Hefti does — maybe it was Basie's band.

2.   Art Farmer Quintet. *Max Nix* (United Artists). Benny Golson, tenor; Farmer, trumpet, composer, arranger; Bill Evans, piano; Addison Farmer, bass; Dave Bailey, drums.

That's a pretty lively sound. That tenor man could have been Benny Golson, and the trumpeter, I don't know . . . It sounded like Art Farmer a little bit.

I enjoyed the rhythm section — they got a nice feeling, but I don't know who they were. The composition was a minor blues — which is always good. The figures on it were pretty good, too. I would give it 3½.

3.   Horace Silver Quintet. *Soulville* (Blue Note). Silver, piano, composer; Hank Mobley, tenor; Art Farmer, trumpet.

Horace . . . Is that *Soulville*? I've heard that — I think I have the record. Horace gave me that piece of music some time ago . . . I asked him to give me some things that I might like to record and that was one of them. I've never got around to recording it yet, though. I like the piece tremendously — the composition is great. It has more in it than just "play the figure and then we all blow." It has a lot of imagination. The solos are all good . . . I think it's Hank Mobley and Art Farmer. I'll give that 4½ stars.

4.   Coleman Hawkins. *Chant* **(Riverside). Idrees Sulieman, trumpet; J.J.Johnson, trombone; Hank Jones, piano; Oscar Pettiford, bass.**

Well, the record had a genuine jazz feeling. It sounded like Coleman Hawkins . . . I think it was Clark Terry on trumpet, but I don't know. The 'bone was good, but I don't know who it was. I think the piano was very good . . . I'll venture one guess: Hank Jones. It sounded like Oscar Pettiford and was a very good bass solo. And Bean — he's one of the kind of guys — he played well, but I wanted to hear some more from him . . . I was expecting some more.

When I first started listening to jazz, I heard Lester Young before I heard Bean. When I *did* hear Hawkins, I appreciated him, but I didn't hear him as much as I did Lester . . . Maybe it was because all we were getting then was the Basie band.

I went through Lester Young and on to Charlie Parker, but after that I started listening to others — I listened to Bean and realized what a great influence *he* was on the people I'd been listening to. Three and a half.

5.   Ben Webster - Art Tatum. *Have You Met Miss Jones?* **(Verve).**

That must be Ben Webster, and the piano — I don't know. I thought it was Art Tatum . . . I don't know anybody else who plays like that, but still I was waiting for that thunderous thing from him, and it didn't come. Maybe he just didn't feel like it then.

The sound of that tenor . . . I wish he'd show *me* how to make a sound like that. I've got to call him up and talk to him! I'll give that four stars . . . I like the atmosphere of the record — the whole thing I got from it. What they do for the song is artistic, and it's a good tune.

6.   Toshiko. *Broadway* **(Metrojazz). Bobby Jaspar, tenor; Rene Thomas, guitar.**

You've got me guessing all the way down on this one, but's a good swinging side and lively. I thought at first the tenor was Zoot, and then I thought, no. If it isn't Zoot, I don't know who it could be. All the solos were good . . . The guitar player was pretty good. I'd give the record three stars on its liveliness and for the solos.

7.   Chet Baker. *Fair Weather* **(Riverside). Johnny Griffin, tenor; Benny Golson, composer.**

That was Johnny Griffin, and I didn't recognize anybody else. The writing sounded something like Benny Golson . . . I like the figure and that melody. The solos were good, but I don't know . . . Sometimes it's hard to interpret changes. I don't know whether it was taken from another song or if it was a song itself.

Maybe the guys could have worked it over a little longer and interpreted it a little truer. What I heard on the line as it was written, I didn't hear after the solos started . . . It was good, though — I would give it three stars, on the strength of the composition mostly, and the solos secondly . . . I didn't recognize the trumpeter.

(Copyright © Down Beat *reprinted from* Down Beat, *Feb. 19, 1959, page 39, by special permission.)*

Down Beat, March 31, 1960, p. 26

There seems to exist some feeling that John Coltrane, while granting him his importance as a major tenor influence, is a harsh-sounding player to whom it is difficult to listen. This LP, if it does nothing else, should dispel that idea quickly. There are times here when Coltrane is remarkably soft, lyrical and just plain pretty. For instance on *Naima*, which is an original as are all the tunes in the LP, JC starts out calling the title almost, on his horn (it's his wife's name, by the way) in a hauntingly beautiful passage. Then again at the end of the same tune, JC cries wistfully and poignantly on the horn. In *Syeeda's Song Flute* there's a throw-away phrase just before Tommy Flanagan's piano solo that is exquisite in its beauty.

Of course, the usual Coltrane forceful playing is present all over the album. The title song (which has echoes of *Tune Up*) is an example of this and so is *Countdown* which has a particularly intriguing tenor and drum duet in the front of the tune, as well as a great soaring ending.

Paul Chambers works particularly well with Coltrane and on the final track there is some hard digging by PC which is the kind of thing you put the arm back to over and over.

It is no wonder that JC is making such an impression on tenor players. He has managed to combine all the swing of Pres with the virility of Hawkins and added to it a highly individual, personal sound, as well as a complex and logical, and therefore fascinating, mind. You can tag this LP as one of the important ones.

(R.I.G.)

(Copyright © Down Beat, reprinted from Down Beat by special permission.)

Below, and the remainder of the Appendices,
illustrate pages from John Coltrane's original workbook,
courtesy of Naima Coltrane.

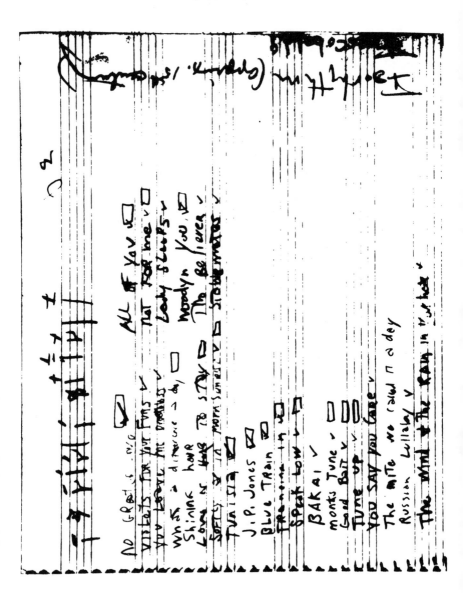

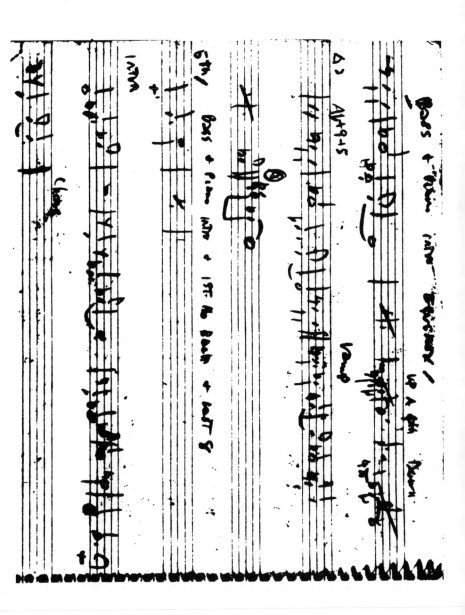

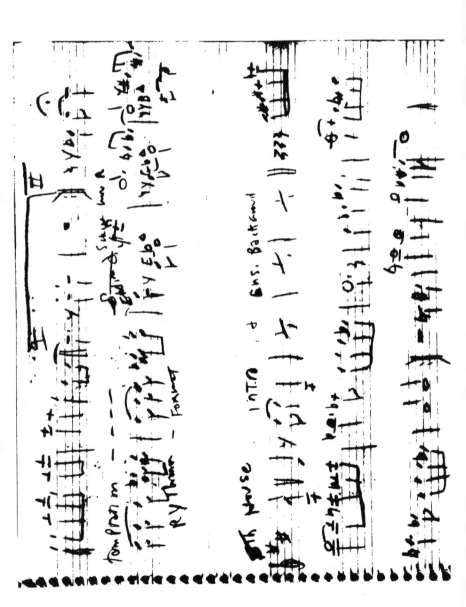

AFTER 32 Bar Rev - REPEAT Sequence AT ending chorus

Little sonay - Temptation - I'll wait & pray — Little boy

Something Blues - There To by love - mad about The Boy —

Human 1810 — | Equinox show here - 5th House

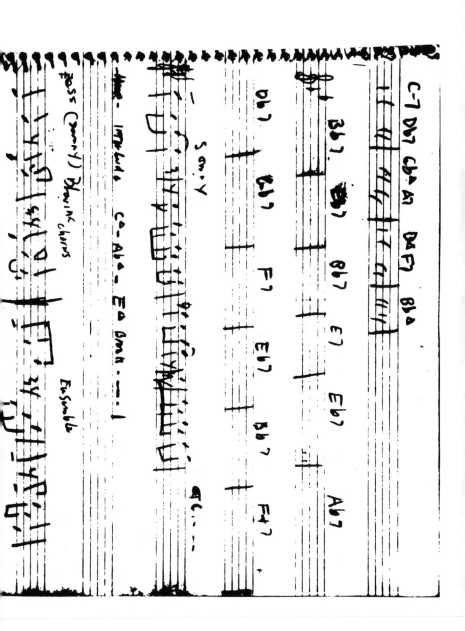

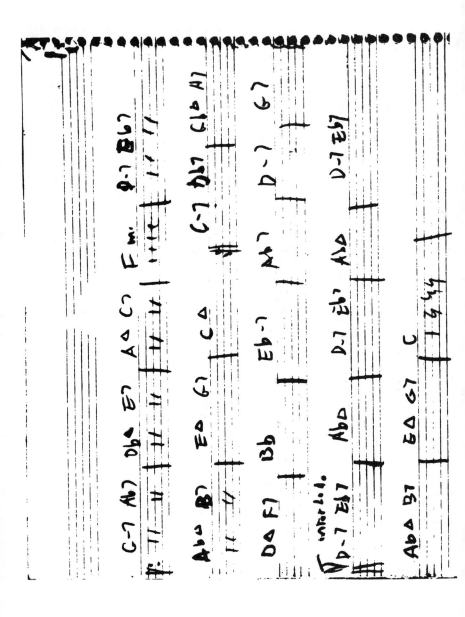

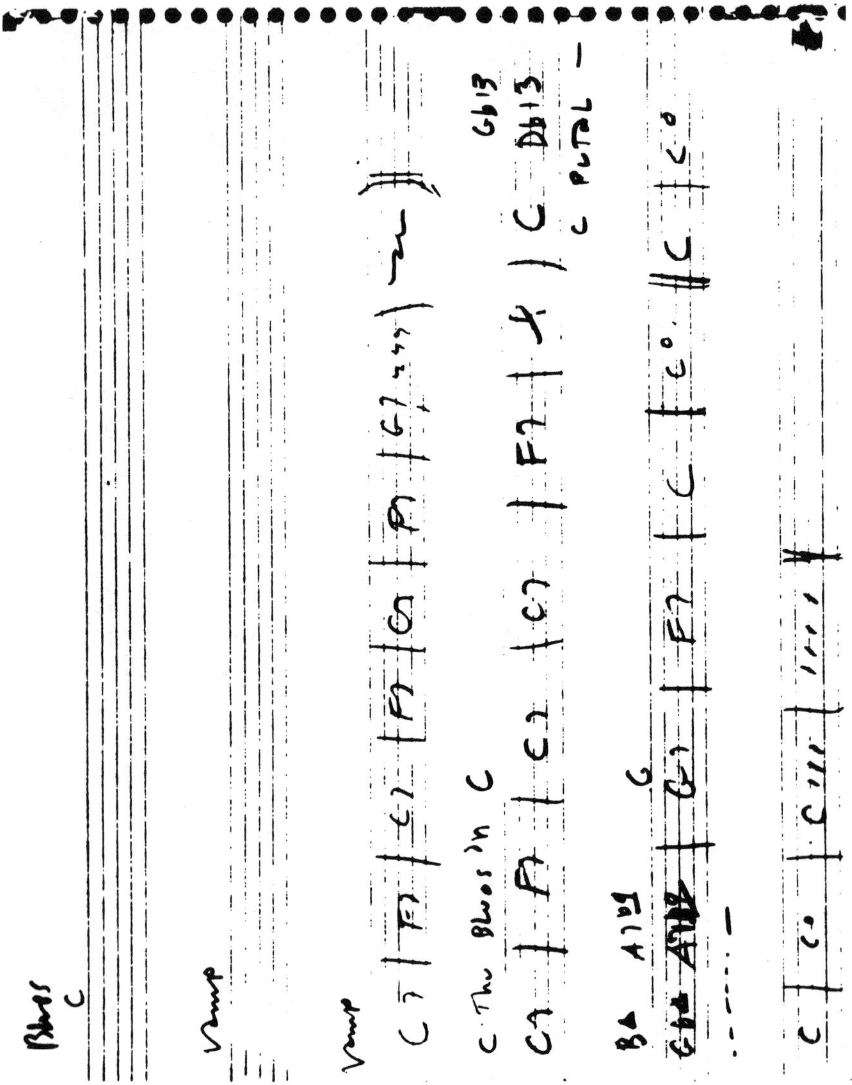
Blues
C
Vamp
Vamp
C Thru Blues in C
Gb13
Db13
C PEDAL

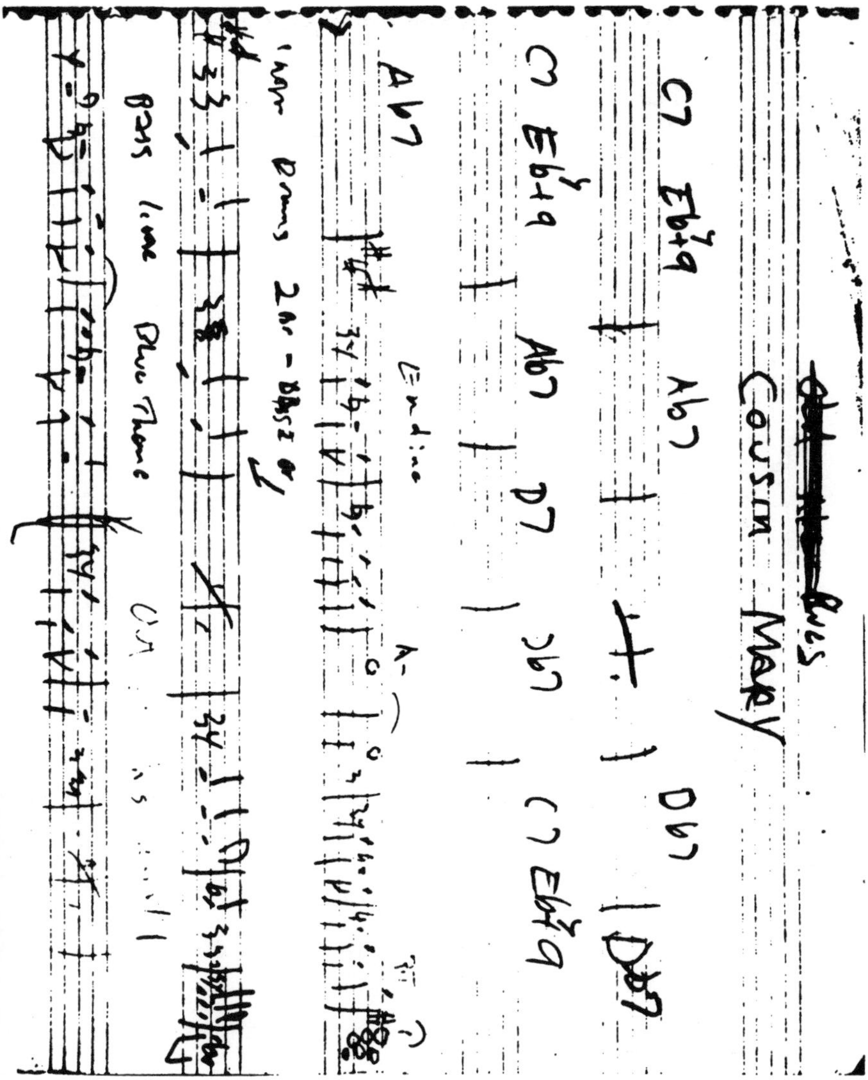
Cousin Mary
C7 Eb7+9 Ab7
Ab7 D7 Db7
Db7 C7 Eb7+9
Ab7

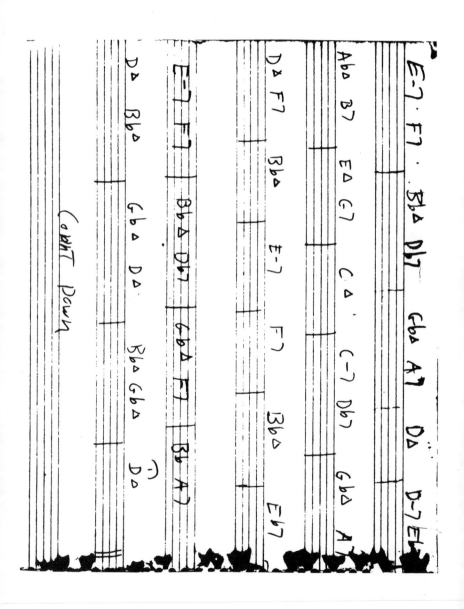

Index

Index

Index

Index

Index